A
SENSE OF
THE WORLD

14. 6. 31

A
SENSE OF
THE WORLD

How a Blind Man
Became History's
Greatest Traveler

JASON ROBERTS

HarperCollins*Publishers*

Frontispiece: James Holman, R.N., K.W., F.R.S, The Blind Traveler

HarperCollins books may be purchased for educational, business, or sales promotional use. For information, please write: Special Markets Department, HarperCollins Publishers, 10 East 53rd Street, New York, NY 10022.

FIRST EDITION
Designed by Joseph Rutt
Printed on acid-free paper

Library of Congress Cataloging-in-Publication Data

Roberts, Jason.
A sense of the world : how a blind man became history's
greatest traveler / Jason Roberts.—1st ed.
p.   cm.
ISBN-10: 0-00-716106-9
ISBN-13: 978-0-00-716106-5
1. Holman, James, 1786–1857. 2. Travelers—England—
Biography. 3. Voyages and travels. I. Title.

G246.H65R63 2006
910'.92—dc22
[B]
2005058166

06 07 08 09 10 /RRD 10 9 8 7 6 5 4 3 2 1

for
Eden Elise
&
Anthony Kalani

arrivals and departures

There is no cheerfulness
like the resolution of a great mind
that has fortune under his feet.
He can look death in the face, and bid it welcome;
open his door to poverty, and bridle his appetites;
this is a man whom Providence has established
in the possession of inviolable delights.

—Seneca
Of a Happy Life

Contents

The World and Its Multiplying Delights

All facts, description, and even dialogue in these pages are drawn entirely from the historical record. This story may at times seem improbable, but it is true.

UNTIL THE INVENTION of the internal combustion engine, the most prolific traveler in history was also the most unlikely. Born in 1786, James Holman was in many ways the quintessential world explorer: a dashing mix of discipline, recklessness, and accomplishment, a Knight of Windsor, Fellow of the Royal Society, and bestselling author. It was easy to forget that he was intermittently crippled, and permanently blind.

He journeyed alone. He entered each country not knowing a single word of the local language. He had only enough money to travel in native fashion, in public carriages and peasant carts, on horseback and on foot. Yet "he traversed the great globe itself more thoroughly than any other traveler that ever existed," as one journalist of the time put it, "and surveyed its manifold parts as perfectly as, if not more than, the most intelligent and clear-sighted of his predecessors."

In an era when the blind were routinely warehoused in asylums, Holman could be found studying medicine in Edinburgh, fighting the slave trade in Africa (where the Holman River was named in his honor), hunting rogue elephants in Ceylon, and surviving a frozen captivity in Siberia. He helped unlock the puzzle of Equatorial Guinea's indigenous language, averting bloodshed in the process. In *The Voyage of the Beagle*, Charles Darwin cites him as an authority on the fauna of the Indian Ocean. In his commentary on *The Arabian Nights*, Sir Richard Francis Burton (who spent years following in Holman's footsteps) pays tribute to both the man and his fame by referring to him not by name, but simply as the Blind Traveler.

James Holman was justly hailed as "one of the greatest wonders of the world he so sagaciously explored." But astounding as his exploits were, a further astonishment is how quickly he was forgotten. The public's embrace, driven more by novelty than genuine respect, did not endure. Critics dismissed his literary and scientific ambitions as "something incongruous and approaching the absurd." One bitter enemy, another professional adventurer whose expedition was eclipsed by Holman's, leveled a charge that took root in public perception: *His sightlessness made genuine insight impossible.* He might have *been* in Zanzibar, but how could the Blind Traveler claim to *know* Zanzibar? He was rarely doubted—his firsthand facts were unassailably accurate—but he was increasingly ignored.

The fame diminished, and curdled into ridicule, but Holman didn't slow down in the slightest. Impoverished, increasingly threadbare, and still in debilitating health, he kept to his solo travels, even as his works fell out of print and his new writings went unpublished. His few steadfast admirers lost track of him, presuming him dead in some distant corner of the globe. His true end came suddenly, in a scandalously unlikely corner of London, interrupting both his fervent work and plans for further voyages.

Holman dreamed that future generations might appreciate his life's work, but they weren't given the chance. His eclectic collection of artifacts was scattered and discarded, his manuscripts destroyed or lost. If he could be said to have a monument at all, it was a brief biographical sketch in the *Encyclopedia Britannica,* an entry that dwindled in subsequent editions. By 1910, it was a single paragraph. By 1960, it had disappeared altogether.

M Y O W N J O U R N E Y S in Holman's faded footsteps began three years ago, with a flash of turquoise. Like most writers who work self-sequestered in the halls of a library, I was in the habit of taking wander breaks. I'd weave idly through the aisles, pick out a book at random, and leaf through it for ten minutes or so before getting back to work. Usually it was the title that caught my eye—*My Life as a Restaurant, Caring for Your Miniature Donkey*—but one afternoon I was drawn to a small book more by its bright turquoise spine than its title, which was *Eccentric Travelers.*

It was an aptly named book, with one important exception. *Eccentric Travelers* profiled seven wanderers of the eighteenth and nineteenth centuries, most indisputably crackpots. One moonlighted as an exorcist. Another brought back hoaxed "specimens" of fictional animals. But despite the fact that sightlessness hardly qualifies as an eccentricity, there was also a chapter on the Blind Traveler. Slim as it was, the volume had apparently needed some filling out.

It was only a brief, frustratingly incomplete profile, but it was that incompleteness that drew me in. I launched a search for a book devoted to this singular individual, a search that started with adjacent shelves and continued to escalate over the course of several weeks, until it was clear that no such book existed—not in any library, in any language. That single chapter in the little turquoise book was, I would discover, the most extensive writing on the Blind Traveler ever published.

I managed to track down a few volumes of Holman's own writings, antiquarian rarities, but reading them only tantalized me further. His published work begins in 1819 and ends abruptly in 1832, leaving most of his life effectively veiled in silence. Even these surviving narratives are notably lacking in autobiographical detail. He does not explain his blindness, because it was an enigma even to himself—the final symptom of a mysterious illness that struck him in his early twenties. He is, uncharacteristically for a professional adventurer, seemingly incapable of self-promotion, racking up a series of unprecedented achievements but almost never bothering to note them as such. He is also discreet to a fault, obscuring most of the identities of people he encounters during his adventures—especially those of women, who were drawn to him, and whose attentions he returned with gentlemanly ardor.

A medical mystery, a modest hero, a series of cloaked affections. How could my fascination *not* become an obsession, and finally a quest? I went to England, to decipher the faded ink of ships' logs, and brush the crumbling wax from broken seals of once-secret documents from Windsor Castle. I traced the fate of the Holman River, long disappeared from maps, and of the African settlement he'd helped to found (now the capital of a sovereign nation). After a century and a half of obscurity, the full tale of the Blind Traveler began to emerge. It proved to be even more extraordinary than I could imagine.

James Holman was a whirlwind of incongruities: an intrepid invalid (at times simultaneously incapable of standing up and standing still), a poet turned warrior turned wanderer, a solitary man who remained deeply engaged with humanity. His adventures were neither acts of machismo nor self-aggrandizing stunts—they were, as he put it, a means "to enter into the business of life . . . communion with the world and its multiplying delights."

This book documents not just a profoundly inspiring figure, but one of history's most richly lived lives. No one, before or since, has experienced our world quite so vividly and completely.

Jason Roberts
San Francisco

A
SENSE OF
THE WORLD

Vesuvius in the eruption cycle of 1821–22.

I See Things Better with My Feet

THE BLIND MAN paused to feel the end of his walking stick. It was scorched and blackened, a few moments shy of bursting into flame. He rolled the tip in the abundant ash to cool it, then continued his progress upward, toward the mouth of the volcano.

His friend, a young Irish surgeon named Robert Madden, looked on with both clinical interest and personal fascination.

The great eruption of June, 1821 was witnessed by me. I accompanied to the mount the celebrated blind traveler, Lieutenant Holman, the evening of which the violence was at its greatest height.

From a distance, thirty-four-year-old James Holman didn't look blind. The prodding of his stick seemed more like a bit of swagger than an act of orientation. Despite his condition he was still a uniformed officer of the British Royal Navy, although that uniform was at the moment irreverently topped with a broad straw hat. He cut an attractive figure: lean, above middle height, clearly accustomed both to command and to life outdoors. His bearing was straight-backed and confident, and his youthful features radiated an intelligent enthusiasm. Jane Austen would have recognized him immediately as a Military Gentleman, dashing yet soulful, suitable for a central role in one of her romances.

> *He insisted on walking over places where we could hear the crackling effects of the fire on the lava beneath our feet, and on a level with the brim of the new crater, which was then pouring forth showers of fire and smoke, and lava, and occasionally masses of rock of amazing dimensions, to an enormous height in the air.*

There was nervous talk of halting the ascent, but Lieutenant Holman remained in firm command of his miniature expedition. He had begun the climb quite willing to proceed alone, and from his two companions he "rather looked for amusement and information than guidance and protection." Signore Salvatori had offered to take them part of the way on muleback, but Holman had insisted on hiking the full distance.

"I see things better with my feet," he explained.

Decades later, when Dr. Madden had abandoned medicine and drifted into hack writing, he recounted that evening in a memoir. It wasn't even his memoir. He was churning out *The Literary Life and Correspondence of the Countess of Blessington* when a chapter set in Italy moved him to slip a personal reverie into the pages:

> *A change of wind must inevitably have buried us, either beneath the ashes or the molten lava. The huge rocks generally fell back into the crater from which they issued. The ground was glowing with heat beneath our feet, which often obliged us to shift our position.*

They arrived at the very edge of the crater. Salvatori, of a family that had served as field guides on Mount Vesuvius for generations, announced that Holman had just made history. Attempts on the volcano were few enough that the king of Naples received a personal report on them all, and Salvatori looked forward to informing His Majesty of the first sightless man to reach the summit. But now it was time to turn back. The air was scarcely breathable, the ground audibly unstable. They were shifting their stances, almost hopping. Too much contact with the fuming ground could burn their feet through their shoes.

Holman lingered as long as he could, savoring the scent of sulphur, the sounds of earth in motion, the very omnipresence of the heat.

When at last they retreated a few yards, Holman shook the ashes from his shoes. Then he calmly pointed out that this was the summit of the *active* volcano—not of the mountain itself. Another, dormant crater awaited higher up the slope, and he intended to climb until there was nothing further to climb. After they cleared the active lava fields it would get quite cold, and he hoped to keep a brisk pace. He had neglected to bring a coat.

It was time for Salvatori to declare an impossibility. Perhaps the lieutenant was forgetting that it was well past midnight. The moon was setting, and outside of the eruption's glow there would soon be nothing but a dangerous darkness. This was, of course, a handicap to Madden and Salvatori, not Holman, who gracefully conceded the point. A quiet settled over them as they began to retrace their steps.

The view of the bay of Naples and of the distant city, from the summit of Vesuvius on a beautiful moonlight night without a cloud in the sky, such as we had the good fortune to enjoy, was almost magic in its effect; such serenity and repose and beauty in perfect stillness, formed a striking contrast with the lurid glare of the red hot masses that were emitted from the volcano, and the frightful bellowings of the burning mountain on which we stood.

It was still dark when they reached the nearest shelter, a hermit's cabin four miles distant. The occupant, something of an entrepreneur-monk, aggressively priced and freely poured cupfuls of a local wine called *Lachrymae Christi*, Tears of Christ. A group of Austrians slumbered on couches, waiting for sunrise and their shot at the summit. In the warmth of the fire and the wine, Holman allowed elation to win out over exhaustion. *The first, the very first.*

It was a triumph, not so much of his courage as of his ability to charm a path in a given direction. Vesuvius was at its most violent in living memory, and yet he had managed to deflect the grave concern of his friends, circumvent Salvatori's professional caution, and march to the very precipice, accompanied but at his own pace, under his own power. Such reasserted freedom wasn't just a sop to his dignity. It was, in his opinion, the only thing keeping him alive.

TWO YEARS EARLIER Holman had been a bedridden invalid, slowly retreating from life. Unable to cure either his blindness or the wracking pain that made an agony of motion, his physicians decided that a warmer climate might provide, if not a cure, then at least a comfortable setting for his remaining days. Left to find his own attendants to convey him to the Mediterranean, the patient— acting out of poverty, pride, or sheer self-destructiveness—did nothing of the sort. Instead he hobbled onboard a ferry bound for France, quite alone.

Six months later he emerged at the Mediterranean coast, bruised and wearied by the journey but also reinvigorated. Solitary travel, he'd found, was the collision of chaos and momentum, a constant, welcome assault on his senses and attention. It distracted him from his pain, and sparked new energies within. Instead of lingering at his supposed destination he'd chosen to keep moving, to cling to the road like a lifeline.

It had led him here, to the volcano's edge. And now he was savoring the realization that it could lead him anywhere.

The monk kept a visitors' book, and Salvatori urged him to

make an entry. A quill was dipped in ink and placed in his hand, then gently guided to the page. Holman, a poet long before he was an officer, thought for a moment, then made what he hoped was a legible approximation of writing:

Some difficulties meet, full many
I find them not, nor seek for any.

He handed back the book and quill, not realizing he had just composed his lifetime's motto. Years later, at the height of his fame, he would make a habit of adding this scrap of verse to his autograph, as if it were a private pact with the world. *I wish to pass through, not vanquish. Do not vanquish me.*

Holman rose from his chair, not needing to ask the hour. The monk was no longer feeding the fire. The Austrians were stirring more in their sleep. Without touching, he knew precisely where the cabin's windows were—he could tap them with his walking stick if he wished—and now a new warmth was faintly radiating from the panes. The sun was rising. There was sufficient light on the path for his companions.

It was time to go.

The medieval "Exeter Elephant," with extraneous ears and webbed feet.

ONE

The Child in
the Compass

JAMES HOLMAN WAS unequivocal about his first and deepest dream. "I have been conscious from my earliest youth of the existence of this desire to explore distant regions," he would recall, "to trace the variety exhibited by mankind under different influences of different climates, customs and law."

The genesis of such a dream can be readily understood. It arose from his childhood universe, from the engine of all his family's ambitions. An apothecary shop.

If you wished to voyage the world in a mindflight instant, you needed only to step into the Exeter establishment of John Holman, Chymist & Surgeon, close your eyes, and breathe deep the mingled scents of all known continents. It was an apothecary in the very latest mercantile fashion, selling not only medicinal products but just about anything that could be powdered, dried, or otherwise prepared for transport from afar. Cayenne pepper and soy from India, tapioca from the West Indies, Arabian cashews, Brazilian cocoa and coffee, Cathay tea, Spanish capers, even Italian macaroni—those were only the foodstuffs, arrayed in open barrels and bins, on offer by the pound, ounce, or pinch. Behind the counter, in Latin-labeled glass and earthenware jars, were the essentials for compounding prescriptions in legal accordance with the *London*

Pharmacopoeia, fragrant esoterics like galbanum from Persia and myrrh from northern Africa. It was not the cheapest apothecary in town—the store's public notices were frankly addressed "to Nobility, Gentry, and others"—but that was no impediment to a healthy tide of trade.

Young James, born on the premises and raised underfoot, was the fourth of six boys, but the first Holman son to know no home but the shop, which had opened in 1779. He knew intimately the rarity and provenance of each item. And for a reinforcing sense of the wideness of the world, he had only to look out the window.

Exeter, a metropolis of fifteen thousand in southwestern England, was second only to London as the nation's busiest inland port, and almost all offloaded cargo flowed overland within sight of the storefront. Fittingly, Exeter had grown in the rough plan of a compass, with the centuries-old city walls pierced by four cardinal-pointed main streets: North, South, Fore, and High. Holman's apothecary owed much of its success to a literally central location, at the crossroads formed by the four streets' convergence.

For the young and adventurous-minded, the city was full of further inspirations. The nearby cathedral held the famous "Exeter Elephant," delighting and intriguing children since the thirteenth century. It was (and remains) a choir stall with a fantastical rendition of an elephant, complete with webbed feet and an extra set of ears, carved by a medieval woodworker who had clearly never seen one. Off the cathedral green was the Ship Inn, looking as it had in Elizabethan days when it served as Sir Walter Raleigh's informal headquarters. Nearby was Mol's Coffee House, equally ancient and unchanged, the preferred haunt of Sir Francis Drake. Both mariners were proudly claimed as native sons of Devonshire (of which Exeter was the capital), and as progenitors of Exeter's secretive and powerful Guild of Merchant Adventurers, which by 1588 was trading as far afield as Senegal.

A little farther down South Street were the Quayside docks, the terminus of England's first artificial shipping canal, where in 1714 a visiting Daniel Defoe had marveled at how "the ships come now quite up to the city, and there with ease both deliver and take in their lading." Woolen cloth was a regional specialty, and the docks were particularly convenient for textile merchants, who saved on warehousing by building their weaving houses within a few yards of the water, loading bolts into holds as soon as they emerged from the loom. Much of the British Army marched in uniforms of sturdy Exeter serge, as did the armies of Holland, Portugal, Italy, and Spain.

But by James's youth, the international bustle of the Quayside was unmistakably on the wane. England was at war against France—had been since 1790, when he was three—and the spreading scope of the conflict had choked off many foreign markets. Even sailing to other English ports, via the shipping canal and the English Channel, was a risk that only a diminishing number of shipowners chose to run.

The taverns on South Street were filling with merchant sailors, hoping to wait out the war. As a commercial inland port, Exeter was an easier place to remain a civilian than coastal naval ports like Plymouth or Portsmouth, where roving press gangs were forcing men into His Majesty George III's service. The Quayside's idled sailors had little to do but bide their time, and revisit past adventures. To an open-eyed child, growing up in the center of the civic compass, it wasn't difficult to hear their tales, and fill with wonder.

Wonder, not hope. The sons of the apothecary had been assigned carefully interlocking destinies. One Holman boy was indeed being readied for an intrepid, seafaring life. But it wasn't James.

AFTER ACHIEVING a solid and public prosperity, John Holman had tried his hand at importance. He kept a large phaeton carriage, a status-symbol vehicle, and ran successfully for a seat on the Exeter city council. But as he was soon forced to acknowledge, these constituted the boundaries of his own upward mobility. A "Chymist & Druggist," or "Surgeon and Apothecary, of genteel Practice," as he variously advertised himself in the Exeter *Flying Post*, could be successful, even prominent. But he could not be a gentleman.

In the eighteenth century, the term *gentleman* conveyed not just good manners and politeness, but a very real social status. A gentleman did not require a title, a noble ancestry, or even much money, but he did need to be beyond the indignity of working with his hands. Even surgeons were regularly excluded from polite society, on the grounds that they performed a manual skill and were therefore servile. John Holman had risen from chymist's apprentice to proprietor of one of Exeter's busiest apothecaries—which made him not only a surgeon without a medical degree but a shopkeeper waiting on customers, and thus beyond the pale. True local gentry, such as the Viscount Courtenay or the Bishop of Exeter (who happened to be brothers), might esteem his skills, perhaps be genuinely grateful for a timely curative, yet such goodwill would never translate into acknowledgment on a social level. He might be able to afford a carriage, but that carriage would still be directed to the tradesmen's entrance.

John Holman ceased burnishing his own image. He sold the phaeton, served out his term of office, and shifted the burden of familial ambition to his sons. There was not enough money to make gentlemen of them all, but together they would be the generation to vault the barrier of class.

The eldest son, also named John (neither father nor sons bore the patrician mark of a middle name), was the child on whom that burden weighed heaviest. Groomed to succeed his father, he would inherit not only the apothecary business but the obligation to underwrite the careers of his younger brothers—in effect, dedicating himself to making them his social betters. The process would not be short, or cheap.

The costliest career was that of secondborn Samuel, who was

to be a soldier. Not a common musket-carrying sort, but an officer (an officer was automatically a gentleman). This was an expensive proposition, since officer's commissions were not won on merit but bought and sold on the open market. The government not only approved of these transactions, it set the prices. The single gold star of an ensign, the lowest of the officer ranks, commanded an official price tag of four hundred pounds, an amount roughly equivalent to the soldier's first seven years of salary. The cost was borne, and the newly minted Ensign Holman, fitted out in powder wig, ceremonial sword, and red coat cut from local cloth, marched off to join his regiment. The real price of this investment in instant gentility would be paid over the course of many years, since the family was expected to make up the gap between Samuel's meager salary and the expenses of an officer's lifestyle. The costs of subsequent promotions would be more expensive still.

William, the third son, was the one destined for the sea. Becoming an officer in the Royal Navy was a less expensive, but significantly slower, path to equivalent social status. There were no price tags on naval officers' commissions, at least not official ones. In theory, everyone entered the sea service at the lowest rung of the ladder, as a simple Able Seaman, then put in at least six years of active duty before becoming eligible for entering officer ranks as a lieutenant. That didn't keep rampant influence-peddling (and the occasional discreet transfer of funds) from short-circuiting the system. Given sufficient motivation, many captains would agree to carry a boy "on the books," which meant that his presence was falsified on the ship's roster. It was a time-honored fiction, letting a boy as young as five rack up sea time when he was, in truth, still playing at his nursemaid's feet. Many teenagers had more than a decade of illusory experience before first setting foot on a ship. Such string-pulling was beyond the Holman family's finances, scruples, or social gravity, so William was fitted out in comfortable clothes (an Able Seaman wore no uniform) and obliged to spend his sea duty actually at sea.

The next son was James. Already an adventurer in his imagination, wanting only, as he would later recall, "to investigate with unwearied solicitude the moral and physical distinctions that separate and diversify the various nations of the earth." This, of course, hardly qualified as a serious ambition. If it was expressed at all to his father, it was summarily ignored. To judge by the tenor of James's education, it seems likely that the senior John intended him to follow the third—and unfortunately, most sedentary—path to gentility, which was the clergy. The Anglican church offered a modest but steady income, and more importantly entrée into polite society (Jane Austen and the Brontë sisters were all clergymen's daughters). Even if the child's clear intelligence led him in a more academic direction, he would still be well served by taking holy orders. Most professors, including the entire Oxford and Cambridge faculty, were required to be clergymen as well. He might rise only to the meager status of a rural vicar, but at least he would be the social peer of the local squires.

By the age of seven, James was already attending private day school in nearby Theatre Lane—an early start, and an added expense. A few years later his father stepped up the investment, enrolling him in the more academically ambitious Alphington Academy. The financial toll of the Holman's ambitions was already starting to show. The Alphington Academy was a school of solid scholarship but minimal prestige, known as a place for "the sons of petty tradesmen in Exeter, or of persons who got for their children a cramming of Latin and Greek as cheap as they could."

Each morning the boy made his way to Alphington Cross, three miles distant. His route took him down South Street, past the dwindling Quayside traffic of ships.

IF JOHN HOLMAN had intended the rigorous new school to extinguish a daydreaming nature, he was not entirely successful. The Alphington Academy taught "all the Polite Arts," which included, in addition to "a little Latin & Greek," Arithmetic, Astronomy and the most reverie-inducing subject of all: Geography. Most cartographers had stopped decorating their work with fanciful creatures such as sea dragons and hippogriffs, but it was still an imaginative profession. As the maps of the day made abundantly clear, much of the planet remained enticingly unknown.

Geographic knowledge was discontinuous and often sketchy, shaped more by the need to navigate trade routes than to gain a comprehensive understanding of the world. Coastlines of trade-rich regions like India or Sumatra were well mapped, but with an accuracy that degraded rapidly away from the principal ports. Outside of Europe and pockets of the New World, interiors were still largely uncharted, with rivers running vaguely through guessed-at regions.

To understand the full measure of this uncertainty, it's useful to examine the sort of map young Holman was studying. *Lumsden's New Map of the World, from the latest discoveries* was incorporated into several schoolbooks of the day; in it North America, Russia, and the North Pole are conjoined, a planetary skullcap of white signifying both ice and ignorance. The Spanish colony of Florida is set in the Mississippi Valley, a thousand miles from its true location. Below an almost-empty Africa (but far from the still-undiscovered Antarctica), a wedge-shaped and imaginary Terra Australis hovers. This is not Australia—that's labeled New Holland, and melded together with what we know as Tasmania. New Zealand is not even an island, only a tentative squiggle of partial coastline floating in the South Sea.

Documents like these were more than maps. They were invitations.

But the task before James was to shed fantasies of adventure, and develop more acceptable outlets for his natural romanticism. And for this a suitable role model was standing right before him, at the head of the class. Doctor Laurence Hynes Halloran, headmaster of Alphington Academy, was in his late twenties, darkly handsome, well dressed, well spoken, and impeccably mannered—in short, perfect emulation material for young gentlemen in the making. This was because of a slight tinge to the headmasters' reputation. It was whispered about that he had stood trial for accidental manslaughter in his youth. He'd been acquitted, of course, but even this slight irregularity prompted the students at other schools "to look down with sovereign contempt on Mr. Halloran's boys."

Still, he was a charismatic educator, capable of deeply inspiring his charges, and a poet of genuine gifts (his verse is still anthologized today). While maintaining his status as a respectable pillar of the community, he was also publishing slim, much-admired volumes, such as *An ode (attempted in Sapphic verse) occasioned by the proposed visit of Their Majesties to the city of Exeter.*

Soon James had a new dream: to be like Halloran. He would pursue a necessary profession, but in his spare hours indulge his growing interest in literature, and poetry in particular. And inspiration willing, he would become a genteel, part-time poet himself.

But then came 1796—the year a French soldier changed the spelling of his name from Buonaparte to Bonaparte, in order to sound more Gallic than Corsican. It was the year of Mozart's death, and of George Washington's farewell to public life. It was also the year when Alphington Academy's greatest scandal irretrievably changed the life of a ten-year-old boy.

IT BEGAN WITH Laurence Hynes Halloran's abrupt disappearance. The headmaster, it turned out, had not left legal transgressions entirely in his youth. Halloran abandoned the academy and went into hiding, both because "he was obliged to leave Alphington for debt," and more seriously, because he was accused of acts of "immorality."

The specifics of his alleged crimes fled with him. Details would have been entered into public record, had he been arrested and tried, but there would be no trial. Still, further truths emerged:

Halloran was a fraud. His degree, purportedly in divinity, was self-awarded, as were his airs of genteel authority and erudition. In fact he'd grown up an impoverished orphan in his native Ireland, and had very probably been guilty of the earlier charge of manslaughter. As one Exeter resident now understood it, "If his legal advisor had not stopped his mouth on the trial, by preventing his declaring he was drunk when he gave the fatal blow, he would have criminated himself."

While the citizens of Exeter were reeling from these revelations, Halloran was already at sea, beginning another life as an assistant ship's chaplain under equally fictional credentials. He would go on to weather further accusations of immorality (in these cases, entanglements with underage girls), before being convicted and transported to Australia for the pettiest of crimes, the forging of ten-pence's worth of postage on an envelope.

Halloran was, in short, a scoundrel. But he would not be remembered as a villain by young James, who had received from him two gifts. The first was what would become a lifetime love of literature. The second was the chaos in the wake of Halloran's flight, during which—much to the boy's private joy—James's future was hastily retooled. The Alphington Academy was not the only place where a clergy-level education might be obtained, but a different sort of advancement was suddenly a possibility. The disappearance of "Doctor" Halloran happened to coincide with the reappearance, after five years' absence, of Governor-General John Graves Simcoe, Exeter's most famous son. He was returning home under a dark cloud of his own.

JOHN GRAVES SIMCOE'S fondest hope was that history would remember him as both the nemesis and antithesis of George Washington. During the Revolutionary War and in the thirteen years since, his career had been one of continuous and very personal opposition to the American general and statesman.

Simcoe was a career British soldier, but not a redcoat. He was the illustrious commander of the greencoats, the militia formed of Loyalists, Americans who'd chosen to remain faithful to the crown. Unlike the imported British troops, tradition-bound and fighting in a foreign land, the native greencoats (officially called the Queen's Rangers) were free to employ both Simcoe's formal military education and the improvisational American way of fighting. The result was what we now call commando tactics: daring raids, thoroughly planned but executed swiftly, with an emphasis on freestyle combat instead of lockstep marching. Simcoe had aimed not to defeat the Continental Army but to demoralize and destabilize it, and to provide a rallying presence for the estimated one-third of the American population still Loyalist in their sympathies. He masterminded a stealth operation to kidnap General Washington, a not-strictly-ethical scheme that would have changed the course of the war—had not conventional British forces insisted on tromping in at the last moment, noisily tipping off the prey.

The Queen's Rangers fought with a singular ferocity, at least in part because they knew themselves to be the other American army's most hated enemy. A captured redcoat was almost always treated in accordance with the rules of war, while a captured greencoat was often summarily shot as a traitor. This explained Simcoe's dismay at war's end, when the articles of surrender provided no protection for the Americans who had backed the wrong side. He knew retaliation was inevitable, that his beloved Rangers would soon be "fined, whipt, banished and hanged without mercy." Washington's position on the matter was already on record. As he watched the British retreat in 1781, he noted with satisfaction that, among the Loyalists, "One or two have done what a great many ought to have done long ago—commit Suicide."

In counterpoint to his old enemy, Simcoe cast himself as the founding father of an alternative America. Loyalist colonials were streaming into Canada, part of the British Empire but predominantly French in its laws and culture. To accommodate the exiles, a new province of Upper Canada was created, with Simcoe as its first leader, a largely unsurveyed wilderness, dotted by Indian tribes and the occasional trapper. Simcoe set out to make it as resolutely and reassuringly English as possible. He changed the name of the river La Tranche to the Thames, established a Parliament and dreamed of the day it would convene in a grand new capital called London. His ambition soared: not only would he welcome the Loyalists who straggled over the border, he would create an irrefutable demonstration of the superiority of British government, a beacon of benign monarchy compelling enough to trigger a mass exodus of those secret sympathizers, the silenced one-third, still in the newly renamed United States.

Simcoe and his loyal Rangers were busily laying out a new city, in a Lake Ontario cove called Toronto, when reality intervened. The government in London—the actual London—had little taste for a second attempt at New World nationbuilding, and once the extent of his plans was understood, they were promptly stopped. The loud protests of Simcoe, who saw this as a second betrayal of his Loyalists, served only to convert him into a figure of fun.

There was little to do but retreat to his hometown of Exeter, and await reassignment. It was expected to be a short stay (he would find new employment in a few months, as the governor of Haiti) and under the circumstances his return was not marked by public celebration.

It's impressive that John Holman was able not only to secure a private interview with the sulking, nearly secluded Simcoe, but to win his sympathetic attention. Despite his many years among the Americans, their informality had never rubbed off on the governor-general. He was famously fond of pomp, and almost as notorious for his snobbery as for his exploits. Dealings with social inferiors were often formalized rituals of submission. At his estate, tradesmen with business to discuss were expected to line up before the gates in double file and, when summoned, march two-by-two into his study.

What, then, was John Holman's calling card? His very presence was an unspoken reminder of an uncomfortable fact: Simcoe owed his career to the generosity of an Exeter apothecary. Twenty-four years earlier, Simcoe's widowed and impoverished mother had needed money to purchase his captain's commission, money which she borrowed from William Pitfield, her local druggist. Pitfield was now dead but he and Holman had been amiable colleagues, both charitably active in the leadership of the Devon and Exeter Hospital. Simcoe could never receive John Holman as an equal, but he could greet him as a friend of an old friend. And perhaps unbend enough to grant a favor.

Simcoe's clout in the army was at an ebb, and besides there was no getting around the expense of purchasing a commission. Fortunately, he had a second set of connections: his father had been a naval man, captain of the HMS *Pembroke*. The senior Simcoe had died when his son was only seven, but he was fondly recalled by his contemporaries, many of whom now ranked high in the Royal Navy. If anything, Captain Simcoe's stature had increased after his death. He was best remembered as the man who had taught navigation to a young James Cook.

England had now been battling France for six years, and stepped-up demand for fresh officers had led to the creation of a new naval rank, the Volunteer First Class, decreed "to consist of young gentlemen intended for the sea service (whether the sons of officers or not)." This was a fast-track position, the equivalent of joining as a Midshipman but eliminating the obligation of three years' prior service—no more preliminary sea duty, real or shammed. It was a highly desirable posting, and despite its announced egalitarian purpose a hard one to win, since it required, at minimum, a captain's personal sponsorship.

John Graves Simcoe, ever status-conscious, seems to have made a show of enlisting the most exalted patronage he could muster. After a few discreet enquiries, the fourthmost Holman boy was accepted not only as a Volunteer First Class, but one under the sponsorship of none other than Lord Bridport, Admiral of the

Blue, Commander of the Channel Fleet, and the fourth highest-ranking officer in the entire Royal Navy. His service would begin late the following year, not on some minor vessel but on the HMS *Royal George*, the admiral's own flagship.

At last, James Holman could satisfy both his father and his deepest dream. He would be a gentleman, and a voyager.

· · ·

YOUNG JAMES WOULD remember the next year and a half only as a blur, "crammed with geography, astronomy, algebra, geometry, navigation, et cetera." The Exeter apothecary shop was a memory. He was now a boarding student at a private naval preparatory school in the port town of Gosport, by the broad anchorage waters known as Spithead. He had to hurry to catch up. Many of his new classmates, like him "destined to the naval service," had begun their vocational education a full two years earlier.

But he was an intelligent child, with a talent for attention. The late start proved no handicap, and formal enlistment in the Royal Navy came three weeks after his twelfth birthday. It was a day auspiciously marked by a brilliant early-morning display of shooting stars. He may have seen the last of them from the thwart of his shore launch in Spithead harbor, were he not too intent on watching the *Royal George* loom closer with each stroke of the oars.

His naval career would officially begin the moment he first stood on the ship's deck. An event carefully noted since it would forever fix his seniority in the Naval List, the precise ranking of all officers and candidate officers in the Royal Navy. Just prior to reporting for duty, he appears to have taken a last liberty with his own chronology. It was a freshly twelve James who mounted the boarding ladder, but by the top rung he was Volunteer Holman, reporting his age as thirteen to the recording officer.

It was December 7, 1798. Napoleon had conquered Italy, Malta, and Egypt, and was laying the groundwork to declare himself dictator of France. Now three Holman sons were fighting a war that would prove to be the deadliest in human history (later conflicts would claim more lives cumulatively, but none have offered worse odds of individual survival). Yet the first son to be mourned wore not a uniform, but an apron. Only four days after James's enlistment, John, the eldest, died suddenly in Exeter at the age of twenty-four.

It was clearly a rapid and unexpected death, as it blew apart the senior John's master plan. Had the tragedy occurred just a few days earlier, there's little doubt that James would have been tapped to take his brother's place. But enlistment was not reversible; no extenuating circumstances would release him, or Samuel, or William from serving for the duration of the war.

The elder John Holman might have entertained thoughts of running the shop single-handedly until a fifth son (Robert, then nine) came of age, but ultimately it was more practical to offer a partnership to one of his apprentices, John Ham. This decision carried significant consequences. The profits from the apothecary shop, already declining along with Exeter's economy, would now be split two ways. There would be few funds available for career-boosting. The boys were on their own.

James mourned his brother. But rocking in his sea hammock, late at night, he also considered himself fortunate to have barely dodged the burden of the family shop. "I felt an irresistible impulse to become acquainted with as many parts of the world as my professional avocations would permit," he would recollect, "and I was determined not to rest satisfied until I had completed the circumnavigation of the globe."

TWO

Scarcely Worth
Drowning

BETWEEN MOONSET AND sunrise, on the cusp of middle watch and morning watch, Young Master Holman took bracing great gulps of night air and fought a private battle with sleep. Since the moment he first stepped onboard the flagship of the Channel Fleet, he'd been kept furiously busy. It was a tonic against homesickness, and the final obliteration of childhood. On top of mock combat, drills with the great guns, navigation practice, and miles of rope to knot and splice and rig, there was late-night duty as a human alarm clock. His task was to respectfully rouse the lieutenants for each change of watch, then stand by should the need arise for further awakenings. In the meantime there was little to do but pace the darkened quarterdeck, watch the twice-an-hour ceremony of the ship's bell *(eight tolls, four a.m.)*, and take stock of his surroundings.

As befitting a ship named for the sovereign himself, the *Royal George* was vast. One hundred guns, both cannons and smaller carronades, were staggered and stacked four decks high, sheaved behind square shuttered ports that glared a blood red when open. Lifting the anchor required the strain of almost three hundred men. The sails alone, more than two acres of cloth put to the wind, weighed nearly ten tons. It was a vessel grand enough to

Holman's patron Lord Bridport, unwilling and
unloved commander of the Channel Fleet.

serve as the headquarters not only of a captain, but of an admiral and vice-admiral. Twelve-year-old Volunteers First Class, stiff and self-conscious in new cocked hats and ruffled white shirtfronts, were swallowed up whole.

Holman should have been beside himself with awe, and a sense of adventure unfolding. But the first light of each day revealed a dispiriting reality: the flagship was still firmly anchored in Spithead, well in sight of the shore. Having joined the navy afire to see the world, he'd landed on the one ship least likely to go anywhere at all.

THE REASON WHY was sleeping fitfully two decks below: Admiral Lord Bridport, head of the Channel Fleet, white-haired, besieged by gout, desperately wishing for his command and career to come to a merciful end. He was sixty-seven years old, a dodering, grandfatherly type, his powers of leadership long faded. Even his own officers had a hard time taking him seriously, chafing against his aversion to risk and privately dismissing him as "scarcely worth drowning . . . a mixture of Ignorance, avarice and spleen." Only one year earlier, Bridport had been the focus of a devastatingly ignominious event. He'd inspired the largest mutiny of all time.

As the sailing force closest to France, the Channel Fleet had evolved into Britain's largest fleet, comprising roughly one-fourth of all the battleships in the entire navy. Anyone joining its ranks might logically expect to soon be sailing the English Channel, keeping the enemy at bay, but under Bridport's command this was rarely the case. He practiced what was called, oxymoronically enough, "open blockade"—sending out only a few patrols to keep an eye on French ports, and keeping the rest of the fleet swinging at anchor in the sheltered home waters of Spithead. This gave the admiral ample time to enjoy his extensive estates ashore, but it alienated his officers, who wanted action, and glory. And it made virtual prisoners of his noncommissioned crewmen, who were given almost no shore leave at all.

The confines of a ship were difficult enough to endure at sea. When the same ship floated, for years at end, within sight and sound of the port towns of Plymouth and Gosport, the proximity was tantalizing. When that ship was surrounded by dozens of other ships, also idled, the situation was ultimately intolerable.

The Great Spithead Mutiny unfurled with a startling degree of organization on Easter morning in 1797, and quickly grew to encompass the entire Channel Fleet. Far from a rowdy, desperate lot, the mutineers wrested command with respectful demeanors that bordered on the apologetic. All shipboard duties continued as usual, even while the officers were expelled from their vessels, or confined to quarters.

It was a brilliantly conceived and executed mutiny, one that had somehow remained secret while recruiting thousands of sailors—gunner's mates and quarters and loblolly boys, all communicating furtively from ship to ship. There was clearly a talented, charismatic leader behind it all, but to the navy's frustration he remained anonymous. All grievances were issued through an Assembly of the Whole Fleet, with mutineer delegates elected from each ship. Refusing to deal with Lord Bridport, they chose to negotiate with his predecessor, a far more popular admiral, who had to be pulled out of retirement for the task.

The mutineers' complaint was not entirely with Bridport. In addition to shore leave, they asked for a raise in pay—not unreasonable, as wages had been frozen at ten shillings a month for 150 years. They also wanted better food, and more of it. The victualling office had stretched supplies by declaring that on shipboard, a pound of food weighed only fourteen ounces. What they did receive was often scarcely edible. Some salt pork was so old the crewmen gave up trying to eat it, and instead carved it into decorative boxes.

The Great Spithead Mutiny was, ultimately, so unusual that even two centuries later it seems almost to reside outside of history. Despite their best efforts, the navy could not break the mutineers' solidarity. They could not even glean the identity of the anonymous leader. After four weeks of a standstill—during which the English coast was almost entirely undefended against invaders—the Admiralty blinked first. They made the necessary concessions, including a "full and irrevocable" pardon for all involved, and the world's largest and most successful mutiny ended in a fleetwide chorus of cheers. All parties joined in a round of "Rule Britannia," then everyone got back to work.

SEVEN MONTHS LATER young Holman, whose school had been within earshot of the cheering mutineers, was standing watch on the one ship where the mutiny's aftermath was most deeply felt. The humiliated Bridport would gladly retire—he had tried to quit during the height of the uprising—but the Admiralty had demanded a show of continuity. So he remained, going through the motions, his daily life made even more uncomfortable by the onboard presence of the man who still claimed no credit, but whom almost everyone now believed to be the mutiny's mastermind: Valentine Joyce, a mere quartermaster's mate. Under the terms of amnesty Joyce had reclaimed his job on the *George*, keeping provisions stowed and cables coiled. That was the curious inversion of Holman's first ship: one of the least effective naval leaders of the waning century was unwillingly at its helm, while one of the most naturally gifted was in the hold, contentedly returning to obscurity.

Bridport's policy of hugging port had made the mutiny possible, but the issue of open blockade was not among the matters negotiated. The mutineers did not think it their place to second-guess naval strategy. When command was again thrust upon him, the admiral carried on, almost defiantly, exactly as before.

• • •

ACTION, OF A sort, came at last in April of 1799, when twenty-five French ships took advantage of an unseasonable fog and slipped out to sea. Bridport was, predictably, reluctant to chase them, especially after a patrol ship picked up a known French spy in a rowboat, hiding on his person a secret naval dispatch. The ships *seemed* headed toward the Mediterranean, but the dispatch revealed this as a ruse of war. It stated that this was the first wave of an invasion force for Ireland's Bantry Bay, which they planned to approach in a roundabout fashion.

Such an invasion had long been a fear of Bridport's (and of many in the Admiralty), since Irish insurrectionists against British rule could be counted on to give French troops a warm reception. Soon the Channel Fleet was once again at anchor, this time in Bantry Bay in County Cork, lying in wait to ambush the invaders.

Two months later, they were still waiting.

The intercepted invasion plans had been a hoax, written and dispatched by the French Minister of Naval Affairs with every intention of their capture. He had known that Bridport was by nature more cautious than skeptical, needing only a rationale to cling to home waters. The French ships were bound for the Mediterranean, just as their heading had indicated. In fact, they were already there.

What passed for morale aboard the *George* now plunged past dismal. The fleet would likely have erupted in a second mutiny, had Valentine Joyce given the signal, but Bridport's crowning indignity was the Admiralty's response to his miscalculation. Instead of relieving him of command through a face-saving retirement, they kept him at the helm—but stripped him of 60 percent of his ships. On June 1, he watched as sixteen of his twenty-six line-of-battle vessels sailed away, redeployed to join Admiral Nelson in the Mediterranean.

HOLMAN WAS WATCHING as well. He'd come to the conclusion that the *Royal George* was perhaps not the most advantageous starting point for a naval career. True, it placed him under the eye of those in highest rank, not a small consideration in a profession ruled by patronage. But it was hard to imagine much more influence emanating from the admiral, or his second-in-command Sir Charles Pole (privately denounced as "equally an old woman" by one of their captains).

The mood in Lord Bridport's cabin, cheerless enough before the fiasco of the false French spy, was now a study in gouty aggrievance. The once-great man was someone to steer clear of, not to seek out for a personal favor. But Holman seemed not to grasp this, or perhaps he remembered his father's success with Simcoe at a similar career-low point. Displaying either foolhardiness or an early, brilliant audacity, the boy sought and won a face-to-face audience with the admiral.

Lord Bridport probably had to be reminded who he was. There were at least a dozen just like him, swarming the gunroom and quarterdeck, and this one looked to be among the youngest and greenest. But Holman quickly imprinted himself on the admiral's memory, for as soon as formalities were observed the boy came to the point: would his lordship be so kind as to arrange a transfer to another ship?

Despite his lowly status as a recent arrival to the service, the request was not a small matter. The Royal Navy itself had no say over Volunteers First Class; they were taken on strictly at the individual initiative of a high-ranking officer. A new posting would require finding a similar officer willing to assume the responsibility. Holman was effectively asking Lord Bridport not only to step aside as his patron, but to take the time to seek out his own replacement.

Beyond the mention that it occurred, no record of this meeting survives. But Holman must have forged his language with inspired care, since his request was not taken entirely as an affront. He was, of course, turned down flat. Yet the admiral's dismissal was not so vehement as to bar the boy from future audiences.

•   •   •

HOLMAN'S FIRST BATTLE was Lord Bridport's last. In July, the winnowed-down remnant of the Channel Fleet departed Ireland and at last sailed into view of the enemy: a five-ship squadron from Spain, now France's ally, moored in a line off the Isle d'Aix and protected by a floating battery of French bomb-boats—small craft carrying little more than mortars, shells, and a dangerous abundance of gunpowder.

Bridport sent in his own bomb-boats, the all-too-appropriately named *Sulphur*, *Explosion,* and *Volcano*, beginning a battle that was bizarre from the first salvo. Both sides struggled to find the range for their fire. The British mortars were too weak to reach their targets, while the Spanish and French had the opposite problem: theirs were too powerful, sending shells flying not only well past the bomb-boats but safely over the masts of the larger British ships. Yet shortening a trajectory was easier than increasing one, and soon the enemy assumed the offensive, detaching some of their ships to attack the attackers.

Watching from a safe distance, the *Royal George* hurriedly hoisted the signal flags for *weigh and stand out*, retreat. The enemy gave just enough chase to claim it as a victory, although in truth it qualified as "a harmless action," not even a draw. Both sides had failed to inflict any damage at all.

For Holman the incident underscored another disadvantage to serving on the *Royal George*: the ship itself. As one of the larger battleships afloat it was a formidable foe, but also an enormous target. Encounters with the enemy would almost always be like this one, conducted from behind a bodyguard of lesser vessels, at a necessary but inglorious remove from the fray. While they sailed back to Spithead, he summoned the courage to once more seek out the admiral's attention.

His transfer request was denied just as summarily as before.

LORD BRIDPORT HAD his own rejected requests to worry about. His heartfelt wish for retirement continued to go unheeded.

Since the Admiralty seemed intent on forcing him to die on duty, he decided that he might as well embrace that fate with aplomb. Slowly, he began to loosen the doctrine of open blockade. His fleet was fewer in numbers now, but they spent far more time at sea. Studiously avoided by his captains, the admiral had little to do but tend to his swollen ankles and relive a career of fifty-nine years. It was ending on a sadly muted, diminishing note, but it had not been without its marvels, and perhaps its most marvelous aspect was its very beginning. His career, his estates and titles—all could be traced back to a traffic accident.

Six decades previously, a Royal Navy captain had been traveling through the Somerset countryside when a wheel on his carriage broke. While waiting for repairs in the minuscule village of Butliegh, he'd stayed with the family of the local vicar. Impressed by their threadbare but sincere hospitality, he'd sought to return the favor. He became professional sponsor of two of the sons, giving them their start at sea.

Now both brothers were not only admirals but lords, with peerages created for their benefit. The elder was now Viscount Hood of Whitley, enjoying his estates and the reflected glory of his former protégé Horatio Nelson, who credited his most successful tactics to him. The younger bided his time reminiscing in the great cabin of the *Royal George*. When one of the stripling boys—what was his name? Holmes? Holman?—mustered the effrontery to make a *third* request for a transfer, the response this time was not indignation. It was impossible to forget that his own life had hung on a single act of kindness

In the final week of the last September of the century, Young Master Holman, still twelve, left the flagship of the fleet and the patronage of its master. He was shifting from a first-rate ship to a fifth-rate one, and the prospect filled him with a quiet delight.

His new ship, the HMS *Cambrian*, was a frigate, one-third the tonnage of the *Royal George* but under fair winds half again as fast. With a single deck of armaments and a long, sleek waterline, frigates were built not for massed fleet actions but for speed and self-sufficiency. They sailed under a separate set of rules, respected by the enemy: larger ships were not supposed to fire on them, unless provoked to do so by an opening salvo. They, on the other hand, could pick and choose their fights, sailing away with honor if outnumbered or outclassed. When they did fight it was usually a duel, against another single ship on the open sea.

They were the scouts, the dispatch runners, the convoy escorts and lone hunters of the fleet, as versatile as they were indispensable. Horatio Nelson relied on them more than any other class of ship, quipping that if he dropped dead, the surgeon would find the words *More frigates!* carved into his heart.

Adding to the allure of the *Cambrian* was the fact that it usually sailed under sealed orders. Not even its captain knew their destination, as he was commanded not to open those orders until they were well out to sea. Holman had not the slightest idea where his new ship would take him. He hoped it was somewhere far, far away.

THREE

The Very Height
of Expectation

T HREE YEARS LATER, a lost ship began an accidental battle with a lighthouse.

The harbor of Halifax, Nova Scotia, was not a friendly port for
newly arriving vessels. The fog was often blindingly dense, "lying
on the ocean like a huge stratum of snow," in the words of one
sailor stationed there, calling for "nerves stout enough for such a
groping kind of navigation, perilous at best." In 1803, that same
sailor witnessed an awkward, nearly disastrous passage through
"the abominable haze":

> The Cambrian, lost in the midst of this fog bank, supposing herself
> to be near the land, fired a gun. To this the light-house replied; and
> so the ship and the light went on, pelting away, gun for gun, during
> half the day, without ever seeing one another.

Captain Beresford of the *Cambrian* understood that the lightweight shot hitting his ship was meant as a guidance signal. Perhaps he already knew that more experienced Halifax hands could
use the echoes of the cannon fire, along with their mental map of
the harbor, to find their way home. But he could not manage such
a fleet. He decided instead to wait out the weather, and ordered

Holman's first two frigates, the HMS *Cambrian* and
Leander, pursuing an American blockade runner.

the ship to a point he imagined to be safely offshore. The crew was
sitting down to dinner when suddenly

> *the bowspirit shot into daylight—and lastly, the ship herself glided
> out of the cloud into the full blaze of a bright and "sunshine holy-
> day" . . . the men, as they flew on deck, could scarcely believe their
> senses when they saw behind them the fog bank, right ahead the
> harbour's mouth, with the bold cliffs of Cape Sambro on the left,
> and farther still, the ships at their moorings, with their ensigns and
> pendants blowing out, light and dry, in the breeze.*

The Halifax so abruptly and embarrassingly revealed to Midshipman Holman—one of the scrambling young men on deck—
would be his home port for the next seven years. It was not the

smallest, coldest, or most isolated naval base in the empire. Those honors went to tiny Newfoundland Station, six hundred miles to the north, but in each respect Halifax ran a close second. It was a modest fishing village, a thousand miles from anything resembling a city, but Holman didn't care. It was a foreign shore, the New World.

He was now a sunbrowned, lanky fifteen-year-old, striding confidently across the frigate's deck as if it were a private world, which, in a sense, it was. He'd spent almost all of the past three years confined to it at sea, far from the sight of other ships. Holman had hoped the *Cambrian* would take him to distant lands, but they'd encountered almost no land at all.

Those years had been spent hunting privateers, civilian ships engaging in a lucrative, sanctioned form of piracy. Enemy privateers carried a license from the French authorizing them to prey on Atlantic merchant traffic at will, so long as they confined their conquests to ships from England and her allies. The English issued equivalent licenses with the reverse stipulation, and both sides sent their fastest ships to protect their trade by hunting the hunters. As glamorous as it sounded, the duty was not particularly dangerous—the privateers they stalked carried less firepower than naval ships, and were notably reluctant to stand and fight. Finding them, however, was a tedious business, and mostly a matter of luck.

The *Cambrian* had not been particularly lucky. Despite cruising continuously for more than a year at a time, stopping only for supplies, they'd managed to capture exactly two French privateers, and reclaim a British one. It was no surprise that the ship was now being reassigned, from individual predation to squadron patrol.

For Holman, the years of perpetual patrol were not without their advantages: the ship was smaller than the *Royal George* but the individual living quarters larger and better supplied with light. The busywork of the new recruit was in his past. There were long watches, but also ample time to learn and read. He emerged from the experience a seasoned mariner, albeit one with a well-indulged appetite for literature; (he was still a poet at heart). But it was frustrating to voyage thousands of miles to nowhere, to float seemingly forever on a featureless sea. He'd dreamed of seeing the wide world but it had shrunken, until he could take it in at a single glance. It was one hundred feet long and forty feet wide, and made of wood.

Halifax, when it emerged from the fog, was a welcome sight.

THE NEW BASE was home to the North American Squadron, the most thin-stretched British fleet on the planet. The *Cambrian* was joining only seven other ships, all modestly sized, in patrolling a region that encompassed the entire Atlantic seaboard. The next nearest station, Jamaica, was almost as distant as England itself.

Far more impressive than the home port were the *Cambrian*'s other expected ports of call. One advantage to being on North American duty was the friendly reception one received in Boston, New York, and Norfolk. The Americans were not allies in the war against France, but neither were they enemies. Their official stance was that of neutrality, a policy based less on political sentiment than on the young, export-rich country's desire to do business with both sides.

Having only a minuscule, thirteen-ship navy of their own, the United States welcomed Britain's policing of the seas—providing the rules of neutrality were respected. Under those rules, any merchant ship could sail to France and its allies with impunity, so long as both its ownership and its cargo were entirely American. The same ships could return laden with French and allied goods, so long as they delivered those goods directly to America. This arrangement required the slight indignity of British officers boarding and inspecting these ships, to confirm they were indeed American and in compliance, but that was usually conducted with a formal cordiality all around.

The *Cambrian* became a familiar sight to Bostonians and New Yorkers, sailing in slow loops just offshore, regularly launching rowboats of inspection crews to greet incoming ships. Shore leave was not too difficult to come by, and Holman became well acquainted with the seaboard cities and their hospitality (he would remember Boston with particular fondness). But with each subsequent leave, one fact became increasingly clear: the British welcome was rapidly wearing thin. Americans were growing increasingly unhappy about the scrutiny of their ships, and for good reason. They were cheating.

NEUTRAL TRADE WAS profitable, but the money to be made by skirting the rules was spectacular. There was the growing collusion of "broken voyage," in which shipments from non-neutral countries were imported to the United States, then recertified as American goods and promptly shipped out again; often the cargo was offloaded just long enough for the ship to undergo "repairs," then returned to the hold. These weren't just occasional transgressions— they comprised a black market that, in dollar value, exceeded legitimate exports. Under the guise of neutrality, American merchants were conveying to Europe entire crops from French or French-allied colonies and possessions: sugar from Cuba, coffee from Venezuela, indigo from South America.

And then there was the ownership-for-hire angle. Yankee merchants from obscure seaport towns were suddenly emerging as titular owners of vast fleets of ships, all of which flew fresh sets of American colors. This arrangement proved so efficient that soon not a single merchant ship flew the flags of France or its allies, Holland and Spain. Why bother risking capture by the British when your ships and cargo could be temporarily and safely Americanized? "Nothing appears to be so easy as to forge a ship's papers, or to swear false oaths," grumbled one British sailor on inspection duty, who even knew the going rate for reflagging a ship: four shillings and sixpence, roughly equivalent to a day's wage for skilled labor. This, for documents he knew to be spurious, but was usually forced to honor just the same.

As pointed out by an increasing number of alarmed Britons, in pamphlets like *War in Disguise; or, the Frauds of the Neutral Flags*, these circumventions were tantamount to making the United States the worst kind of enemy: an undeclared one.

A crackdown was inevitable. Where once the North American squadron had zeroed in on blatant acts of contraband smuggling—like the ship found ballasted not with rocks but with Spanish gold bullion—it now moved toward the wholesale seizure of any ships, and shipments, that aroused suspicion. In the summer of 1804, both the *Cambrian* and the HMS *Leander* were in tight formation, intentionally blocking the entrance to New York Harbor. The inspection process was no longer universally cordial. British sailors were the subjects of sneers and cold shoulders when they ventured ashore.

A fellow midshipman of Holman described their routine:

Every morning, at day break, during our stay off New York, we set about arresting the progress of all the vessels we saw, firing off guns to the right and left, to make every ship that was running in to heave to, or wait, until we had leisure to send a boat on board, "to see," in our lingo, "what she was made of." I have frequently known a dozen, and sometimes a couple of dozen ships, lying a league or two off the port, losing their fair wind, their tide, and worse than all, their market, before our search was completed.

If the inspection seemed "to justify the idea that the cargo was French and not American, as was pretended," no efforts were made to resolve the matter on the spot. Instead, the ship would be taken into custody and sailed the thousand miles to Halifax, where it would be mothballed until the matter would be judged in Admiralty Court. There was no appealing this confiscation: holds were hammered shut, and the bridge handed over to a "prizemaster" dispatched from the Royal Navy. For the duration of the voyage to Halifax, the prizemaster was captain of the ship.

Prizemaster duty was typically a rare, sought-after honor for ambitious lieutenants, eager for experience at the helm. But the North American squadron was soon confiscating dozens of ships each week—so many that demand for prizemasters outstripped the supply of available lieutenants. Over the next six years, an estimated two thousand American ships would be sailed northward under British control. The majority of them would be commanded not by officers, but by an improvised corps of youthful midshipmen.

At sixteen, Midshipman Holman was abruptly promoted to acting captain of not one but a string of ships. His surviving writings are silent on this period, but a faithful record was kept by his shipmate Basil Hall, a fifteen-year-old Scottish midshipman also elevated to prizemaster status. He remembered it as the crowning experience of his young life, but was shocked at how quickly the role was thrust upon him:

> *The happy but anxious young prize-master has his orders to proceed, and in the course of an hour, or it may often be much less, he finds himself alone and with a fluttering heart in the middle of the wide ocean, with a rich and important vessel in his charge, and a long voyage to make . . . He learns practically, for the first time, what it is to be implicitly trusted.*

The simple act of navigating through some of the stormiest waters of the planet was challenge enough. Having to do so on an unfamiliar ship with a shoestring crew made it a sleepless, white-knuckle passage. Prizemasters had to steer far out to sea, since Americans spying them from the shore were known to launch interception raids to "liberate" both the prisoners and cargo. Adding to the tension was the onboard presence of the ship's original captain, and at least a portion of the original crew. They were prisoners, but under the lightest confinement, if any at all. One could count on them to bitterly critique every command decision—and, if opportunity presented itself, to launch a violent retaking of the ship.

Most boy-captains inevitably spent little time in their cabins, choosing instead to keep an open-air vigil on the command deck. Some mastered the skill of catnapping standing up, clutching the wheel or tiller, as if an endurance contest were underway. It was both exciting and exhausting, an ordeal, as Hall wrote, of "the constant play of hopes and fears, anxieties during a foul wind and ecstasies when it is fair." They were young and eager to prove themselves impervious to the rigors of the task. But there would be lasting consequences.

WHILE HOLMAN AND Hall were plying their new trade, a physician named William Turnbull was finishing up the first comprehensive study of sailors' health in the Royal Navy. In it, he divided the diseases of seafaring into two basic types: those of heat and those of cold. Sailors in warmer climates, he concluded, were prone to ailments that "assume chiefly nervous and putrid form," such as dysenteries, fevers, and any of the myriad nauseas and diarrheas lumped together as "fluxes." Their common traits were rapid onset, and swift progression to a point of crisis. You would either recover or die, but you would probably do so in a matter of days.

Sailors afloat in more frigid weather had a notably high number of conditions with opposite characteristics: illnesses that took months, if not years, to develop, and were more chronic than crisis-driven. These included catarrh—a swelling of the throat and other mucous membranes—and consumption, later labeled pulmonary tuberculosis. But most prevalent were "inflammatory complaints," which meant reddening, soreness, and swelling of the soft tissues. It usually struck first in the hands and knees, but could manifest in any part of the body. The catchall term was rheumatism.

Today rheumatism, and particularly arthritis (a rheumatism of the joints), is widely perceived as a sign of aging. But in the Royal Navy of 1805, it was predominantly a young man's illness. Turnbull noted that it "generally attacks the younger part of the crew, or all those whose ages do not exceed thirty-five years." He offered no explanation for this, but did speculate that the problem was not the cold so much as the wet. "A long train of rainy and stormy weather," he warned, "renders the body particularly liable to this form of the disease."

Hall and Holman could have provided Doctor Turnbull with a further insight: the young suffered the most because they were the most exposed to the elements. On every Royal Navy vessel, tradition dictated that the semi-sheltered "weather" half of the command deck—the side raised up by the tilt of the ship—was the exclusive province of the ship's elite. "No one but the captain, the lieutenants, the master, surgeon, pursers, and marine officer, is ever allowed, upon any occasion, to walk upon the weather side," noted Hall, adding that the restricted region was "certainly the most convenient to walk upon when the ship is pressed with sail; it is also the best sheltered from wind and rain." In contrast, the midshipmen "found themselves jammed imperiously over to the lee-side, to get drenched by the rain, and chilled by the wind out of the odious mizzen-staysail, the abomination of all poor middies!"

Those were their ordinary conditions. The midshipmen on prizemaster duty, Halifax-bound, had even less respite from the elements. Confiscated American merchant ships were smaller, with little shelter on either side of the mast. Most were built for fair-weather cruises in the southerly latitudes, not for the infamously thick Nova Scotia fogs, which Hall declared "even worse than rain, for they seem to wet one through sooner." It was somewhere in the expanse of New England and Nova Scotian waters, far from the sight of land, that Midshipman Holman began to feel a dull, deep aching in his joints.

It's almost certain that he mentioned it to no one. Rest, or even retreat from the elements, was not an option. There was no ship's doctor onboard. And back in sight of his superiors, in New

York Harbor and in Halifax, his strongest motivation was to project an image of rude health. The next phase of his career depended upon it.

PRIZEMASTER DUTY HAD one lasting side effect: it ruined a midshipman for midshipmen's work. It was hard to return to subservience after tasting command, and now that Holman was fulfilling his sixth year in the service, he would soon be eligible for his lieutenancy examination. But "passing for lieutenant" and actually obtaining a commission were two separate matters. Promotions were made only when vacancies arose within the squadron, and the choice was keyed not to seniority but to the whim of Vice Admiral Sir Andrew Mitchell, commander of the North American fleet. It was necessary to get noticed by Mitchell, so Holman campaigned for a reverse of his earlier reassignment: a transfer from a frigate back to an admiral's flagship. He rowed his belongings across New York Harbor to the *Leander* on April 16, 1805.

The *Leander* was no *Royal George*. It was only a little larger than the *Cambrian*, and crowded with midshipmen vying, in the words of one of them, "to get, if possible, directly under the shadow of the flag itself." Competition for Mitchell's favor was particularly pitched, because everyone knew that fresh rounds of commissions were imminent. Two months earlier, the *Leander* had recaptured the *Cleopatra*, a Royal Navy frigate earlier taken in battle off the coast of Bermuda by a French man-of-war.

The *Cleopatra* was a drifting hulk when they found her, with two of her three masts toppled and the bowsprit splintered into the sea. One quarter of her crew had died defending her, and although they'd fought a losing fight, they'd succeeded in damaging their attacker, the *Ville de Milan*—to the point that when the *Leander* happened upon them both, the French surrendered without firing a shot. Now both ships were undergoing repairs in Halifax, and crews would be appointed as soon as they were seaworthy. A few fortunate midshipmen, passed for lieutenant, were about to become officers in deed as well as name.

ON THE THIRD day of December, Holman walked into an Admiralty chamber in Halifax, trying hard to mask his nervousness. Adherence to protocol meant that he carried his cocked hat protectively, harbored in the curl of one arm. His other hand held a sheath of required papers: service records, certificates from past captains, and an affidavit that he "appears to be more than twenty one years of age." *Appears* was the loophole through which he hoped to squirm. He was eighteen.

Seated before him were Captain Beresford of the *Cambrian*, Captain Talbot of the *Leander*, and Captain Tyrell, soon to assume command of the *Ville de Milan*. As they bade him be seated, Holman understood why there was a term for this specific moment in a naval career. Old sea-hands called the lieutenant's examination "making buttons," because, under a salvo of questions from a chorus of captains, the natural reaction was to fret mightily with the numerous brass buttons of one's uniform.

As he struggled to summon the proper mix of composure and accuracy, he was bolstered by the knowledge that, should he pass, he had a ship awaiting him. Despite Holman's relatively short time aboard the flagship, Vice Admiral Mitchell had been sufficiently impressed with the youth to include him in the second tier of new assignments. The admiral's first-tier favorites got a coveted billet on the *Ville de Milan* (soon nicknamed the "Wheel 'em Along"), the new prize of the fleet. For Holman, Mitchell had in mind the smaller, salvaged *Cleopatra*. She needed a replacement for a lieutenant who had emerged from the losing battle with the *Milan* alive but "dangerously wounded" and unable to serve.

Two days later, Holman, clad in a new uniform, reported for duty as the *Cleopatra*'s new third lieutenant. To his new captain, John Wight, he presented a document attesting to his "Diligence,

Sobriety and obedience to Command," as well as his ability to "work a Ship in Sailing, shift his Tides, keep the reckoning of a ship's way by Plain Sailing and Mercator [and] observe by the Sun and Stars."

Those were the standard skills he'd demonstrated during his exam. Of more interest to Captain Wight was Holman's now-substantial intimacy with American coastal waters, as it was probably superior to his own. Wight was new to the station, having spent most of his career assigned not to a specific fleet but to the Transport Board, which ferried personnel and prisoners from one naval station to another.

THE WEATHER IN Halifax on the following day—the date of *Cleopatra*'s departure, and Holman's first full day as an officer—was well documented by a midshipman on a neighboring ship.

> *A fresh north-westerly wind, in a day so bitterly cold that the harbour was covered over with a vapour called "the Barber", a sort of low fog, which clings to the surface of the water, and sweeps along with these fierce winter blasts in such a manner as to cut one to the very bone. The Barber is evidently caused by a condensation of the moisture close to the water in this severe temperature. As the thermometer, when we sailed, stood at eleven degrees below zero, nothing but the violence of the wind, which broke the surface into a sheet of foam, prevented our being frozen up in the harbour.*

That night, the "Barber" ice-fog was more cuttingly frigid still. Until four in the morning, the lone figure on the *Cleopatra*'s windward deck was Holman, pacing out of nervousness, excitement, and a futile effort to keep warm. As third lieutenant it was his duty to stand the last watch, hailing the night lookouts every fifteen minutes, shouting out sail trim instructions, and conveying course corrections to the helm.

The ships sailed into a squall. For three unrelenting days, gale-force winds scattered the squadron over hundreds of miles. The *Cleopatra*, losing sight of the others, kept heading southeast out to sea, through sheets of rain that fell with stinging force. The new third lieutenant had an oilskin to place over his woolen watch cloak, but even this arrangement kept him far from dry. It was pointless to change clothing—a new outfit would be equally wet within minutes—nor could he go belowdecks to warm himself in the galley. That would be a dereliction of duty, and at any rate the rules of wartime dictated that the frigate's galley fires be extinguished at night, and not relit until dawn.

All he could do was wrap the collar higher around his throat, and wait for his body heat to warm the soaked wool against his skin. Still, exhilaration trumped misery. Holman was an officer at last, with the favor of his admiral and the trust of his captain. The storm blew straight in his face, but fortune seemed to be at his back. He would remember this time as "the very bloom" of his career.

It was the watch officer's prerogative to walk the weather deck alone. An attentive midshipman stationed on the opposite rail, looking on from a respectful distance, might have noticed that Lieutenant Holman had a slight stiffness to his step. Instead of striding fluidly he set his boots down heavily, as if to minimize the flexing of his ankles.

FIVE MONTHS LATER, Great Britain and the United States were a hairbreadth away from war, thanks to a misadventure of Holman's prior ships. Both the *Cambrian* and the *Leander* had returned to their old pacing grounds a few miles offshore New York Harbor, resuming their inspections with a heightened degree of scrutiny. Now they were not only inspecting holds, they were quizzing arrivals about any French ships they might have spotted at sea—information that the American captains were under no obligation to provide.

But the biggest rankling point was the stepped-up confiscation not of ships, but of men. Desperate to fill their ranks after decades of war, the Royal Navy was resorting to impressment, the forcible drafting of seamen who happened to be British citizens, regardless of the nationality of the ship they were found upon. These were often former Royal Navy men, either discharged or deserted, drawn to the American ships by better working conditions and pay that was often twice their Admiralty wages. American merchants were loath to see these experienced sailors marched aboard the British frigates, especially since many of the impressed men carried papers attesting that they were now naturalized American citizens.

The British usually ignored these papers, because many were patently forged—and because even if they were legitimate, His Majesty did not recognize the right of his subjects to renounce their citizenship. "Once an Englishman, always an Englishman" was the long-held policy, with the Revolutionary War standing as a single massive-scale exception. Growing numbers of Americans viewed these impressments as an assault on their young country's sovereignty. The fact that some of those swept up were native-born Americans or immigrants from other countries—men who had never been English by any definition—did not help matters.

The incident that tipped American sentiment decisively against the British came one April afternoon, when the *Cambrian* closed in on a cluster of merchant vessels approaching from the New Jersey shore. As was standard procedure, the frigate fired a gun to signal *prepare for boarding*, but this time only some of the vessels stopped their passage. The others kept on toward New York, so the *Leander* cracked on sail and gave chase. It took several warning shots to bring them all to a halt, but once inspections began, it became clear why they'd tried to run. At least two (one captained by a nephew of John Paul Jones) were guilty of breaking neutrality by carrying full cargoes of contraband from the West Indies. When the British boarded one of the smallest ships, the coasting sloop *Richard*, they found the body of the helmsman John Pierce. One of the *Leander*'s warning shots had accidentally found a target.

Pierce's body was soon ashore in New York City, where it happened to be an election day. Local politicians were already mobilizing voters in the usual fashion, with liberal quantities of liquor. The election crowds coalesced into an unruly, macabre parade with the corpse carried at the fore, angrily eulogized as an instant martyr. Both political parties, the Federalists and the Democrat-Republicans, found themselves temporarily united in outrage. The furor was such that within a week President Jefferson issued a Proclamation Against British Ships, declaring the captain of the *Leander* a murderer and calling for his arrest for "sundry trespasses, wrongs, and unlawful interruptions and vexations on trading vessels." Both ships were banned from American waters, as were any ships their captains might command in the future.

Such measures were politically opportunistic (Jefferson, a lifelong Francophile, had never been a fan of the British), but they accurately reflected the depth of enmity now crystallized by the death of Pierce. Even a quarter-century later, British sailors would return to New York to find "our good old ship the *Leander* . . . still held in detestation."

Jefferson's action had the effect of rendering the entire Royal Navy *non grata* in all the harbors of the American shore. The ships of the North American Squadron continued to enforce neutrality—it was too important a part of the war effort to abandon—but now they had to do so without touching port. The nearest landfall after Halifax was now Bermuda, not a naval station but a sparsely staffed supply base. The cruises of the *Cleopatra* became continuous loops, from Nova Scotia to tropical latitudes so hot that, at nighttime, the ship's candles began to melt even before they were lit. The passage from one extreme to the other was usually accomplished in about ten days of sailing, and the interval between cruises was either brief or nonexistent. The ship simply took on supplies and turned around, usually without dropping anchor.

THE TWINGES IN Lieutenant Holman's bones weren't going away. If anything, they seemed to be exacerbated by the constant shuttling between hot and cold climates. Little else could be expected, according to the medical wisdom of the day. One well-respected treatise, *Buchan's Domestic Medicine*, lay the blame for "very obstinate rheumatisms" on "sudden changes of the weather, and all quick transitions from heat to cold," going on to state that "the same effects are often produced by wet clothes [and] traveling in the night." This was practically a description of Holman, whose pain now seemed to manifest itself most strongly in the lower extremities, particularly in the ankles and feet.

In the earliest stages, this was easy enough to disguise. The pitch and yaw of the ship made unsteady gaits a part of daily life. A discreet clutch of railing hardly warranted notice. Holman, spending most of his waking hours alone and in darkness on the weather deck, seemed to have called little attention to himself, stoically enduring the progress of his affliction for several months.

It is hard to imagine him doing otherwise. A lieutenant aboard a frigate at sea placed himself on the sick list only under the most severe circumstances, as there was no replacement officer or means of bringing one aboard. The sick man's duties would have to be temporarily assumed by the two other lieutenants—or, worst of all, by the captain himself. It was a burden one did not place lightly upon one's fellow officers.

There is no better indicator of the extremity of his condition than Holman's frequent appearance, in late 1806, on the *Cleopatra*'s sick list. James Nesbitt, the ship's surgeon, noted "evident enlargement of the Heads of the Bones of the Ancle [sic]," to a degree that rendered the lieutenant incapable of even putting on his boots, much less hobbling about. Nor could he comfortably lie still. His condition had progressed to what *Buchan's* identified not just as "exquisite pains" but "lying pains, which are increased by the least motion." Even a hammock offered no respite from the constant rocking of the ship. Holman also admitted to other pains that shot through the rest of his body, but seemingly from no consistent source. They flared up haphazardly, although they seemed more prevalent on his right side than his left.

Nesbitt hesitated to offer up a definitive diagnosis. Holman's long exposure to the weather made acute rheumatism the obvious culprit, but that conclusion had one practical complication: almost none of the standard treatments for rheumatism could be applied at sea. *Buchan's* prescribed the usual regimen of leech-bleeding, but also horseback riding and a diet of fresh fruits and vegetables, specifically "stewed prunes, coddled apples, currants or gooseberries boiled in milk." At the very least, the patient should keep warm and dry, and drink copious quantities of wine-whey, fresh milk coagulated with a bit of wine.

At the time, the North American fleet was subsisting largely on a dish they called "the Old Thing," salt junk (pickled beef) in a thick wheat-and-water sauce that was somewhere between paste and dough. A standard breakfast was a single roll, tapped smartly to dislodge the weevils. Wine was aboard in quantities, but milk was a memory. Since there was little he could do to provide a more wholesome environment for his patient, Nesbitt chose another tack, treating the symptoms as "attacks of the Gout."

Holman was the antithesis of a likely candidate for gout. That condition usually struck the middle-aged, the sedentary and overweight, particularly those who overindulged in alcohol and rich foods. Holman's youth at sea had given him modest habits, and no chance to acquire a taste for high life. He cut a trim figure at 146 pounds, a weight that would hardly vary for most of his life. But gout was commonly marked by swollen feet, and the pain was characteristically severe. One sufferer of the time said it felt "as if I was walking on my eyeballs." *Buchan's* describes it, almost poetically, as "different kinds of torture, as if the part were stretched, burnt, squeezed, gnawed, or torn in pieces ... the part at length becomes so exquisitely sensible, that the patient cannot bear to have it touched, or even suffer any person to walk across the room."

Holman was beginning to fit this description. And conveniently, gout could be treated onboard the *Cleopatra* just as well as anywhere else, since the treatment consisted of little more than being left alone. Standard care was "a glass of generous wine," aside from which "there is little room for medicine during a regular fit of the gout." If the doctor was mercifully inclined, he might add thirty or forty drops of laudanum, liquid opium, to the wine.

As unlikely as the gout scenario was, Nesbitt had reason to congratulate himself. The enforced rest seemed to abate the swelling and bring new strength to his patient, who was soon not entirely cured, but anxious to put the entire episode behind him.

The length of his convalescence is not documented, but two things are clear: Holman recovered sufficiently to resume his duties as officer of the watch. And the recovery did not last.

IT BECAME A cycle of struggle. Holman kept to his night watches, hobbling about, bearing the rising pain until it could no longer be borne. Then he reported once again to Nesbitt, submitted to whatever treatment the surgeon wished to try this time, and rested until he could walk once more. By the spring of 1807, he was, according to Nesbitt, "repeatedly in the Sick List," and despite his best efforts to remain stoically dutiful, it was time to admit the obvious: he no longer belonged aboard the ship. The next time *Cleopatra* touched port in Halifax he was eased ashore, helped into a bed in the naval sick ward, and wished well by his now-former shipmates. By now his condition was grave enough to leave him there effectively immobilized for six straight weeks.

The desperate course of Holman's illness is summed up in a single physician's notation, written at the end of those six weeks:

He has latly [sic] been blistered and is now rather better.

Holman was now entirely in the realm of what was called "heroic medicine," a term that summoned shudders from those subjected to its principles. Heroic medicine did not seek to identify the malady or match it to a cure, but simply to force it out of the body via a fresh set of ordeals.

In 1807, most physicians were humorists. This meant they subscribed to the dogma of bodily humors, a notion little changed since the days of Hippocrates. There were supposedly four humors—phlegm, blood (including semen, seen as purified blood), yellow bile, and black bile—ethereal substances that could manifest themselves as fluids, but might also invisibly suffuse any part of the body.

Illness was only an imbalance of those humors' natural proportions, and heroic medicine an attempt to restore the balance using one of two techniques, Depletion or Disruption. Depletion was the process of systematically introducing deficits in each humor, in hopes that when the body restored itself, it would do so in new, proper proportions. Shedding blood required only a lancet or a leech, while expelling phlegm or the biles usually called for a draining procession through a spectrum of aperients (mild laxatives), purgatives (strong laxatives), clysters (enemas of liquid or smoke), and nauseants and vomitories (self-descriptive).

When those failed to work, the physicians moved on to Disruption. This was based on the belief that the "disorder" of the humors could only take one form at any given time—that the body could be tricked into forcing out one malady by introducing another. That was the point of blistering. Second-degree burns were inflicted on the skin, either with a hot poker, splashes of boiling water, or the application of acids, with every intention of causing violent pain. The body, it was postulated, would rush to heal the new affliction, "forgetting" the older one in the process.

In its brutal way, blistering worked—at least, it caused a lot of patients, like Holman, to announce themselves "rather better" and assure the physicians that no further treatment of the sort was necessary.

But brief rallying periods were not the same as genuine healing, a fact that Nesbitt had to face when he returned to the Halifax ward to look in on his charge. On June 20, he performed the last task he could for Holman. He convened a medical review board, consisting of himself and the surgeons of the *Milan* and the *Mermaid*, for the purpose of conducting "a strict and Careful Survey of the Person." After an examination, they jointly stated that the patient "in our opinion, will be subject to the same Complaint, on being exposed to Cold and Wet," and passed down a verdict of Unserviceable.

This was Holman's ticket home. The *Mermaid* was departing shortly for England, and there are indications that he was bundled hurriedly aboard. Exactly one month later, he was back in English waters, floating at anchor in sight of Portsmouth but trapped aboard the ship. His invalidation papers had gotten him on, but there were no arrangements for getting him off. He was compelled to write the Admiralty from his sick berth, "to request you will inform me whether I am to remain here [at] their Lordships' pleasure, or am at Liberty to go into the Country, for the restoration of my health."

Leave was granted, but once on land Holman found another, crucial loose end: he had dropped off the navy's payroll. Sick midshipmen were paid nothing. Invalided officers were entitled to draw half their normal salary, until discharge or return to duty. But he found, to his dismay, that his appointment to the *Cleopatra* had never been registered on the Naval Lists. He was, in the eyes of the Admiralty, an acting lieutenant, not a real one. No lieutenant's pay, or fraction thereof, would be forthcoming.

This was both a social and financial embarrassment to Holman.

It also at least partly hindered his hopes of a convalescence in the countryside, since eight months later he was living in temporary lodgings in London's bustling Piccadilly district, plaintively petitioning the Navy Pay Office for restoration of status and his missing wages. It was only when the matter was partly settled in his favor—he was given half-pay, but his official lieutenancy began in London, not Halifax—that he could give his full attention to the task of recuperation.

THE QUESTION WAS, recuperation from what? The three ship's surgeons had been required to append an official diagnosis to his invalidation papers, and they had settled on *Diseas'd ancle joint and flying Gout*. It was difficult to determine a course of action from this, as it essentially meant nothing. A "flying gout" only described a pain that obstinately refused to stay in one place, but instead "flew" about the body. The poet Robert Burns had cold saltwater baths prescribed for his flying gout, and consequently died soon after taking up daily plunges into the sea. In contrast King George III, in the throes of what his physicians believed was a flying gout that had started in his feet and "had flown to his brain and lodged there," was kept indoors as much as possible. Other sufferers took the mineral waters at Bath, or devoted themselves to self-administered quantities of red wine. Madeira was thought to be particularly therapeutic.

Whatever treatment, or series of treatments, Holman pursued, he pursued in a hurry. His post on the *Cleopatra* was lost for good, but there was still the chance he could resume his career without a major stigma attaching to him—if he recovered quickly enough to mark the illness as a single episode, decisively overcome. Within weeks of settling his status with the Admiralty, he was already looking for a new ship.

Circumstances clearly called for a fresh start. With the doctors' warning against re-exposure to "the Cold and Wet," Holman would likely have had little trouble obtaining a new assignment to a warmer climate. Moreover, his patronage had already all but disappeared. Admiral Mitchell had died soon after signing Holman's commission, and the new admiral had his own cadre of favorites. Captain Wight had transferred off the *Cleopatra* after only a few months at the helm, and his replacement, Captain Simpson, knew Holman primarily as a struggling invalid. From both medical and political standpoints, there was little reason to return. But North American waters were the ones he knew best, and that experience might balance the blot upon his record. There was also the personal triumph that could only come from picking up where he left off.

Holman's brother Samuel, his army career truncated by the change in family fortunes following their eldest brother's death, was now working as a victualling officer at the naval shipyards in Chatham, thirty miles southeast of London. He was well positioned to inform his brother about vacancies arising on the ships stationed there for repairs. The most enticing of these was the *Guerriere*, a prize of war captured two years earlier off the Faroe Islands near Greenland. The name was kept as a taunt to the French, but the ship was being refitted with an impressive set of English guns. It was bound for the North American station, where it would take its place as one of the most powerful ships in the fleet.

Its new captain was Alexander Skene, a Scotsman made wealthy a few years earlier by the fortunate capture of a particularly rich French merchant ship. His previous command was on the Ireland station, however he was unfamiliar with New World waters, and the subtleties of dealing with thorny Americans.

Skene was no doubt made acquainted with Holman's deeply relevant expertise. It is not to be expected that he was equally enlightened about the lieutenant's recent medical misadventures, but he may have learned about them anyway, or they may have been apparent from Holman's physical appearance. The details of the lieutenant's campaign to wrangle a post on the *Guerriere* have not been recorded, but the end result is clear. When the ship sailed for Halifax by way of Jamaica in the early weeks of 1808, Holman was not onboard.

This was a blow, not only to his pride but his pocketbook. The ship proved lucky on its maiden voyage, vanquishing two French privateers and freeing a captured British merchant. Holman, stuck in London, still convalescing but convinced of his readiness to serve, could only have winced when the details emerged in the *Naval Chronicle*. As a midshipman his share of prize money had been nominal—an odd pound or two—but as a lieutenant he was entitled to approximately two percent of the proceeds from such captures. Depending on the market value of the privateers' cargo, that sliver of this single run of good fortune could equal several years' salary.

A fresh and fleet ship, with a captain already rich on prize money and now enriching his crew, barreling through what Holman now considered his home waters. There was no place he more fervently wished to be.

It's easy to imagine his jubilation that autumn, when a post from the Admiralty brought the most welcome news possible: a lieutenant's berth had come open on *Guerriere*, and Captain Skene was holding the post open for him. October found him scrambling to hitch a ride on the HMS *Comet*, hurrying to Halifax as quickly as possible, only to wait another two months for the *Guerriere* to complete its patrol and make port. The ambitious young man joined his formidable new ship in January 1809—the height of winter, and prime Barber weather. As the least senior officer, it was once again his duty to stand the coldest watches of the night.

THE WAR WAS elsewhere. The American shore was off-limits, and given the widest of berths. Holman's world was once again reduced to a featureless horizon and endless pitching, frigid seas. In time, despite his best show of stoicism, the old complaints began to reassert themselves. Before the year was out, he was compelled to report yet again to the ships' surgeon. The cycle of bloodletting, purgations, and blistering began anew.

By 1810 he was once more confined to a bed in the naval hospital at Halifax, the subject of still another medical board of review. The proceedings of this second examination have not been preserved, but the tenor of their diagnosis can be discerned from Captain Skene's subsequent action. Lieutenant Holman was formally removed from the ship's complement, and a new lieutenant registered in his place.

Two months later, he was back in England, pursuing a cure even more strenuously than before. He knew that his prospects of future employment on the North American station were virtually nil—indeed, a captain on any station known for extremes of weather would likely be reluctant to take him on. But the Mediterranean or Channel fleets were still possible, given a quick enough recuperation. This time he took up residence in Bath, the venerable spa city on the River Avon in western England.

A pilgrimage for the infirm since Roman days, and a fashionable resort since the 1700s, Bath was not only a source of soothing mineral waters. It was also one of the epicenters of Regency culture, renowned as a place where social distinctions were slightly blurred. Class barriers were still firmly in place—tradesmen would not mingle with gentlemen, of course. But a well-spoken, well-mannered lieutenant might find himself in the relaxed company of captains, perhaps even an admiral or two.

Joining the ranks of Bath's convivial convalescents could inestimably enhance one's career. If Holman could recuperate and revive his career, there was also the possibility of making a suitable match with a young woman from a good family; the town was crowded with marriageable daughters and chaperoning parents. Holman would be an attractive matrimonial prospect: he was twenty-five, a man of the world (or at least a man of the open sea), who had made the most of the opportunities handed him in life.

He was, as he would later describe, "in the very height of expectation." True, he was an invalid officer without a ship, drawing half-pay. But Horatio Nelson had been in identical straits in 1781, when he retreated to Bath to shake off the "exceeding ill health" that had plagued him during his own service on the North American station.

Holman could not afford the cachet that came with staying in the finer hotels, but he had the face-saving option of staying with friends. A further economy was the green, steaming water itself. He could choke down draughts of it for free (Dickens would later describe the taste as a "strong flavour o' warm flat-irons") or, clad in the requisite bathers' uniform of white cotton drawers and a smock, float in it all day for the cost of a few shillings.

Happily, his stiff-swollen joints responded well. His strength and range of motion began to improve. He would henceforth consider himself a connoisseur of mineral waters, not only eagerly soaking in them but analyzing their chemical constituents, trying to better understand their soothing properties. There was every reason to look forward to a second recovery, a renewed profession, and better times ahead.

Then he discovered a new kind of pain.

CLEAR EYESIGHT IS a requirement for every Royal Navy lieutenant. Holman had experienced no prior problems with his vision—had never even required spectacles—yet on an otherwise ordinary day he found himself cupping his face in his hands, struggling to maintain his composure. Something was wrong with his eyes.

It was likely first thought to be an infection of some sort, contracted in the communal waters—an all-too-common scenario, given the absence of segregation between the openly diseased and the merely infirm. But infection almost always manifests in an unsightly fashion, transforming the eye into a bloodshot mess, either predominantly pink or solidly red. Holman's condition seemed not external to the eyes but internal. There were many doctors on hand, but all they could confirm were the symptoms of ophthalmia—another medical catchall, meaning simply *inflammation of the eye.*

What nature wishes us to guard with care, it wreathes abundantly in pain receptors. The delicate, vulnerable tissue of the eye is no exception. It is crowded with nerve endings, and responds with acute sensitivity to pressure. When that pressure arises from within the eye itself, the pain is diffuse, profoundly deep and impossible to relieve. For reasons no one could quite explain, Holman's eyes were rapidly, agonizingly, increasing in internal tension.

The affliction progressed rapidly. Soon he was lying in a darkened room, his face swaddled in cold compresses, trying hard to "quiet" his eyes by keeping them closed, or focused only on stationary objects. "Some hope was entertained that his sight would be preserved," says one account, "but that hope gradually gave way under the painful progress of the terrible malady."

Within a short time—weeks, if not days—it was no longer necessary to darken the room. He was completely blind.

FOUR

Nor Sun Nor Moon

IT WAS A curious phenomenon. There were no signs of external damage, no visible changes to the eyes themselves, nothing beyond his attestations that they simply no longer worked.

Even years later, words failed Holman. "It is impossible to describe the state of my mind at the prospect of losing my sight," was all he would say about those first days of darkness. His one surviving comment on the trauma is written, uncharacteristically, in the third person, reading more like an obituary than an autobiographical passage:

> It is sufficient to say, that at the age of twenty-five . . . his prospects were irrecoverably blighted by the effects of an illness, resulting from his professional duties, and which left him deprived of all the advantages of "heaven's prime decree"—wholly—and, he fears, permanently blind.

Holman had a habit of concealing his most profound emotions in sidelong literary allusions. "Heaven's prime decree" was a quote from John Milton's *Samson Agonistes*, in which the newly blinded Samson bewails his exclusion from God's first command: *"Let there be light."*

The permanence of the condition was not yet a certainty. After all, his rheumatic pains had waxed and waned. Perhaps this was

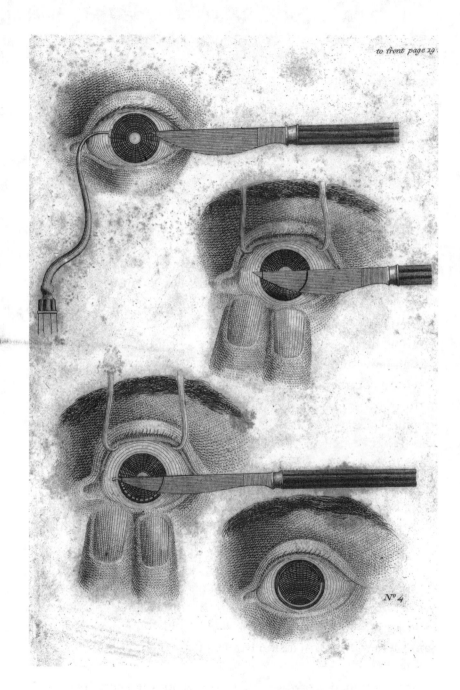

Optical prods, clamps, and scalpels, circa 1811.

yet another symptom of duty-related exhaustion, something to be washed away with still more rounds of the baths at Bath. More optimistically, the blindness might even be a positive sign, a disturbing but transitory indicator of healing. *Buchan's Domestic Medicine*, one of the most respected and bestselling medical texts of the day, attributed extreme ophthalmia to, among other things, "the stoppage of customary evacuations; as the healing of old sores, drying up of issues, the suppressing of gentle morning sweats, or of sweating of the feet."

But *Buchan's* also warned that "this is one of those diseases wherein great hurt is often done by external applications. Almost every person pretends to be possessed of a remedy." Bath was home to the greatest concentration of medical men in Britain, most of whom routinely touted miraculous cures. As the weeks went by and the blindness persisted, Holman subjected himself to a procession of such treatments. The common first course of action in such cases was already grimly familiar to him: leeches and bleeding.

Standard practice was to inflict them as close to the site of the affliction as possible. Leeches were applied directly under the eyes and on the temples. ("The wounds must be suffered to bleed for some hours . . . it will be necessary to repeat this operation several times.") Lancet-induced bleeding, incredibly enough, targeted the neck. ("An adult may lose ten or twelve ounces of blood from the jugular vein, and the operation may be repeated according to the urgency of the symptoms.")

Less bloody but more painful was the installation of a seton, a thin strip of foreign matter—usually linen, horsehair, or silk—threaded underneath the surface of the skin and left in place. This was inserted vertically, between the shoulder blades and near the base of the neck, to draw down the head's malignant humors, like an inverted wick. Setons were, of course, a regular source of infection, exacerbated by the usual dressing of yellow basilicon, a profoundly septic mix of lard, wax, resin, pitch, and olive oil.

Only slightly more benign were the poultices and ointments applied directly to the eyes themselves. Paste of bread and milk, soggy with sweet oil. Diluted brandy. Diluted vinegar. Mutton suet and camphor. The searing concoction Collyrium of Lead, ammonium chloride and "sugar of lead" (lead acetate), made bearable by the addition of forty or fifty drops of tincture of opium. Other methodologies, all perfectly respectable: shaving the head three times a week, then dunking the newly shorn scalp into cold water. Doses of *aethiops mineral*, a condensation of mercury and sulphur that stained the teeth and tongue quite black. It was later recognized as a pigmenting agent for rubber, and a potent poison.

THERE IS NO record of the specific treatments endured by Holman, nor their sequence. We do know that he stopped short of being "electrified," a technique employing state-of-the-art medical technology, in which "a strong stream of the electric fluid was . . . applied to the eyes, and continued for about ten minutes or a quarter of an hour." Not small shocks but a continuous surge of voltage, kept below the threshold of electrocution only by the crudity of generating mechanisms. The process was torturous, but not without attributed successes. Holman's forgoing of it was more likely a lack of funds than of courage.

He soon found it prudent to withdraw from Bath. The waters still soothed, but he was mindful of his meager finances and unwilling to wear out his welcome. It was one thing to be an ailing houseguest, another to be a completely helpless one. There was a further benefit to quitting the town: it stopped the wagging of tongues.

In Bath's intricate society of the sick, an officer with service-related pains was a sympathetic, even dashing figure. But there was a stigma attached to blindness in a young man. It was a common marker of late-stage venereal disease, and as such readily recognized as unmistakable proof of divine retribution against sin. In the book of Leviticus, God's threat to transgressors is quite specific:

I also will do this unto you; I will even appoint over you terror, con-
sumption, and the burning ague, that shall consume the eyes, and
cause sorrow of heart.

Holman had no other outward signs, no suppurations, boils, buboes, or gleet, but syphilis could manifest itself without them. Until the discovery of a definite diagnosis—or, better yet, a cure—circumstances seemed to call for a tactful retreat from public convalescence. He went home. Exeter offered the insulative comforts of family, the informed medical advice of his apothecary-surgeon father, and proximity to a sea spa, Jefford's Baths, in the fashionable coastal hamlet of Lyme Regis, twenty-five miles distant.

Providentially, Exeter was also one of the few places in the world where a new approach to the treatment of eye diseases was taking hold. Only three years earlier, the West of England Eye Infirmary had opened on Holloway Street, right on Holman's childhood route from shop to school. It was the first such specialized hospital outside of London, a pioneering outpost in the slow but accelerating process of stripping centuries of quackery from ophthalmic medicine.

IN 1811, EVEN the most enlightened medical professional knew no more about the eye than might a curious butcher. It was an orb with a single nerve disappearing into the gray depths of the brain. Slice one in half and you'd find three nested pockets of slightly different kinds of transparent substances, which were, of course, labeled "humors." Directly beneath the cornea, the touchable outer window, was the aqueous humor, a thin, waterlike fluid. Under that was the crystalline humor, more solid but pliable, intriguingly shaped like a lens. Beneath that, plumping out the rest of the sphere, was a gelatinous goo dubbed the vitreous humor.

Most everything else was a mystery. Were these humors three aspects of a single substance? Did the crystalline purify, magnify, or condense the streamed-in light? What made the pupil expand and contract? None of these questions could be answered. Nor was there even a rudimentary reply to the biggest question of all: how does an eye work? The lens seemed to direct the light to the orb's back wall, but how that translated into vision was anyone's guess. The network of tiny retinal rod- and cone-shaped light receptors would not be discovered until 1834, when the microscope was first used to systematically explore the eye's interior.

Blindness, then, was understood purely as an obstruction to the stream of light. If the cornea itself was not scratched or otherwise damaged, the inevitable conclusion was that one of the three humors had lost its transparency. Cataracts, the most common visual impairment, were easy to diagnose—a simple close-up examination usually revealed the crystalline middle humor clouding toward opacity. Cataracts were easy enough to treat, too. The time-tested method was called *couching*, a procedure far less comfortable than its name implies. Still practiced today in impoverished and isolated areas, couching is unchanged from Aulus Cornelius Celsus's description of it, circa A.D. 30:

> *Thereupon a needle is to be taken pointed enough to penetrate, yet not too fine; and this is to be inserted straight through . . . The needle should not be, however, entered timidly, for it passes into the empty space . . . When the cataract has passed below the pupil it is pressed upon most firmly in order that it may settle below. If it sticks there the cure is accomplished.*

The couching implement is indeed "not too fine"—it is typically more of a slender spike than a true needle. It is thrust directly into the pupil with considerable force, for the point of the blow is to detach the lens entirely. Otherwise multiple proddings are needed, severing the lens into smaller pieces, then coaxing those pieces to fall into the darkness of the vitreous humor.

In fortunate cases, the puncture wound heals. The remains of the crystalline humor are reabsorbed, and a sort of sight is restored. Spectacles can sometimes compensate for the lack of an organic lens. In more unfortunate cases the end result is grim: loss of the eye, infection, death. For centuries it was one of humanity's most common surgeries, as likely to be administered by an apothecary or traveling oculist as by a physician.

THAT HOLMAN, AN apothecary's son, avoided such willful mutilations was likely to the credit of the West of England Eye Infirmary and Dr. Samuel Barnes, its brand-new chief physician. Barnes, an Exeter native just two years older than Holman, had assumed the post only a few months previously. His predecessor had accidentally slipped his scalpel while conducting an autopsy, and subsequently died of the self-inflicted wound. The Barneses were as well-known a local family as the Holmans: his father was the Reverend Ralph Barnes, resident canon of the cathedral, nick-named with some justice "Old Ugly." The two native sons were likely lifetime acquaintances, if not friends

Barnes was already considered one of the most gifted surgeons in England— except when it came to cataracts. In that regard, he was a throwback. Other practitioners at the infirmary had achieved years of remarkable results with a scalpel-based tech-nique, removing the lens rather than punching it to pieces. But for obscure reasons, Barnes had reinstated old-fashioned couching.

It was an eccentricity that puzzled even his own patients. One, an elderly Quaker woman, quipped that she could have achieved a similar result by stabbing herself with her own knitting needles.

Barnes was quirky but conscientious, and the final mark of his skill was that, in Holman's case, he chose to wield neither the scalpel nor the spike. Other surgeons might have removed the lens (and most couching oculists certainly wouldn't have hesi-tated), but Barnes resisted the temptation. He could see nothing wrong, and he had the presence of mind to consider that perhaps there *was* nothing physically wrong. What had to be weighed and quietly discussed (probably outside the hearing of Holman himself) was the possibility that this sightlessness was a manifestation of the mind alone.

It wasn't an unknown occurrence. In fact, most of Europe was thoroughly familiar with the notion that blindness could be not only transitory, but seemingly conditional upon emotion. The well-known case of Maria Theresia von Paradis had made that clear. She was a teenage musical prodigy (Mozart, Haydn, and Salieri all composed piano concertos for her) supposedly "cured" of her blindness in 1777 by Franz Anton Mesmer, the charismatic hypnotist who gave language the terms "animal magnetism" and "mesmerizing."

Having regained at seventeen the sight she'd lost mysteriously as a three-year-old, von Paradis proved not to be entirely thankful. She found the visual world disorientingly strange. Upon first seeing a face she squealed out, "That is terrible to behold! Is that the form of a human being?" Almost all spatial relations confused her: she'd pick up a biscuit, then refuse to eat it since the act of drawing it toward her mouth had made it grow unappetizingly large. Worse yet, her virtuosity at the keyboard was gone. She could still play, but the assuredness and grace had flown from her hands.

The cure did not last. After a few emotionally turbulent weeks, highlighted by an unseemly personal attachment to Mesmer, von Paradis awoke to find her sight once again snuffed out like a candle flame. To her private happiness, she never saw again—or, at the very least, she managed to suppress future episodes of sight. Her musical gifts soon returned, and she lived a long and busy life, writing operas, opening a music school, and performing widely to great acclaim.

Holman knew, if not the specifics of the case, at least the spirit in which it was remembered. His old disgraced mentor Laurence Hynes Halloran had parodied it in one of his most famous poems, *Animal Magnetism, or The Pseudo-Philosopher Baffled*:

At length enraged, his basilisk-like eyes
He rivets fast upon her orbs of sight:
With greater vehemence he tries,
And pegs her stomach with augmented might.

ONE HALLMARK OF early-nineteenth-century medicine is the abundance of catchall quasi-diagnostic language, terms that, like "flying gout," do not dispel the mysterious so much as encapsulate it. The broad clinical appellation for cases like von Paradis' was *amaurosis*, which meant only blindness with no clear physical cause. When Doctor Barnes grew convinced that the level-headed Lieutenant Holman's affliction was not *amaurosis nervosa* (i.e., psychological), the next culprit to be considered was naturally *amaurosis gutta serena*. This condition's most famous sufferer was John Milton, the towering poetic presence of the seventeenth century. In fact, it was seen as the impetus for his becoming a poet in the first place.

John Milton had reached middle age with no literary ambitions whatsoever. He was a political activist armed with a quill, a pamphleteer thrown into prison for controversial essays advocating divorce, church reform, and regicide. When struck blind in his forties (much to the glee of his enemies), he was compelled to dictate verse to his daughters as a means of making a living. He was describing himself in the third book of *Paradise Lost,* when he wrote:

Revisit'st not these eyes, that rowls in vain
To find thy piercing ray, and find no dawn;
So thick a drop serene hath quenched their orbs

Gutta serena means "drop serene." It was not a figure of poetry but of medicine, understood as a real yet unseen entity. The depths of the interocular fluid were, to the examiner's gaze, impenetrably dark (ophthalmoscopes were not invented until 1851). If sight failed, the thinking went, it must be due to an obstruction hidden deep within the eye itself. Unfortunately, such obstructions proved impossible to locate—not even autopsies of the deceased blind could produce them. So the theory arose of a crystallized "drop" of aqueous humor, perching serenely on the optic nerve, untreatable and ephemeral. The Drop Serene, the doctors presumed, evaporated upon death.

Holman's symptoms were similar to the famous earlier case, but ultimately *gutta serena* was ruled out. Milton's loss of sight had not been sudden but gradual, over a span of years. While medical imagination granted aqueous humor the ability to solidify, Doctor Barnes was not ready to assert that it could do so quickly enough to explain the rapid onset of this particular blindness.

UNCERTAINTY IS ITSELF an affliction. His eyes had failed at the height of summer. By the beginning of spring Holman was desperate, not for a cure so much as a means to rationally comprehend what was happening to him. "The suspense which I suffered, during the period when my medical friends were uncertain of the issue," he would remember, "appeared to me a greater misery than the final knowledge of the calamity itself."

Should he keep faith that his sight might return? Might it be restored, if not by an immediate operation then by an eventual one? "At last I entreated them to be explicit, and to let me know the worst, as that could be more easily endured than the agonies of doubt."

An answer was crafted, perhaps more out of kindness than conviction. It was a poignant balance of hope and nonsense. "Namely, that a cataract existed, but not sufficiently matured, to be operated upon with advantage for the present." In other words: yes, your sight might eventually return. Yes, surgery might help—in the future, perhaps.

To a man not starved for an answer it was a ramshackle assessment, easy enough to demolish with a few salvos of logic. How could his cataracts be substantial enough to leave him in absolute blackness —yet be "not sufficiently matured" for the scalpel? Since when did cataracts suddenly and simultaneously attack both eyes with equal virulence? Why were these cataracts invisible? But Holman had no taste for such questions.

When there was nothing to be done, the medical humorists had a clinical term for doing nothing. They called it *coction*. During coction, the body pursued its own course of "preparing to expel" the disordered humors. It was considered risky, if not foolhardy, to intervene before the process was ended, before the body was ready to let go of its illness.

Holman was prescribed nothing but coction. Perhaps for another season or two, perhaps for the rest of his life. As meaningless as this diagnosis was, Holman took comfort in the certainty with which it was delivered. "Their answer, instead of increasing my uneasiness, dispelled it," he would remember. "I felt a comparative relief in being no longer deceived by false hopes."

It was time to learn how to be blind.

CONTRARY TO POPULAR conception, the remaining senses of a blinded person do not become more acute. They become more eloquent. A blind man hears no better than he did when sighted; the change is wrought in his ability to extract new meanings from familiar sounds. Touch is not increased, but its role is heightened. It is called upon for more than the blunt confirmation of contact. The shift from raw sensation to refined perception arises from a cultivation of attention.

Once hope of a cure is extinguished in the newly blind adult, there is typically a period of self-mourning, in which the individual retreats from ordinary interaction. Often they speak little, respond tersely if at all to questions, and spend long hours sitting almost motionless. It is an insulative emotional mechanism, an understandable grief response to a profound loss, but also an unconscious ritual of passage. As one researcher puts it, "The adjustments that need to be made are so far-reaching that the blind person is a different individual from the sighted person he or she once was: in a way, the sighted person has 'died,' to be reborn as a blind person."

This self-mourning is a signpost of shock and depression, but also a kind of beginning. In the self-imposed silence and stillness, a new way of comprehending the world begins to unfold.

Vision is an indiscriminate, almost greedily swift way of acquiring knowledge. The eye takes in everything in a single gulp—size, shape, position, texture, composition, color. It leaps about, flickering its gaze from your hand to a random corner to the view out the window then back, all in a fraction of a second. The mind patchworks these dartings together into a precise, continuously updated spatial map, one that allows for rapid, assured movement through the assembled landscape.

No doubt this sight-centric consciousness developed as a crucial survival characteristic for our species, but it is not without its drawbacks. Our focus wanders to the bright and vivid. Our assessment of an object is skewed toward the portion facing us. And the spatial map that seems to orient us so firmly is, in reality, a thin thread, which disappears the instant sight is obscured.

IF YOU ARE sighted and wish to experience the limitations of sight-centrism, sit down in your most familiar chair, in your most familiar room. Pick an object across the room, and stare at it as long as you like. Do your best to fix it in your memory. Then close your eyes, rise, and walk toward it.

Chances are your first two or three steps will be natural and confident, but by the fourth or fifth, a certain apprehension will suddenly set in. By the sixth or seventh, your focus shifts from progress to protection; is a forgotten piece of furniture lurking at shin height? Your hands splay out at arm's length, ready to touch a wall or interrupt a fall. Perhaps you can fight the impulse to open your eyes long enough to reach the vicinity of your target object. If you actually succeed in touching it, your motions arise more out of a tentative clambering than a true sense of location. If you're honest with yourself, you may acknowledge at least the slight presence of panic.

No matter how intimately familiar you are with the room— whether you've occupied it for a month or a lifetime—the results will be the same. That's because your visual spatial map begins to degrade with your first step, and in the absence of new data soon becomes useless. It appears to be enduring, but is, in fact, a repeated ephemerality, persistent only because it is continuously updated. Like the screen display of a computer, it needs constant refreshing— pull the plug and it disappears into darkness.

That mild panic, by the way, is a common source of misguided pity for the blind. The notion is that they spend their lives in that uncertain, unsettling state.

They do not. Touch-based understanding, or *haptic* perception, is quantitatively different. Where vision gulps, tactility sips. In the haptic world, an object yields up its qualities not all at once, at the speed of light, but successively over time, and in sequence of necessity. It is not a flash but a process, like the procession from rough sketch to finished portrait.

A blind visitor to your familiar room would probably approach orientation from the bottom up. The floor itself is the first demarcation: where are the surface transitions, the steps and carpet edges? Then the obstacles are blocked out; their precise shape is of less concern than their solidity and permanence. The ones that seem to stay put are recruited as landmarks. Then zones of uncertainty are identified—the variable placement of chairs around a table, or a door that might swing into an arc of random positions. Everything is then connected by the process of physical motion: the movement of one's own body from point to point. Distance is understood not as empty air but as a series of paces and turns. With practice, these are not counted, simply internalized, like dance steps. The blind choreograph their world.

Other details, such as the fabrics of the furniture, the items on the shelves, are filled in at leisure. It takes a little longer to compile— say, five minutes instead of five seconds—but once created, this mind's-eye map takes on a richness quite unlike its visual analog, particularly when sensory input begins to augment and intertwine with haptic knowledge. The presence of windows (and something of the weather) is discerned from the beams of sunlight heating your arm. Those windows are easy enough to locate, even without touching. The sounds of the neighborhood are concentrated through them. The scent of furniture polish announces the table. With time and experience, these coalesce into a well-honed sense of place, far removed from the stumbling uncertainty imagined by the sighted.

In truth, the haptic world is far more varied, and therefore more potentially overwhelming, than the visual one. The bricks of a wall may be painted one color and thereby seen as a unit, but to the blind they are a collection of textures, each unique. A box may look uniform on all sides, but the wood of each cannot be identically grained. And then there are the attributes the sight-centric so often overlook—patinas of dust and grime, the smoothworn of the familiar, any of a myriad other marks of time and use. The newly blind must learn to parse them all.

When it came to acquiring and honing these skills, and piecing together a life afterward, Holman was very much on his own. There were precious few sources for education and support of the blind, and from the standpoint of personal and familial dignity, applying for them was unthinkable. Which was moot, since he was ineligible for them all.

THE WORLD'S FIRST school for the blind was France's Institution Nationale des Jeunes Aveugles, founded in the year of Holman's birth by a man named Valentin Haüy. He'd been moved to action during a visit to the fair of Saint Ovid in Paris, which had a popular attraction: a band of blind men, rounded up off the streets and fitted out as ridiculously as possible with donkeys' ears, peacock feathers, and enormous pasteboard parodies of eyeglasses. The improvised troupe was set on stage with scanty rehearsal and the thinnest pretext of a script. In reality, the entertainment was in watching the performance go wrong.

The crowds laughed themselves hoarse. But Haüy was moved to pity, not by their blindness but by the fact that the troupers were genuinely grateful for the employment. With a few notable exceptions, such as musicians like von Paradis (who came from a wealthy family), the blind were considered suited for little more than rattling a cup at a crossroads. Education—social, vocational, or intellectual—was not wasted on them.

Haüy's school taught simple self-functioning—walking, cleaning, and dressing oneself, navigating stairways and streets. Then it coached habits that made the blind more palatable to the sighted: an upright posture, a composed face (the blind, forgetting or never knowing the niceties of appearance, often settled into protective hunches, and slacked or screwed their features into unsettling expressions). Finally, a trade was introduced, usually a light handicraft like mattress-stuffing or broom-making for the men, brushmaking and knitting for the women.

Reading was not taught. There were a few experiments made in producing books for the blind, usually a series of embossed letters on metal plate, but they were eventually abandoned as impractical (Louis Braille, the institute's most famous student, would not perfect his system until 1829). There were no experiments in teaching them how to write.

England's first school for the blind opened in Liverpool in 1791, operating on the same general principles. It was founded by Edward Rushton, a former sailor, himself blinded by a case of infectious ophthalmia contracted, he believed, from a cargo of slaves he'd been transporting in the West Indies. The concept spread slowly. By 1811, there were only four schools for the blind in all England. All were modest, filled to capacity, wholly reliant on charity, and primarily concerned with those blinded from birth or early youth. Male students were ushered out of the facilities at the age of twenty-five—Holman's age—and expected to shift for themselves. The females were cloistered for life, sheltered from the outside world in fears they'd fall victim to exploitation, sexual and otherwise. Any suitors were met with extreme suspicion by the administrators, who viewed their charges as permanently naive and innocent. A blind woman could expect to be treated like a young girl for her entire life.

Emotional attachments between blind men and women—a natural occurrence, given that they grew up together—were not just discouraged, they were squelched with such vehemence they became a virtual taboo. Conventional wisdom considered intermarriage of the blind "always a calamity," as two helpless people could not possibly help each other. There was also the persistent belief that any child from such a union was destined to be born blind, regardless of whether the parents' own blindness was congenital or accidental.

Even if they had mastered a trade, the men's prospects were permanently dismal. As late as 1886, seventy-four years later, it was not uncommon to see them begging on the very steps of the institution they'd graduated from a few years earlier. Almost no one wanted to hire the blind. There was little need to do so, in an era of unregulated child labor and a surplus of ex-soldiers and sailors. And there was a longstanding social barrier that neither Haüy nor Rushton could demolish—the fact that most sighted people were unsettled by the presence of the blind.

As Dante acknowledged in his *Divine Comedy*, there was an abiding unease in the nonreciprocation of eye contact. In the thirteenth canto of the "Purgatory," the narrator encounters the Envious, who are punished by having their eyes sewn shut. He recoils not from the sight of them but from the fact that they cannot return his gaze:

Somehow it seemed to me a shameful act
to stare at others and remain unseen.

Dark-tinted spectacles, of the kind used by later generations of the blind to obligingly conceal their eyes, were not yet manufactured. When the blind had cause to interact socially with the sighted, it was not unusual for them to tie a cloth around their eyes—which was, of course, unsettling in its own way. Sir John Fielding (1721–1780), one of the few blind persons in English history to hold a position of any importance (he inherited command of London's first police force from his half-brother, the novelist Henry Fielding) improvised a headband out of black cloth, which he would pull down over his eyes for public appearances.

Such dignified blind were few and far between. More common were the street musicians, who learned not to display too much talent on their instruments (pity, not musical appreciation, gathered the most pennies in the cup.) Many took to churning a single tune on a hurdy gurdy all day long, a crude sonic advertisement: "Blind Man Here." For them, donations were an unspoken encouragement to move on, out of earshot.

Others adopted the pseudo-profession of Bible Man: memorizing passages from the Bible and orating them in public, but with the added show of pretending to read from the page. And then there were the tatterdemalions, blind men who called attention to their condition by intentionally dressing in bizarre, clashing colors and mismatched clothing. Green hose and a pink shirtwaist, buttons askew. A boot and a shoe.

It was not inconceivable that Holman would be forced to join their ranks. Abhorrent as the prospect was, even worse was the thought of remaining a burden to his family for the rest of his life. His two elder brothers were still serving in uniform, his parents still supporting three younger siblings, yet English law was clear on the matter: under the terms of the Poor Law Act of 1601, "the relatives of every poor, old, blind, lame and impotent person" were required to provide support for their incapacitated family members. If they were incapable of doing so, the responsibility then shifted—to the public embarrassment of the entire family—to the person's parish church. In Holman's case, that was Saint Petrock's in Exeter, just a few blocks up North Street from the apothecary. This was a prime reason why many of the impoverished blind were itinerant vagabonds. It was less humiliating to go elsewhere and beg than remain an obligatory strain on one's own community.

He was still a lieutenant on half-pay from the navy, but that could end at any moment. Half-pay was technically for those awaiting orders, ready and able to resume duty as soon as the need arose. Holman, like hundreds of other officers permanently unfit to serve, was extended this status as a polite fiction, but it was not a right and could be revoked without notice. There were no entitlements to disability, pensions, or any other form of compensation; the Admiralty only stipulated that "commission officers worn out or disabled in his Service, are considered as their cases may deserve and as his Majesty shall think fit."

Ironically, ordinary seamen were better insulated from infirmity and old age than their commanders. The noncommissioned could draw from a charity called the Chatham Chest, and, if lucky, find a berth at the sailors' old-age homes in Greenwich and Plymouth. Officers, who were expected to have independent resources, were simply declared "superannuated" and left to their own devices.

Holman knew he was superannuated in all but name, and that the fifty pounds a year he was drawing should be considered a temporary bureaucratic oversight. Yet he was not quite ready to begin memorizing the Bible, or misbuttoning his vest.

"The certainty that my case was beyond remedy," he would write, "determined me to seek, in some pursuit adapted to my new state of existence, a congenial field of employment and consolation." In Lyme Regis, in the midst of fashionable seashore vacationers, he remade himself as a most unusual sort of blind man.

•   •   •

HE DID NOT wear a rag around his eyes. Nor did he shirk from the gaze of others. When he ventured outdoors, he did so in full uniform, with as erect a bearing as his rheumatism would allow. After a few months, old acquaintances might have noticed that he was speaking more quietly—one of the hallmarks of someone trying very hard to listen. As he would later explain,

> *Others hear, but not as do the blind. He concentrates his very soul while he listens, and can detect the slightest variations, the finest fractional point of tone . . . they tell minutely all the alteration of welcome, of regard, of coldness, pleasure, pain, joy, reproof, and all that fill the measure of his misery or his mirth.*

Holman began to use his ears not only to read people, but to read the landscape. In this he was unusual, for while sound is crucial to the orientation of all blind, it rarely becomes the primary compensatory sense. Conventionally trained blind were (and still are) taught to rely most heavily on the sense of touch.

Then as now, a standard method for negotiating streets and unfamiliar rooms was to directly detect the presence of obstacles through "sweeping"—swinging a stick through the space ahead in a back-and-forth arc. The canes of the blind were not yet uniform in size, shape, or color, but, in most cases, they were not true canes, too slender and lightweight to bear much weight. Some, like Sir John Fielding, used a simple switch whittled from a tree branch. Others used reeds, or lengths of bamboo, usually cut long, to sternum or shoulder height.

Holman taught himself to navigate with an ordinary walking stick. It was approximately navel height, lathed out of hickory or a similarly sturdy wood, with an unadorned knob and a metal ferrule to keep the tip from splitting—in short, standard strolling equipment for gentlemen of the day. This may have been an effort to call as little attention to himself as possible, but it was a choice that fundamentally shaped his approach to the world.

Such a stick was fatiguingly heavy for constant sweeping. It was also stiff rather than flexible; hitting an object didn't send a gentle pressure to the user, but a solid jolt. Its shortness created a very abrupt field of warning, and Holman diminished that field further still by the way he held it, balanced like a paintbrush in the crook of his thumb and forefinger, not thrusted out with an overhand grip. Deployed in that fashion, a walking stick is good for limited sweeping purposes. But the metal ferrule can be easily bounced up and down, producing an authoritative series of taps. Holman was feeling his way through the streets of Lyme Regis, but, even more so, he was hearing his way.

IMAGINE YOURSELF WALKING through a dense wood, in the dead of a moonless night. You have no light, but you do have two pieces of flint you can strike together to make a spark. Can you navigate by sparklight? Given a great deal of alertness and attention, you can. Each flash penetrates only a few feet of the darkness surrounding you, and only for the briefest of moments, but that can be sufficient information to avoid a misstep, and keep you on the path until the next spark is struck.

A metallic click, like the tip of a walking stick, is the sonic equivalent of a spark. To the sighted it is only a quick burst of noise, but some blind people have learned to interpret it as a compressed definition of ambient space. Just as a chorister singing a single, reverberant note can convey the space of a cathedral, a landscape can be encapsulated in the scarcely perceptible echoes of a single click. And if the source of the sound is consistent, then the way it changes can be understood as dimensional information, even when it is only one part of a busy soundscape.

To the sight-centric, it can be difficult to believe that the blind can detect the presence of a wall, or the branch of an overhanging tree, by listening. It is, in truth, still something of a feat among the blind. But as the French essayist Denis Diderot observed in 1742, well-honed ears can render "The blind man . . . so sensitive to the least atmospheric change that he can distinguish between a street and a closed alley."

Holman's orientation skills progressed rapidly enough to set him venturing into the unfolding soundscape of the town. The streets were cobblestoned, full of clatters and cries, but even the most populated part of Lyme Regis would seem tranquil by modern standards. Horse-drawn vehicles were slowed in city limits to a walking pace, the better to share the streets with pushcart vendors, yoke-bearing milkmaids, and bundle-burdened laundresses and delivery boys.

Holman listened, and began to comprehend just how much could be discerned from what, to the sighted, registered only as a wash of noise. Even from a distance, a carriage made sounds distinct from that of a cart or wagon. They creaked on their springs differently when empty or full. The gait of the horses told if they were concluding a long journey or just starting out. Avoiding other pedestrians was easier than it would be in later centuries—all shoes were hard-soled, and audible. A woman's footsteps sounded different than a man's. Often a profession, or at least a social class, could be discerned in the choice of footwear. With practice, it wasn't hard to sense their approximate size and height. If he so wished, he could salute them in passing.

SOON, HOLMAN WAS an unusual blind man in another respect. He learned how to write.

In the era of featherquill pens, the act of writing required a number of skills. One began by carving the quill out of a raw feather, cutting and sharpening the nib point with a knife. If the inkwell needed replenishing, you crumbled off ink powder from a cake, diluting it to your preferred shade with water. A quill had no reservoir, so one needed to dip into the inkwell frequently—gently and deftly, lest the ink drib, drip, or splatter. Blotters soaked up the excess. The ink itself was quick to smear and slow to dry, so the final step was sprinkling on a fine dusting of sand, then tapping and blowing it off.

In his youth Holman had mastered almost perfect penmanship, but now he could not attempt the process without disaster. For the blind, quills meant indecipherable scrawls, alternately overthick with ink or quite invisible where (unbeknownst to them) the ink had run dry. Lines of script careened and crossed. Blots transferred from the paper to one's hands and face. The sand flew everywhere.

He surmounted all this with an impressive piece of new technology: a "writing machine" called the Noctograph. Invented just three years earlier by one Ralph Wedgewood, it was, as the name implies, a mechanism for writing in the dark. It was designed for military applications, for spying, or encampments near enemy lines, or any circumstances where lighting a candle to write a message could give oneself away. Holman appears to have been one of the very first to grasp its utility for the blind, and to purchase one for his personal daily use. He would become its most prominent user, even endorsing it in the pages of his books, but the device would never come into common use for either soldiers or the sightless.

The Noctograph had no moving parts. It was, in essence, a portable wooden frame with wires stretched across at horizontal intervals, with a handful of metal clips provided to attach sheets of paper underneath. The real technology lay in the special kind of paper it required, dubbed "carbonated paper" by the inventor. These were dark pages, blackened on one side with a dried coating of printer's ink. Instead of a quill the writer used a solid stylus, pressing down and relying on the guide wires for straight lines. The pressure transferred the dried ink onto a second page of normal paper, producing a mark that was fainter and grayer than liquid ink but nonetheless solid and unsmudged.

The Noctograph left no tactile cues, so Holman could not read his own writing. And, while legible, his script bore no relation to the swoops and flourishes of his previous fine hand. The letters were fat and rounded, with small ascenders and, because of the wires, no true descenders at all—a child's writing, but exactly straight across the page. His letter *t* was usually uncrossed, his letter *i* dotted only by an approximate stab, if at all. His punctuation was similarly speculative, the guide wires making commas in particular hard to create.

The writing machine was not strictly necessary. He could have, like most blind, relied on dictating to the sighted, with far more handsome results. But it was liberating to know that he could set down words whenever and wherever he chose. Professional scribes were commonplace, but he needed to keep his expenses to a bare minimum, and while he had no shortage of friends and relations to act as volunteer secretaries, he was loath to increase his reliance on anyone. As unorthodox as the Noctograph was, it got him closer to his goal of self-sufficiency.

By midsummer, his efforts to achieve that goal took on an even greater sense of urgency. England was, against its will and beyond its resources, now fighting two very different wars.

SEVEN YEARS EARLIER, Britain had sealed its domination of the seas by winning the Battle of Trafalgar. But, to their consternation, this did nothing to slow the rise of Napoleon. Always suspicious of his admirals and of naval warfare in general, he had responded to the defeat by simply abandoning sea-based strategies, concentrating on overland attacks instead. He'd conquered Spain, Saxony, Bavaria, Prussia, Poland, and now he was marching toward Russia. It was the largest nation in the world, but the general-turned-emperor was now leading the largest army in the world, and it was difficult to imagine that he would not succeed. "You will see that Napoleon stalks at a gigantic stride among the pygmy monarchs of Europe," wrote one American diplomat to another. "It is even an equal chance if Russia, after all her blustering, does not accede to his demands without striking a blow."

It was American confidence in France's eventual victory that prompted James Madison, the new president, to step up his rhetoric against British policing of the Atlantic. He issued an ultimatum: end the blockades and impressments, or else.

His calculation, that the British had no taste for escalating another fight, ultimately proved correct. The foreign ministry finally rescinded the marine policy, but only after considerable face-saving maneuvers and foot-dragging. Slightly too much foot-dragging. Just five days after they enacted the repeal, the news arrived: America had already declared war.

Diplomacy was moot. Anti-British sentiments were now so strong that not even President Madison could avert a fight, despite the fact that the enemy had capitulated even before being declared an enemy (a capitulation that was now revoked). In time, the war would be named, almost generically, the War of 1812—a misnomer, for it lasted thirty months, but accurate in its lack of attachment to a location or cause. Much of it would be waged in no particular place, on open waters and on barely charted territory, and for no clearly articulated reason other than to vent long-harbored antagonism toward the British. Some American politicians were already calling it the Second War of Independence.

It should have been Holman's war. Suddenly the North American station was not a neglected backwater, it was the front—in fact, the only naval front in the world, since Napoleon's policy of ignoring the sea had forced the other fleets into holding patterns. The small but swift-sailing U.S. Navy was now lying in wait off its home shores, avoiding the Royal Navy ships but hoping to pick off unprotected British merchants and supply vessels. For the moment it was a war of words, not deeds, but it seemed inevitable that shots would soon be fired.

Holman was forced to face up to reality. Britain, nearly bankrupted by one war, couldn't fight two wars for long without cutting back on such fripperies as half-pay for the blind. If he wasn't going to end up on a pallet in the back of the apothecary shop, or subsiding on charity in some mercifully distant city, it was time to act.

He returned to Exeter, and walked up North Street to Saint Pet-rock's, his baptismal church. He had a request to make. Not long afterward, the minister and a few prominent parishioners handed over a set of documents: sworn statements, freshly notarized. Then, in his rented rooms at Lyme Regis, Holman took up his Noctograph and wrote:

> *The enclosed will be sufficient proof of that rectitude of conduct which is so essential to merit the commiseration of those who have the power to alleviate, in some degree, the affliction it has pleased God to visit me with.*

Holman would be neither a beggar nor a burden. He would be a knight.

Travers College, home of the Naval Knights of Windsor.

The Seven Gentlemen

S AMUEL TRAVERS WAS not a sailor. In fact, he could hardly have been a more landbound individual. In the late 1600s, well before the birth of James Holman's grandfather, he was Surveyor-General of the Land Revenue, responsible for managing all the forests, hunting grounds, and tenanted lands owned by the crown. But when he died in 1726, he left behind a strangely nautical will. In it, he bequeathed his own substantial real estate holdings— "manors, lands, tenements and hereditaments,"—to a group that did not exist, and could not exist unless the King agreed to upset the status quo.

His will proposed the funding of a new knightly order, one limited to

> *Seven Gentlemen, who are to be superannuated or disabled Lieu-tenants of English men of war . . . single men without children, inclined to lead a virtuous, studious and devout life, to be removed, if they give occasion of scandal.*

They would be called the Naval Knights of Windsor. Each would have lifetime appointments, and only a single obligation: to daily attend divine service in the castle chapel. The late Mr. Travers endowed a permanent fund for their support, and also allo-cated monies for the building of a special headquarters within the castle grounds, a college—at the time the word had no academic connotations, meaning only that the residents shared housekeeping and kept a common table. Naturally, the building would be called Travers College.

Explicit as his instructions were, this disposition of his fortune seemed so out of character for Travers that his niece hotly contested the will. She launched a lawsuit that, like a real-life version of Jarndyce versus Jarndyce in Dickens's *Dombey and Son*, stretched on for generations. It sputtered on expensively throughout her children's lifetime, and her grandchildren's, until all appeals were exhausted. Samuel Travers had asked George I for the royal charter of the Naval Knights of Windsor, but the request was granted by George III, after seventy-four years of litigation.

WHY DID TRAVERS wish to populate Windsor Castle with praying sailors? It was, he hoped, the solution to a problem that had begun four centuries earlier. England's oldest chivalric order was, and remains, the Most Noble Order of the Garter, invented by Edward III in 1348 as a means of binding potentially rebellious nobles to the crown. The Garter Knights grew to be deeply intertwined with the monarchy itself. The order's motto, *Honi soit qui mal y pense* (Evil to him who thinks evil) also served as the motto of the House of Tudor. Charles I went to his beheading dressed in his Garter insignia. And within the walls of Windsor, Saint George's Chapel is both the royal family's official house of worship and the order's ceremonial headquarters.

In the chapel, each Knight of the Garter has a personal "stall" in the area closest to the altar. These are carved booths that, over the centuries, have grown cluttered with heraldic displays: banners and crests and helmets and swords. From these venerable seats, each occupant is expected to offer up prayers for the souls of the royal departed, as well as for the reigning sovereign and all fellow knights.

That was the first manifestation of the problem. Membership in the Garter Knights is limited to the monarch, the prince of Wales, and an elite of twenty-two. Since the point of the order is to acknowledge and affiliate the important (it is still the most exalted honor the kingdom can bestow), it has, by definition, been almost exclusively comprised of very busy people. Having given over the most prominent portion of the chapel to his knights, the pragmatic Edward III realized there was something dispiriting, if not impious-seeming, about having all those ornate stalls remain empty most of the time.

Just four years later, he founded a second order, the Knights of Windsor. These marched alongside in Garter processions, but, most importantly, they served as stand-ins during church services. When a Garter Knight was absent (which was usually), a Windsor Knight occupied his stall and took up his quota of prayers, thereby assuring a steady heavenward stream of devotion. If there were no vacant stalls, they attended anyway, sitting in the outer chamber.

This secondary order was populated by "soldiers of gentle birth, who, by age or infirmity were grown more fit for prayer than war," men of modest means who had sacrificed a lifetime, if not a limb or two, in service to their country. In a broad sense, they shared the monarch's home, enjoying a lifetime grant of board and lodgings within the castle walls. To distinguish them from their wealthy betters, and because they were drawn from the needy (and likely to remain so; the honor came with a notoriously small pension), they were traditionally called the "Poor Knights" of Windsor.

Despite their relative poverty, their status had its advantages: comfortably spacious apartments in the castle, and outfits matching the Garter Knights in everything but the garter (actually a sort of sword belt). To be a Knight of Windsor was to be a recipient of charity, but of one of the world's most dignified charities. Membership was not an ennoblement—these knights were traditionally not called "sir"—but it was an honor nonetheless to append the initials K.W. to one's name.

Therein lay the next manifestation of the problem. These perks led, almost inevitably, to a straying from Edward's original intent.

His decree specified "impoverished warriors, infirm of body or in needy circumstances . . . who shall be worshippers of Christ permanently." But by Samuel Travers's day, the order had devolved into a "grace and favor" office, a plum benefit for the well-connected. Many of those appointed had no military experience at all. Records show the positions filled by tailors, victuallers, even a Turkish orphan raised as a servant by the Duke of Saint Albans. Nor were they uniformly needy. One knight died leaving an estate so large it endowed yet another charity, a school for poor boys.

Naturally, the obligation of daily worship was also taken less and less seriously. Despite the fact that the knights' apartments were just a few steps away from Saint George's, they made an art of attending a bare minimum of services. Which was why Travers had made his unusual bequest: to once more keep the sanctum of the chapel from looking conspicuously vacant. He was tacitly addressing the laxity of the Knights of Windsor by duplicating the order in a slightly different form, with sailors instead of soldiers. To keep the Naval Knights of Windsor from acquiring their own airs of importance, he specified only lieutenants, not captains or commanders—and, more particularly, only those lieutenants who had served on a man-of-war-class ship. Those were the kind most used to following orders.

Travers's bequest was fully enacted in 1803. Nine years later, when Holman made his application, the Naval Knights were still considered a new element in the daily life of Windsor, a stream of modern navy blue (for they retained their uniforms) filing into chapel twice daily for morning and evening services, their presences only occasionally punctuated by the medieval crimson robes of the two elder orders.

Despite the relative newness of the order, one trend was already clear. As in the navy itself, seniority held sway. Although lieutenants of any age were technically eligible, the knights thus far had been universally geriatric, another bow to pragmatism: The aged seemed more likely to maintain the required life of sedate, bachelor respectability. The royal charter dictated not only the removal of "any knight who should marry or give occasion for scandal," but made it clear that, between church services, they were expected to do little more than sit quietly in their rooms. It admonished

> *that they should not leave the said house or absent themselves for more than ten days in any one year without a license . . . that they should not lie out of their respective apartment, not haunt the town or taverns.*

These were not just rules to be observed, they were components of an oath administered to each new Naval Knight. Which was why most successful candidates were those like Lieutenant John Gardiner, who joined in 1806. "As I am now getting on in years," he wrote in his application, "I thought a situation was no bad retreat for age and infirmity."

FOR ALL HIS pains in its preparation, Holman couldn't rationally assign much hope to his application to the Naval Knights. There was only a single opening, and, while the applicant pool was narrowed by the specifics of membership, there were still thousands of men who met the criteria. Many of them had spent years pursuing an appointment, putting themselves forward time and again. Lieutenant William Jones, far senior to Holman and applying at the same time, would have to campaign through four more vacancies before finally winning admission.

Every single one of the current knights had been lieutenants since before Holman had even enlisted, and most of them since before he was born. He was still a very young man—blind, yes, but only for little more than a year, and with no real means of ascribing that blindness to his naval service. It was a long shot.

Holman seems to have been well aware of the odds, for he took a number of steps to improve them. One was the application itself, a specimen of his newly acquired, still clumsy Noctograph handwriting. This was almost certainly something of a calculated pluck at the heartstrings, for all supporting documentation, submitted in the same envelope, displays someone else's crisp, professional hand. Another was the sworn statement in the accompanying paperwork, signed by the minister and two wardens of his baptismal church:

> We do hereby certify that Lieut. James Holman of the Royal Navy, resident of this Parish, is a Single Man, without Children, inclined to lead a virtuous, studious, and devout life.

The "virtuous, studious, and devout," coming from clergy, served as a discreet assurance that Holman's blindness was not due to venereal disease. But the language was also carefully chosen for its resonance. It was a verbatim appropriation of the words Samuel Travers had used in his will, ninety-one years earlier, to first describe his vision of the Naval Knights.

The application was dated August 16, and logged by the clerks of the Commissioners of His Majesty's Navy four days later. During that time in transit, events half a world away transformed the interpretation of Holman's plight. The *Guerierre*, Holman's last ship, now sailed into history.

THE *GUERRIERE* HAD acquired a new captain since Holman's final sick leave. Now it was commanded by James Dacres, just a few years older than Holman but significantly better connected, the nephew of a captain and the son of an admiral. He was young, headstrong, and impatient for the war of words to give way to actual fighting. To nudge matters along, he'd taken to issuing challenges through the American merchant ships he'd forcibly boarded. In the register of the *John Adams,* he left his compliments to the American commodore, adding that he would be "very happy to meet him, or any American frigate of equal force . . . for the purpose of having a few minutes *tête à tête.*" This was actually a relatively modest bit of martial flair—other captains had taken out advertisements in the American papers, taunting their counterparts into a showdown. But Dacres was the first to get his wish. On August 19, the *Guerriere*, cruising off Halifax, sailed into view of the USS *Constitution*. The inaugural battle of the War of 1812 was underway.

The two belonged to the same class of fighting ships, but were not perfectly matched. The *Constitution* outsized and, more important, outgunned the *Guerriere*. Firing all its guns on one side at the same time, the *Constitution* could deliver a broadside of cannonballs and grapeshot totaling about seven hundred pounds, while the *Guerriere*'s broadside was closer to five hundred and fifty. But Dacres, who had unsuccessfully chased the American ship previously, felt that his greater maneuverability was a compensating advantage. The *Constitution* might blast out more iron, but he would be able to aim his shot more carefully.

While cannonballs could pierce a hull, neither ship was trying to sink the other. The goal was not to send the adversary to the bottom—that lost you a valuable prize, and gave you the burden of taking on survivors. The key targets were the masts and their rigging: knock away enough of them and the ship was dead in the water. To inflict maximum damage above-decks the *Constitution* double-shotted its guns, filling each muzzle with two cannonballs at once. It took a quarter hour of relentless gunning, but finally the *Guerriere*'s mizzen, the rearmost mast, fractured out of its tethers and fell into the sea.

This was not fatal in itself. The ship had two more masts, and, with jury-rigging, could raise sail even on the stump of one. But it wasn't a clean loss. Some of the rigging still held, and the drag of the mizzen in the water was greater than the steering force of the rudder. The ship swung out of helm's control, helpless in the enemy's sights. Captain Hull, eager to keep up the point-blank blasting, steered a shade too close to the target. The *Guerriere*'s foremost point, the bowsprit, speared into the *Constitution*'s hindmost rigging, locking the two ships together into a single mass, slowly winding counterclockwise in the sea.

The entangled bowsprit was the *Guerriere*'s last hope. For a few moments at least, as long as this accidental bridge lasted, it offered the chance to trump the guns with hand-to-hand combat. The first ship to swarm a boarding party over the still-splintering wreckage—under fire, in a heaving sea—might have the decisive advantage. The task of leading this charge fell to Lieutenant Bartholomew Kent, Captain Dacres's second in command, and he hastily mustered all hands forward. He could see the Americans already grouping in their stern, assembling an even bigger boarding party than they hoped to put over first.

Everything depended on Kent. But before he could lead the final desperate charge, the pitch and plunge of the waves worked the bowsprit free, and the two ships careened apart. The force of this final wrenching was enough to topple the *Guerriere*'s two remaining masts. Dacres, severely wounded himself, had no choice but to strike the flag in defeat, but the *Guerriere* was too gravely damaged to be saved by surrender. When the Americans realized it could never be brought to port, they evacuated it and set the hull on fire. The timbers burned until they sank.

THE NEWS STUNNED both the old world and the new. From a military standpoint, the loss was inconsequential: the British had over a thousand battle-ready ships to deploy, while the minuscule U.S. Navy could barely muster sixteen. But the symbolic effect was overwhelming. The *Constitution*, now nicknamed "Old Ironsides" for the way it emerged from the fray relatively unscathed, promptly entered the mythology of the young nation (two centuries later it floats, preserved and still under commission, in Boston Harbor). The loss of the *Guerriere* shattered the British aura of seagoing invulnerability.

Arriving just as the naval commissioners were narrowing down the candidates for the Naval Knights of Windsor, news of the *Guerriere*'s demise cast a particular prominence on one application. The commissioners could now make the observation that, had illness not intervened, Lieutenant Holman would have been the senior lieutenant on the ship—it would have been him leading that final charge, not Lieutenant Kent.

This lent a new depth of sympathy to Holman's story. Here was a man deprived not only of his sight and of his livelihood, but of his chance at glory.

Selection was a complicated process. The commissioners made three choices, which they presented to the office of the Lord High Admiral (at the time not a person but another committee), which narrowed the field down to two. The final determination was left to the King himself—or, rather, to whatever murky group of advisors happened to be making decisions for him at the time. Just a year earlier George III had descended into what would be his final bout of insanity, but even before the madness struck he'd been struggling with another complication. His eyesight had begun to fail. He could still perceive sunlight and vague shapes, but was, for all practical purposes, blind himself.

That fall the commissioners announced that Lieutenant James Holman, late of the *Guerriere*, would become the newest member of the Seven Gentlemen, and the youngest Naval Knight of all.

IN THEORY, IT was a masterstroke of good fortune. Naval Knights were appointed for life and sheltered for life, so long as they obeyed the rules and performed their devotional duties. Like their military counterparts, they could add the honorific "K.W." to their names. After deductions for room and board, Holman's annual share of the Travers trust would come to thirty-four pounds per year. Also, so long as he remained a knight he was exempt from being declared superannuated, which meant he could hang on to his reserve-duty status and his half-pay. That gave him a total income of about eighty-four pounds a year—an extremely small sum for someone expected to maintain the trappings of respectability. In contrast, physicians called in to attend any member of the royal family at Windsor charged a standard retainer of twenty pounds for a single day's consultation. A midlevel government clerk could earn around six hundred pounds a year. The isolated keeper of the naval semaphore station in Norfolk was paid one hundred and ten pounds per year.

But it was preferable to begging. Besides, there were advantages beyond the financial. It would permanently silence any whispers about Holman's blindness being caused by venereal disease; moral impeccability was implicit in the honor. And as someone still adjusting to blindness, he'd benefit from an ordered world of predictable routines, bounded scope, and little change. The circumscribed, placid grounds of an ancient castle provided precisely that. The company of his fellow officers could only be a comfort, and sitting through services was no more onerous than standing watch had been. In all, it "afforded him an easy retreat from the turmoil a person in his circumstances might be supposed desirous of avoiding," as a later anonymous account would put it.

That was the pleasant prospect of Holman's new knighthood. The reality, as he soon discovered, was somewhat less idyllic.

Travers College was a finely built, commandingly solid edifice of yellow brick, more stately than ostentatious. The *Naval Chronicle* called it "neat and handsome." Its prominent features were a slender, clockfaced cupola for ringing out the hours (the old sailors were used to their bells), and a colonnaded long veranda to mask the confusion of multiple front doors. The edifice was really a sort of townhouse row, a set of seven separate residences smoothed externally to appear as one.

Although modest by Windsor standards, Holman's one-seventh sliver of the College was vastly more private space than he had ever known before. One of the perquisites of his lieutenancy had been a cabin with thin, removable walls, no bigger than a closet.

Now he had the lifetime tenancy of no less than three rooms, linked fore to aft. As was explained to him, the sitting room looked out across a broad lawn, with a garden just beyond. The bedroom drew warmth from the fire in the adjacent private kitchen, where he could prepare his own meals. If he wished to eat in company he could step through the rearmost door, into the communal dining area that Samuel Travers had insisted upon.

That was where the first surprise of his arrival awaited him. There was a common table, and behind that a larger kitchen, staffed and stocked for regular meals. But the knights did not consistently share that table, or much else of their lives. Though cordial enough to Holman and to one another, the residents could hardly be said to constitute a community, much less a brotherly band. "Travers' ideal has, I believe, never been fulfilled," a later knight would observe. "Seven gentlemen as he pictured in his mind's eye are not likely ever to come together here."

Some of the knights were simply too set in solitary ways, others too infirm to venture much from their rooms. But some had strong motives to keep to themselves: they were regularly breaking the rules. Their code forbade them to "haunt the town or taverns," but at least two knights, William Tapp and Anthony Hunt, were carrying on active social lives, even launching courtships of women. Both would soon marry.

The eldest knight, a sixty-eight-year-old Scotsman named Daniel Burgess, was harboring his own secret. Like the others, he had attested to being both a bachelor and childless, but in fact he was practically a clan patriarch, not only a husband and father but a grandfather; his family remained discreetly behind in the Orkney Islands. Whether his wife was alive at the assumption of his knighthood is undocumented, but the distinction was immaterial. Knights were supposed to be bachelors, not widowers (there was a clear legal distinction). Having been married made him technically ineligible.

But there was an even greater reason why the knights did not cohere as a group, and discovering it was the dismaying second surprise of Holman's arrival. The generations-long lawsuit against Travers's will had failed in the end, but the seventy-four years of delay had brought about the order's congenital flaw.

In the era of George I, there had been plenty of available space inside the castle walls. Back then Windsor was not the king's primary residence but a country retreat, and a neglected one at that. But George III disliked London and claimed Windsor as his home, filling it with his family and court and embarking on an extensive plan of renovation. By the time the suit played out, the castle was crowded and bustling. So Travers College was constructed just outside—and most importantly, just below—the walls.

WINDSOR CASTLE WAS founded as a fortress, and like most fortresses it occupies high, defensible ground. The towers rise from a steep escarpment, itself emerging from a chalk mound that forms a solitary outcropping of the Chiltern Hills. A carriage path, in time named Thames Street, winds up and around, leading to the several fortified gates of the South Terrace. But the sheer northern face can be scaled only on foot, and only by ascending in the shadow of one of the towers, on a stone staircase called the Hundred Steps.

The name is a misnomer. The gated steps have varied over the years, but never have they numbered less than a hundred and thirty. Travers College was close by the base of the Hundred Steps, and since all seven gentlemen were expected at both morning and evening services every day but Saturday, they had two choices: haul themselves up and down the stairs each time, or take the longer, less steep but equally exhausting roundabout march up Thames Street. "To a fit man, this is merely a pleasant exercise," observed one visitor to Windsor. "But to old and rheumatic limbs the double journey made twice daily, could be a painful ordeal and indeed become impossible." Nor could they take too many liberties in their attendance, since it was meticulously noted in a volume called the Knights' Check Book. Whether or not they took the sacrament during the service was also noted. Lest they be tempted to put in a token appearance and wander off, the royal charter specified that their presence "must continue to the end of the same service." The Check Book was also supposed to document "all other neglects and defaults" of the knights, inside and outside of the chapel. In short, the daily act of devotion had been converted into a humbling, painful chore, matched with a rankling degree of scrutiny.

Under such circumstances the true commonality of the Naval Knights was cantankerousness, and complaint. The records of Travers College are replete with grievance, and requests for exception to the rules. Burgess, the eldest, sought and eventually won the personal privilege of four months' absence each year, presumably ample time to scurry back to his family in Scotland. Even Tapp and Hunt, the ones who married, fought a pitched but ultimately losing battle to keep both their knightly status and their wives.

HOLMAN MADE NO such claims against the status quo. For the first several months at least, the structured days conferred a welcome independence. After a brief orientation, the routine was easy enough for him to manage by himself. Early rising, a quiet breakfast, a short path to the gatehouse of the Hundred Steps, then the mounting of the broad steps themselves. This was another advantage to using not the typical blind man's cane but a stout walking stick: he could use it to push his complaining joints up the steps, and to rest when necessary.

At the top he pushed through the bastion of the tower gate, then followed a covered passageway into the arcaded quadrangle of the Dean's Cloister. The clicks of his walking stick began to resonate, a lopsided echo: on one side, arched Gothic traceries, open to the weather. On the other, a stone wall that six centuries had converted into a marble patchwork of memorial plaques. He knew he was approaching the chapel itself when the floor went irregular with inset tombstones.

Instead of proceeding to the formal entrances, he stepped through a modest auxiliary door. Now he was in a soundscape of soaring reverberation. The swelling chords of an organ, but also the pneumatic wheeze-clicks of its hand pump and the conspiratorial whispers of small boys: the choristers of Saint George's, chosen from the purest young voices in the land. He threaded past the vestry, past numerous small chapels, then down a checkerboarded floor that marked the center of the Garter sanctum called the Quire. He paused short of the altar, waiting for a guiding touch to direct him to a particular vacancy. He might be led to any Garter Knight's personal stall, with the exception of the one with purple curtains. That was the King's stall, which these days was only fitfully occupied. Then services began.

THE WEEKS WORE on. The novelty of the castle, of opulence and history and proximity to royalty, faded into familiarity. The closest thing to excitement came on the first day of April, when workmen discovered the centuries-lost bodies of Henry VII and Charles I, both in tombs directly beneath the Quire's checkerboard floor. But even this did not disrupt the routine—the bodies were left in place and the floor closed up. Later a plaque would be added as a reminder of their presence, but Holman's haptic awareness needed no such marker. He knew exactly when he was treading on the kings' bones.

In his first half-year of residence, somewhere between bedroom and chapel stall, Holman was forced to quietly acknowledge a new emotion. Not relief at having landed on his feet, but a growing sense of dread. For all his trials he was still quite a young man, just twenty-six years old. He was thankful for the recognition and royal favor, but there was one inescapable fact.

He was expected to do nothing—nothing but sit quietly—for the remainder of his life.

It was hard enough to bear the notion of identical days, stretching out indefinitely, until a final Saint George's service, one featuring his coffin front and center upon the altar (the last perquisite of the order). An even harder reality was the fact of his recurring pain, and the uncertainty it introduced into the equation. In his application he had omitted all mention of flying gout, but now it was clear that this condition could not be concealed in perpetuity, not with the Hundred Steps looming twice daily. It was a cruel quirk of the Naval Knights that, although its members were chosen from the aged and infirm, they were expected to resign when ill health kept them from fulfilling their daily obligations. One had already done so; two would soon follow. Most hoped to keel over before it came to that.

The irony was that Holman had now honed his perceptive powers to the point that independent movement, even travel, was no longer daunting. As he would later explain (resorting again to the third person), he had "acquired an undefinable power, almost resembling instinct, which he believes in a lively manner gives him ideas of whatever may be going forward externally." His confidence in that power had given him "an almost irresistible inclination to visit different parts of his native country, in quest of knowledge or amusement." Yet he was all but confined to the castle, and surrounding small town.

In the midst of others squabbling over the rules, Holman found himself searching for a means of carving out his own measure of freedom. He found it in the words of the order's founding charter, in the description of the Seven Gentlemen as "studious and devout." The devout part was well attended to. How about studious?

Let the other Naval Knights shuffle toward their graves. Holman resolved to transform himself into a scholar. What's more, a scholar with a private and particular agenda.

His physicians had despaired of finding him a cure. Perhaps it was time to become a physician himself.

A period caricature of a practitioner of "chymical
medicine," the discipline studied by Holman.

SIX

A Smattering of Physic

I T W A S A plan too audacious to unveil all at once. A blind man proposing to pursue *any* sort of university education was far-fetched enough. That the prospective student was Holman, whose non-nautical education had ended abruptly in Dr. Halloran's scandal-ridden classroom, made the idea almost ridiculously implausible. He would not only be at least a decade older than most of his fellow freshmen, but in many crucial areas almost two decades behind them in scholarship. When he did broach the idea to the Naval Knights' governors—a two-person group known formally as the Visitors—it is difficult to imagine that medicine was mentioned at all. Instead the talk was doubtless of his lifelong passion for literature, with abundant evocations of Homer, Milton, and other blind bards.

While Samuel Travers clearly intended "studious" more along the lines of tranquil Bible readings, the Visitors were hard pressed to see much harm in interpreting it in a broader educational sense, particularly on the terms Holman put forth.

He would study literature, but not at relatively nearby Oxford and Cambridge. Both had multiterm academic calendars, requiring students to remain on campus throughout most of the year. In contrast, the University of Edinburgh, three hundred miles away, concentrated most of its classes into a single six-month session. Matriculating there would still leave half the year for his Windsor duties.

The University of Edinburgh's literature curriculum was well respected, although massively overshadowed by the medical program—throughout the Western world, an "Edinburgh doctor" had the highest cachet of all physicians. Still, Edinburgh itself was renowned as a literary center. It was the home of Sir Walter Scott, the English language's best-selling author, of several publishing houses, and of the *Edinburgh Review*, the most influential literary journal of the day.

Holman's request had a certain force of logic. It was clearly an act of folly, but some follies are easier to indulge than dispel. Since there was every reason to expect the experiment to sputter out in a session or two, the Visitors agreed to an unprecedented academic leave of absence, with the understanding that he pay his own way.

After months of enforced, sedate predictability, Holman was at last blissfully busy. The leave was granted just two weeks before classes began, which gave him scant time to travel to Edinburgh, secure lodgings and, most dauntingly, learn how to live independently in a crowded, unfamiliar city. He departed on the morning of October 15, 1813, a day he already considered personally auspicious. It was the fifteenth anniversary of the beginning of his naval career, and his twenty-seventh birthday.

The carriage ride was wearisome. Four days of perpetual jostling later, he disembarked to discover a town where a blind man might not feel entirely out of place. Culturally, Edinburgh was renowned as a city of enlightenment. Physically, the capital of Scotland was a place of enduring darkness.

THE SCOTS LANGUAGE boasts the word *reekie*, roughly translated as "fouled with black smoke." Edinburgh was nicknamed Auld Reekie, because it was, in the words of poet Robert Southey, "the finest smoke-scape that can anywhere be seen . . . you might smoke bacon by hanging it out the window." Most of the city was built in the bottom of steep-sided ravines, which confined the smoke and haze, and added deep, encompassing shadows of their own. One of Holman's fellow freshmen, arriving at the same time, described the strange atmosphere:

> *Everywhere—all around—you have rocks frowning over rocks in imperial elevation, and descending, among the smoke and dust of the city, into dark depths which leaves the eye, that would scrutinize and penetrate them, unsatisfied and dim with gazing.*

The university itself was in Old Town, the densest and dingiest part of the city. Holman sought out cheap lodgings in the crowded lanes that Edinburgh native Robert Louis Stevenson would later describe as "so narrow that you can lay a hand on either wall; so steep that, in greasy winter weather, the pavement is almost as treacherous as ice." These aspects of the close quarters were not as hard for Holman to tolerate as the accompanying odors and vapors. Three years of blindness had honed his sense of smell to the point that even tobacco smoke was difficult to tolerate. Yet a cramped, ramshackle life was all he could afford on eighty-four pounds a year.

How, exactly, did a blind man of small formal education win admission to one of the world's most prestigious universities? He didn't, nor did he have to. There was a matriculation fee, but no entrance requirements. In theory, anyone could simply show up and start attending classes, given they had the financial wherewithal and appeared to be male (and the key word was *appeared*—James Miranda Stuart Barry, who graduated from the medical school in 1812, was a woman masquerading as a man). This lack of standards was, in fact, a point of pride with the faculty, who had for centuries resisted any notions of an entrance examination. Not only would administering such tests be beneath their dignity, they considered it pointless to impose standards of learning on incoming students, when their prior education hadn't been standardized in the first place.

As Laurence Hynes Halloran had demonstrated in Exeter, anyone so inclined could simply launch a school, take on pupils, and teach them what they wished. As a result, many young men arrived in Edinburgh with heads full of wildly varying degrees of misinformation: scrambled Greek grammar, historical half-truths, crackpot notions passed off as gospel. It was an unspoken assumption that one's real education started here.

There was another reason the professors were adamant to accept all comers: their lifestyles depended on it. Most of the instructors' income came in the form of box-office receipts—i.e., tickets sold for admission to the lecture hall. Anyone not purchasing and possessing a class ticket was immediately ejected by a staff of watchful janitors who shared in the proceeds. In consequence, it was not unusual for the more popular professors to address a packed crowd of up to five hundred students, all straining to get their money's worth.

Because it was the most crowd-friendly format, most classes were conducted solely as lectures. Tests were almost never administered. When they were it was usually not at the end of the term but the beginning, to give the lecturer a better sense of his audience. Texts were not assigned. Instead, most professors treated their lecture notes as a sort of verbally delivered textbook, read out loud over the course of each year, usually without additions or improvement. The worst instance of this in Holman's time was demonstrated by Alexander Monro, known as Tertius because he was the third generation of Alexander Monros to occupy the chair of Anatomy. He was notorious for simply reading out loud, word for word, the lectures his grandfather had written, right down to the phrase "when I was a student in Leyden in 1719 . . ." It was a tradition for students to await the annual recital of this sentence, and greet it by pelting Tertius with smuggled-in dried peas.

This reliance on the verbal, not the visual, made for an educational experience that would hardly be recognizable as such by today's university standards. But it also made the dreams of a blind student not entirely impossible. To learn was to listen.

• • •

THE UNIVERSITY OF Edinburgh offered three main courses of study: literature, medicine, and divinity, although students were free to take most any class once their core competencies had been well established. Before he would be allowed to tackle medicine, Holman needed to do well in literature—a subject close to his heart, but also in sheer practical terms the most difficult. It required not only becoming colloquially conversant in Latin and Greek, but demanded a deep command of any number of source texts. His sighted fellow students had access to one of the most extensive libraries extant (publishers were commanded by the king to send free copies of all their books to Edinburgh), but he would have to commit his books to memory. What's more, he'd have to find people to read them to him in the first place.

Fortunately, many students were reliant on rote memorization, so much so that a whole subclass of mercenary scholars had sprung up. These freelance tutors were called "grinds," because they specialized in grinding data into students' heads, usually by repetition and mnemonic tricks. This was another expense, but a notably effective one. Even good students submitted themselves to being "polished by a grinder," not because they were insecure in their learning but because "everyone did it." Even before his blindness, Holman had been accustomed to memorizing long swathes of poetry. Now he honed in himself the capability of retaining massive amounts of information—not only works of fiction, but texts of history, rhetoric, and natural philosophy—in minute and correct detail. "The whole work of my experience is mental," was how he described his deepening powers of memory. "Consequently whatever I retain, I retain permanently."

He flourished as a student of literature, returning for the winter session of the following year, and the next. "Throughout this protracted day of darkness, the book of nature has been largely opened to his mental view," he wrote of himself, again resorting to the third

person. "Nor has he failed to cultivate the pleasing fields of literature." In fact, he quoted Milton's meditation on blindness (*So thick
a drop serene hath quenched their orbs*), only to cite the redemptive
subsequent lines:

> *"Yet not the more*
> *Cease I to wander where the Muses haunt*
> *Clear spring, or shady grove, or sunny hill."*

THE EUROPEAN WARS ended at last in 1815, with Napoleon
consigned to Saint Helena in the south Atlantic sea, a bleak, water-
less island Holman remembered glimpsing during his endless
cruises on the *Cambrian*. That same year, the second conflict—the
American War—ground to a stalemate, then ended with a mutu-
ally face-saving treaty hammered out in Belgium. After a quarter
century of fighting, Britain was at last entering into what had every
indication of being an enduring peace.

A generation that had known nothing but war scrambled for
fresh futures. Edinburgh was swamped with former soldiers and
half-pay sailors, seeking to take up or resume long-deferred educa-
tions. This was fortunate for Holman—he was less conspicuous in
the growing tide of older, uniformed students, and, since he had
completed his foundation coursework, it was time to expand his
course of study. The registration book for that year lists him as "Lit
& Med," a student in both the schools of literature and medicine.

A blind medical student would seem to inspire at least a few raised
eyebrows, but these were the most crowded classes of all. He was
now used to calling as little attention to himself as possible, easing
unobtrusively in and out of the lecture halls. Holman himself took
pains to minimize its significance, in the future referring to his medical education offhandedly as a "smattering of physic."

This was disingenuous. Holman studied medicine with a thor-
oughness and persistence that made his earlier academics seem
trivial by comparison. His courseload, running concurrently with

his literary studies, was equivalent to that of full-time medical students. The cost of these classes was a far-from-trivial expense, equivalent to about one third of his available income. He had every right to be accepted as a peer of the other physicians in training, but that was the opposite of his intention. He wanted his presence to be tolerated, so as not to attract unwelcome inquiries into his plans and purposes—or, worse yet, well-intentioned meddling.

To achieve this, he adopted a policy that would prove invaluable in years to come: inviting others to not take him seriously by acting decidedly unserious himself. The more daunting the task, the more disarming it was to undertake it with a casual air. If you had been a fellow student in a well-packed lecture hall, you'd be forgiven for noticing Holman, then dismissing him as an idler with both time and money to burn. He was just one of the few figures in the crowd not frantically taking notes.

Holman never set out to fulfill all the requirements for a medical degree, only to pursue a highly individualistic course of study. But that was no measure of the extent of his learning. Just as there were no rigorous standards of admission, there was also no clear-cut means of exit, of becoming an "Edinburgh doctor." Obtaining an actual degree was considered only one method, adopted by the meticulous or those in no hurry to begin a medical career. Many students who qualified for a diploma never bothered to pick one up (there was a ten-pound fee for formal graduation). Others simply studied as much as they felt like studying, then went home and hung out their shingle. The rule of thumb, according to the local handbook *Guide for Gentlemen Studying Medicine*, was that three years of study were usually sufficient to gain the skills for a successful practice.

Holman's medical studies lasted three years. It is not difficult to see in them signs of a personal agenda. He steered clear of the lectures in anatomy and surgery, which relied heavily on visual aids, instead studying *materia medica* (the practical pharmacology of the day) and chemistry (at the time considered a subgenus of medicine). In short, he was learning diagnostic forensics—under-standing the cause and course of illness—and the mechanistics of medicine—how a treatment was discovered, tested, refined, and put into general use. If there had been any treatments for ophthal-mia he had not personally endured, he learned them now as well.

Holman's first class was held at eight o'clock in the morning, an uncomfortably cold and dark hour during the Scottish win-ters. But the lecture hall was usually standing-room only, since Dr. James Home, professor of materia medica, was one of the school's more popular teachers. As one classmate put it,

> . . . although the lectures were not enlightened by well-defined gen-eral principles, or illustrated as now by experiment and demonstra-tions, or enlivened by any of the flowers of oratory—they were a mine of useful facts, laboriously collected, sifted with care, and well put together. His delivery was quiet, but earnest; and his whole soul was evidently in his duty.

Professor Home was popular for another reason. Almost alone among the medical faculty, he voluntarily administered exams at no extra charge. This offer was eagerly accepted by many of his students, as a rare opportunity to display their knowledge. It's unlikely that Holman was showy enough to step forward in such a fashion, but he was compiling an encyclopedic knowledge of medicines, their origins and uses, building on what he'd already gleaned as an apothecary's son. Persistent coughs called for orchil-la weed, harvested in the Canary Islands. Gum camphor, from Bra-zil, was thought to lessen sexual desire. Zanzibar was the source of *tinctura capisici*, a treatment for seasickness.

Frustration over the passive nature of learning led some students to extreme measures. Nowhere was that more evident than in the other classroom Holman frequented, that of Dr. Thomas Charles Hope, the university's sole chemistry professor. "Dr. Hope . . . seems to have abruptly and unaccountably deserted the tempting field of chemical research," one student wrote. "Neither did he encourage experimental inquiry among his students. His laboratory was open to no one but his class assistant." This lack of hands-on experience compelled twelve of his students to form a clandestine Chemical Society, buying the raw materials from a nearby druggist and performing their own experiments in a rented attic room.

Holman was not among the secret members of the Chemical Society. He compensated for the limitations of the lecture format in his own way, by doggedly attending the entire one-year course of study for a second time. And then a third.

THE CONTEMPORARY MIND is acclimated to the notion that scientific and medical knowledge are both perpetually expanding frontiers. But in Holman's era, these fields were small and closely bounded. It was entirely possible for one of his classmates to write, without exaggeration, that he

> *knew almost all that was then known in chemistry, botany also well, mineralogy and geology also fairly, anatomy and physiology thoroughly, and so much of the practice of physic as enabled me, at the age of twenty, to undertake with some sense of security the duties of Resident Medical Officer in the Royal Infirmary.*

Holman was temperamentally incapable of making such self-congratulatory statements. But after immersing himself in chemistry for three years straight and materia medica for two, he could rightly claim to be as much an authority on the "practice of physic" — "physic" meaning nonsurgical medicine — as it was possible to be. Many successful physicians had founded their careers on far less experience, also without the formality of degrees. No one would have thought twice about his leaving Edinburgh, establishing a practice, and assuming the honorific "doctor"—had he been able to see.

By 1818, Holman's medical studies had gone as far as they could go. That all along he had one patient in mind, himself, is not confessed in any surviving statements. But it's worth noting that, at the age of thirty-one, he abandoned both Edinburgh and medicine simultaneously. He gave up the discipline at the very moment he could be assured of fully understanding its abilities and limitations. And quick on the heels of this departure came another attack of debilitating illness.

According to Holman, it was attributable to "causes which it is unnecessary to mention," a strong hint that this time the malaise had both physical and emotional components. He explained the breakdown only circumspectly. "In the cultivation of those pursuits which were pressed upon me by the tasks I had prescribed to myself," he wrote, "my health suffered severely, and I was compelled to seek in my native air (Devonshire) the usual means of restoration."

THERE WAS A systematic sapping of strength, and a reoccurrence of pains so familiar the logical course was to treat them as they'd been treated seven years before: an aquatic convalescence at Bath, an extended stay in Exeter, a return visit to the Lyme Regis shore. But in 1811 those earlier rheumatic complaints, already on the wane, had been thrust almost entirely out of his consciousness by the shock of sudden blindness. This time they were not to be denied. By 1819 he was back at Windsor, in no shape to venture far from his rooms at Travers College. His physicians began to contemplate radical measures.

"At the time my health was so delicate, and my nerves so depressed by previous anxiety," he would write, "that I did not suffer myself to indulge in the expectation that I should ever travel." But that was exactly what his doctors proposed. Now that peacetime had opened the continent to British citizens, a restful, sun-soaked residence in "the more favoured clime of the southern parts of Europe," i.e., the Mediterranean coast, seemed like his only recourse for recuperation. He was granted a one-year leave of absence from both the Royal Navy and the Naval Knights, and left to make his own travel arrangements.

The physicians doubtless envisioned a leisurely sail to the Mediterranean, sea transportation being by far the least stressful for the invalid. But such trips were expensive and difficult to organize; there were no passenger ships regularly bound for that area, so Holman would have to charter a boat, or piece together a passage out of several short jaunts on merchant vessels. And then there was the issue of an escort—who would accompany him on this journey, to care for him and monitor his health? More wealthy invalids would have hired a nurse, or at least paid for a relative to come along. To leave the country, Holman was required to obtain a formal leave of absence from the navy, and, significantly, Admiralty records show his younger brother Robert (now twenty-eight and a lieutenant himself) applying for a year's leave at nearly the same time, and with the same destination: France.

This may have been the arrangement that satisfied the doctors, but if so, it did not satisfy Holman. As the planned day of departure approached, he'd received his leave, but his brother had not. Robert's leave would ultimately arrive three weeks later, but that was clearly longer than Holman was willing to wait.

By now Holman was displaying the best evidence that this bout of illness was, at least in part, psychological: the very prospect of the journey was already proving something of a tonic. He was impatient to go. He was still sick, but strengthening, and in far better spirits. In fact, he was experiencing a surge of elation. "I know not what might have been the consequence, if the excitement with which I looked forward to it had been disappointed," he wrote. Whether driven by that excitement, a necessary frugality, or a wild underestimation of the challenges involved, he made two fateful decisions. To proceed overland, via public transportation. And to travel quite alone.

• • •

CONFIDENT OF A "greater facility of locomotion than he could have anticipated," Holman hobbled onboard the Dover-to-Calais packet ship on October 15, 1819. It was the morning of his thirty-second birthday. The sail across the Channel was uneventful but ill-timed: currents prevented the ship from safely docking, so it hove to just off the Calais shore, waiting several hours for the tide to turn. Holman, invigorated by salt air and anticipation, was so eager to begin his adventure he paid a passing mailboat five francs—the equivalent of half of his fare from England—to take him the final few yards to land.

> Behold me, then, in France! surrounded by a people, to me, strange, invisible, and incomprehensible; separated from every living being who could be supposed to take the least interest in my welfare, or even existence.

It was his first taste of the freedom of abandon. Of the seductive power of plunging into the utterly unknown.

SEVEN

A Whimsical Invalid

THE FIRST OBSTACLE was young Virginie, a *fille de chambre* in the Grand Cerf Hotel. That evening, she entered Holman's room and proceeded to make herself useful, easing him toward the bed and loosing his clothes with a practiced flutter of hands. He had to seek out an interpreter to assert that he wanted no help in disrobing, and needed not so much as a candle for company. Locking the door behind her, he tried to dissipate the day's excitement into sleep. Tomorrow was a festival day, and Calais city gates would be locked for much of the morning, the better to encourage attendance at mass. He hoped to be well on his way to Paris before they swung closed, and he knew the journey would be far from relaxing.

The dominant European notion of overland travel was that it was an ordeal to be endured, and therefore best pursued in a headlong rush. The faster the journey the higher the fare, for speed required the frequent expense of changing horses. There were no concessions to comfort, much less enjoyment: you were, in a sense, underwriting your own abduction from one point to another. Stops were irregular, dictated by the horses' needs, not the passengers'. You pursued meals and hygiene during those pauses—or not at all. The carriage kept rolling through the night and you were expected to sleep where you sat, usually shoehorned in, crushed up against the other passengers.

Anonymous 1817 lampoon on the hazards of coach travel.

Not that sleep came easily. Even on well-traveled routes, most roads were either wheel-rutted dirt, loose jagged stone, haphazardly spread gravel, or a combination of all three—surfaces that might strike the modern eye as more suitable for a garden path than a busy thoroughfare. Decades of war had also transformed the landscape: roads once proudly maintained for centuries had been worn down by invading forces, torn up by retreating troops, and left unrepaired by war-burdened economies. On the whole, it was more taxing to travel Europe in 1819 than it had been a hundred years previously.

Holman's progress to Paris was typical of its day. The morning carriage was a cabriolet, named for its resemblance in motion to the jittery skipping of a *cabra*, Portuguese for she-goat. It was a light, two-wheeled affair with a basket-shaped back and room for only six. It was also inherently unstable, as they discovered that midnight. All the passengers jumped out so quickly that the vehicle fell forward—a sudden shift of weight that staggered the horses to their knees. Their rush to disembark was understandable: it was their first stop in ten hours. The horses' distress gave them a chance to awaken three or four local households, finally finding one sleepy housewife willing to sell them some cold meat and wine. Until then, they'd been subsisting on sour apples, knocked off roadside trees in passing. There would be only two more stops during the trip's thirty-five hours.

NOT SURPRISINGLY, HOLMAN spent his first evening in Paris recuperating. This meant a solitary meal and an early retreat to a hotel chamber, decorated with an opulence lost on him. The stone floors and marble tables gave only a hard coldness to his touch, and he found himself fighting not just fatigue but the first tinges of gloom. The road had rattled away his euphoria, and he was beginning to experience that particular kind of loneliness that only a crowded city can provide.

To shake it off he relocated to Mr. Fetherstone's boardinghouse, a less prestigious but more companionable establishment, where he hoped to launch a conversational approach to learning French. In this he was more successful than he wished to be, for a spate of cold and wet weather kept all twenty of Fetherstone's tenants confined to the parlor for days on end. Like countless beginning francophones before and since, he was soon stumbling on the vast gap between the language's stated meaning and actual usage. Assured that *toute à l'heure* meant "immediately," he observed that, when used by Parisians at least, a better translation would be "perhaps sometime today."

He made no effort to brave the weather and explore one of the world's great cities. He was, after all, not a tourist but an invalid, in transit to a warmer climate. After a week he felt strong enough to press on, but found it was not an easy thing to arrange. So much foreign traffic was centered on Paris that travel beyond the capital was seen as a separate matter entirely, requiring registry with the police and a special passport signed by the British ambassador. This time he booked the slowest route available, and climbed onboard the carriage with a basketful of what would become his standard traveling fare: a bottle of wine, a supply of fruit, and cow tongue—a tough but dense meat, not easily given to spoiling. He was bound for Bordeaux, which meant four days of around-the-clock confinement and motion.

He tried to practice French with his carriagemates, but such efforts soon petered out into silence. It was a small, enclosed space, overpacked knee-to-knee with passengers, at least one of whom puffed obliviously on a steady stream of cigars. The constant rain kept the windows closed. Holman was relieved to at last hear the cry "Voilà Bordeaux!" but apparently this was just a glimpse of the outskirts, for it was three more hours before the coach halted and everyone—except him—trundled out. Suddenly he was alone.

In as civil a shout as possible, he called out. Tired and weakened, he needed a hand disembarking, and someone to at least point him in the general direction of shelter.

"*Toute à l'heure,*" he heard a voice reply, then the sound of footsteps retreating.

He later wrote:

> . . . *what could I do? Had I jumped out, I should not have known what step to have taken next, and the rain was falling in torrents. There appeared no remedy, but to sit patiently until it might please some one to come to my assistance.*

The carriage doors opened, but not to retrieve Holman. Instead, hands prodded him first in one direction, then another, "as if they were using me for shifting ballast."

> *In a while I heard at least thirty people around the coach, talking a loud and unintelligible gibberish, quite unlike any language of the*

country which I had hitherto heard; soon afterwards I perceived the carriage undergoing an extraordinary, and irregular kind of motion.

He also heard the noise of water splashing, perhaps the sound of the wheels traversing particularly rain-soaked ground. But he suspected, paradoxically, that the vehicle no longer had any wheels—the motion was strangely smooth. He let his shouts become more strident.

"Toute à l'heure!" was the only response.

An hour later the doors again flew open. This time the passengers blithely bundled back in, taking care to resume their original seats. They explained nothing.

Fifteen minutes later he was in the actual coach station, piecing together what had just happened. The first halt had been on the banks of the Dordogne River, which in this rain-swollen season was best crossed by boat. All the other passengers had ridden over on a ferry. The carriage, along with its cargo and Holman—effectively categorized as human baggage—had floated across on a shallow raft, a downstream voyage of four miles. They had, in fact, been using him for ballast.

Blindness, compounded by silence, had made Holman all too easy for everyone to ignore. He was used to the unease of strangers back in England, but now he grasped that the commonplace manifestation of that unease—a willful oblivion—could have real consequences. Henceforth he cultivated the skill of subtly reaffirming his status as a human being, observing every wordless courtesy and taking pains to speak with a geniality that needed no translation. Decades later, fellow travelers encountering him for the first time would be struck by how easily and quickly his voice assumed "the earnest tone of an ancient friendship." It was a genuine sociability, but also a measure against slipping into invisibility.

•   •   •

BORDEAUX, AS SOGGY as Paris, was no place to recuperate. On Holman's single social call there, to a friend of a friend, he had his first taste of what would become a familiar tribulation: well-meaning, over-earnest efforts to restore his sight. First he was introduced to "an eminent oculist of this place," who fortunately concurred with the earlier diagnoses that an operation was premature. Holman received this news with equanimity, but his unsatisfied new companion promptly dragged him off to another medical expert—the wife of a local umbrella maker. He graciously endured her examination and the details of her surefire herbal cure, but as her course of treatment required a long-term stay he respectfully declined. The road to Toulouse held the prospect of a new means of transportation, and he was eager to try it out.

It was a carriage that, innovatively enough, actually paused at the end of each day. What's more, there were advance arrangements for lodging at each stop, so every passenger could expect a mattress and a meal. This sounds luxurious compared to the usual heedless hurry, but in fact it was a downscale alternative— the line saved money by cutting down on the need to change horses. The relaxed pace took five days, as opposed to the usual two, to travel the 125 miles to Toulouse, but, even with food and shelter included, the fare was a full third cheaper. Holman was concerned that the low price meant traveling in rough company, but the proprietor assured him that a French officer and his wife would be on board as well.

The "officer" turned out to be a bootmaker in a cavalry regiment—perhaps an honest mistake, as even bootmakers in Bonaparte's army were splendidly attired in great cocked hats. His wife, however, proved a most agreeable friend, particularly at the end of each day's travel, when she would take Holman by the hand and lead him to his private chamber.

"After having assisted in my arrangements, and warmed my bed, she permitted me to lock her out," he noted, in true gentlemanly fashion. "I cannot but express myself grateful."

The flirtation was almost certainly chaste, but it stirred Holman enough to admit that "the attentions of the softer sex are peculiarly acceptable under my present affliction." Between ships of war, palace chapels, and lecture halls, he'd had precious little sustained exposure to the pleasures of mixed company. Now he was discovering a happy disparity in the attitudes of male and female strangers.

Men, he found, almost automatically assigned him a sort of eunuch stature. Being blind, he was hardly a threat, and presumably incapable of perceiving a woman's attractions anyway. The women, however, often had a very different reaction. The bootmaker's wife would prove only the first of those unabashedly drawn to him, intrigued by his trust in touch, aware of his heightened awareness. They responded to him with sympathy, an emotion poles apart from pity. Other qualities—the fact that he was handsome, an officer, a war hero, a learned and well-spoken man given to reciting poetry—also did not escape their notice. Yet in the eyes of men, his blindness almost uniformly induced a different sort of blindness.

THE SLOW, AMBLING trip to Toulouse marked the true beginning of Holman's recuperation. Self-reinvention is one of the freedoms of the solo traveler, and with the Windsor physicians well behind him he felt emboldened to set some of his own unorthodox medical ideas into practice. First, nutrition. While everyone else started the day with a typical "fortifying" breakfast of bread and brandy, he consumed only fresh fruit. Then exercise: the carriage's typical speed was barely that of a brisk walking pace, so, when weather permitted, he would jump out, unwind a length of cord from his pocket, tie one end to the vehicle, and grasp on to the other.

"I then followed, in this way, on foot for several miles," he noted, "to the no small amusement of the villagers, who laughed heartily, and even shouted after me."

It was fortunate that witnesses were entertained rather than alarmed, for his regimen—spare diet, intentional exertion to the point of exhaustion—was the opposite of what was commonly considered wholesome for a healthy man, much less an invalid on medical leave. But it bore immediate results, allowing him to sleep soundly and banishing the severe headaches that had plagued him. By the last full day of the journey, he was in excellent spirits, particularly when the bootmaker's wife volunteered her hand as a substitute for the string. She led him away from the meandering carriage to a spot where, she assured him, the view was most inspiring—and where she endeavored, through touch and words, to make him understand that her choice of husband had been disappointing.

Holman did not record his response, only that "The air at this spot I found so soft, balmy, and exhilarating, that I felt assured I had now reached the south of France."

He decided to winter in Toulouse. In February, news arrived from England: the blind, delusional George III had passed away at the age of eighty-two. Holman's absence would not go unnoticed at the elaborate, moonlit state funeral, attended by thousands. The Naval Knights of Windsor marched at the very head of the procession, and it was apparent to many that the Seven Gentlemen were missing one of their number.

MARCH MELTED THE snow, and April dried the snowmelt mud to render passable the southern roads. Holman departed toward the Mediterranean coast, thanking those who had welcomed him as "a whimsical invalid." In the carriage, he befriended a fellow passenger, a gentleman who promptly offered to share his home in the town of Montpellier. They arrived to a compounded unpleasantness.

This new acquaintance, clearly generous to a fault, had in his absence loaned his home to a group of friends—one of whom, he now found, had died on the premises. The others, solemnly observing a local custom, burned the deathbed, and somehow managed to set fire to much of the other furniture as well. Now there was a dead friend to mourn, an uninhabitable home, and a substantial bill from the landlord. But the misfortune was serendipitous for Holman: his sudden need for lodgings sparked an offer of hospitality from a prosperous noblewoman, the Countess de M——.

Each era has its stylistic trends and literary conceits. One of the frustrations of accounts from the early 1800s is the then-popular fashion for concealing full names, as if there was something undignified about appearing in someone else's reminiscences. Holman observed this convention wholeheartedly, either rendering his acquaintances entirely anonymous—as with the bootmaker's wife, or his burnt-furniture friend—or by masking them under an amalgam of dashes and initials. Even his bankers, who could hardly have minded the publicity, were cited only as "Messrs. G—— & H——".

At times it is possible to fill in the blanks and strip away the masks, but the Countess—like many of Holman's discreetly described female friends—remains difficult to pinpoint with certainty. We do know that she welcomed him not only into her mansion but into her family, making him a part of their daily domestic life. It was an instant intimacy that would have been unthinkable with a sighted gentleman, particularly since no husband was in evidence. The family consisted of herself, two daughters, and one apparently distant male relation, a Monsieur de C——.

Holman found himself surrounded and suffused by beauty. He walked the fragrant paths of the mansion's terraced gardens, enjoyed the cool of the fountains, and delighted in discovering a secluded thicket where nightingales sang, not only at night but throughout the day. And then there were the daughters, both young and vivacious and eminently marriageable. When the eldest returned from a ball with excited tales of dancing and flirting with an officer, Holman was honored to chaperone the subsequent courtship. When she joyously accepted the officer's proposal, he joined the others in welcoming the new fiancé into the family. In this bower of feminine companionship, now buttressed with the friendship of the fiancé, a fellow military gentleman, Holman pronounced himself "exceedingly happy in this family." Not *with*, but *in*.

THE TROUBLESOME ELEMENT was Clementine, the countess's youngest daughter, just seventeen and a rare beauty, of the sort that inspires stammering and furtive fixation on the part of men.

One night, Holman awakened to the sound of footsteps directly beneath his window. His first impulse was to raise the alarm for burglars, but it turned out to be a young student from Paris, obsessed with Clementine since his first sighting of her near the nightingale thicket, where she'd been languidly leading a goat on a string. Too tongue-tied to address either the Countess or Clementine herself, the young man had taken to stalking the grounds after dark. He wasn't apprehended, nor, it seems, even confronted; no one was much concerned about such foolishness. Monsieur de C—— even attended all-night parties in the town, leaving Holman the sole male in the household.

In early summer, de C—— returned from just such a night out. Strolling through the garden in the dawn light, he found the Parisian student sitting on the lawn almost motionless.

Discovered, the young man reared up, unsheathed a large knife, and plunged it into his own breast.

"*Mon Dieu! Mon ami*, why have you done this!" cried de C——.

"Clementine! Clementine!" was his only answer. At least until a few minutes later, when he was slipping into unconsciousness and slowly bleeding to death. Now surrounded by the entire household, he effused, "Ah! Clementine! For you I die! I feel you can never be mine, nor can I live without you!"

The melodramatic language may reflect Holman's limited trans-

lation skills, or the true tone of the incident. But the end result was
the irrevocable shattering of the peace of the house. Suddenly, the
absence of a more able, protective male was acutely felt. While
no one could conceivably fault Holman for inaction, he was perceptive enough to realize it was time to move on. A week later he
hobbled onboard another carriage—hobbled because one of his
weakened ankles had again wrenched its ligaments. Every jolt in
the road was a fresh visitation of pain. By the time he disembarked
in Nîmes, he was hardly able to walk at all.

NÎMES WAS INTOLERABLY hot, and it was high summer
before Holman felt well enough to proceed to Aix. This was likely
the destination his doctors had in mind when they prescribed a
sojourn in the south of France: it offered not only the celebrated
sunlight of Provence, but a district called the Fauxbourg that
catered to the sick. The Fauxbourg's stock in trade was fresh air—it
occupied the highest part of town— and a mineral spring that Holman soon preferred to those at Bath. The waters emerged at a heat
that nearly matched body temperature, and to float in the buoyant
depths was almost to feel oneself disappear. He tried unsuccessfully to learn their chemical composition, and made them the cen-
terpiece of his residence.

There was little else to do. He had taken too long, nine months,
in transit, and everyone who could possibly afford it had fled to
cooler retreats for the summer. "The town is empty and dull," he
glumly observed, and resolved that when his health permitted,
he'd make a side visit to the port at Marseilles, just fifteen miles
distant. There were no social diversions there, either; it was not
a resort town but a working-class harbor with decidedly seedy
aspects, and not a place to wander about indiscriminately. But
early each morning, people gathered on opposite sides of the harbor—men on the right, women on the left—to bathe in the sea.
If the clubfooted Lord Byron could paddle across the Hellespont

in Greece, already a famous exploit, the least Holman could do was plunge into the Mediterranean.

Somewhere in his past, he'd picked up a rare skill for a naval man: the ability to swim. The men's bathing area was not a beach but a stretch of shallows slightly offshore. Boats carried their passengers to a depth of about five feet, then floated steps into the water. These he ignored; instead he dove in headfirst, directly from the deck. Once in the water he ignored the shallows too, and headed, quietly but deliberately, straight out to sea.

Soon his only orientation was a thread of sound, the occasional exchange of shouts between him and the astonished bathers rapidly diminishing in his wake. He was naked, alone, testing the limits of his newfound stamina, savoring the rewards of risk, utterly happy. Almost lost, but almost free.

At an earlier time, he might have been tempted to keep going, to discover which would fail him first, his senses or his strength. This morning, he made one last defiant stroke in the general direction of Africa, then began a slow loop back to the voices.

IT WAS SEPTEMBER now. His one-year leave of absence expired on the twenty-first, and by every measure it had been a success. Not only had the baths at Aix seemingly washed away most of the pain in his joints, but "my eyes in particular felt lighter, and I fancied that I could occasionally discern a flash of light from the under part of the left one."

The light, or fantasy of light, soon died. After a few more weeks he admitted the obvious conclusion to himself: further convalescence would not significantly improve his condition. Logically, it was time to return to Windsor Castle and resume his knightly duties, thankful for the healing interval.

Holman *was* thankful. But he was also anything but homesick. His journey had reacquainted him with three potent forces: the invigorating embrace of risk, the engrossing immersion in the unknown, and the intoxicating company of women. Life back at Windsor was notably deficient in each of these qualities—and besides, there seemed no particular hurry to expend his repaired constitution by grinding it down, twice a day, on the Hundred Steps.

He stayed in France just long enough for the Admiralty to confirm extension of his leave. If he sent a parallel request to Windsor, or even informal notice that his convalescence was continuing, no record of it survives. Then he moved on.

Sketch of Holman as an attentive traveler.

EIGHT

The Experimental Citizen

ITALY DID NOT exist. There was a patchwork of wobbly, warring states whose only commonality was the Italian language and the memory of empire. Sardinia, an island, now had vast claims on the mainland—or, more accurately, the king of Sardinia was, at the moment, also the king of Savoy, Liguria, and the Piedmont. Austrians were sweeping through, adding as much as possible to *their* empire. Power-seizing plots, combined with the settlement of old scores, were creating a chaotic and bloody tangle of ambitions. Armed secret societies, with cryptic names like the Carbonari and Sublime Perfect Masters, were rising in the aftermath of Napoleonic domination.

This era marked the beginning of the *Risorgimento*, the resurgence of Italian nationalism that would ultimately unify the country forty years later, under the military leadership of Guiseppe Garibaldi. But in the fall of 1820, Garibaldi was barely a teenager, a fisherman's son growing up on the streets of Nice, the same streets that Holman now walked with an air of disappointment. It hardly qualified as a city—even a blind man could make a tour of it in about twenty minutes—and while he understood that there were at least a few notable views, he was annoyed to the point of distraction by the ubiquitous rattles and strokes and thumps of machines extruding macaroni, a constant sonic presence that the sighted found easy enough to ignore.

He found more relaxing lodgings in Saint Rosalie, about a mile and a half out of town. This was a unique fusion of two adjacent edifices, a mansion and an ancient church fused into a vineyard estate. The lady of the manor was Madame Therese M, a "pretty little sensible woman." Her hospitality seemed a reprise of his recent residence with the Countess, as her household also consisted of herself and two daughters. Only this time, the fourth presence was not only female but English, a young governess.

Holman, the solitary male in this ménage, chose not to protest the blind-as-eunuch assumptions that kept this arrangement untainted by notions of impropriety.

Again, the months passed as one extended idyll. In the vintage season he joined in the all-hands hurry of harvest, taking up a knife and laboring through the arbors, cutting down the grapes in their clusters. On the feast day of Madame M's namesake saint, he and the daughters arose early to honor her with the traditional shower of bouquets. Later that evening, Madame M's brother pulled his chair close to the young governess and began to sing pointedly of *ma belle voisine,* my beautiful neighbor. Holman was witnessing yet another courtship.

This time, it evoked in him something more than simple happiness for the couple. "I thought I could have reposed for ever in this semblance of an earthly paradise," he confided to his writing machine. "And yet there was something which, in my situation, I felt was still wanting to make me completely blest."

Too gentlemanly to bluntly express his desires, he resorted to awkwardly quoting the minor poet Benjamin Church:

> *Rapt in the soft retreat, my anxious breast*
> *Pants still for something unpossessed;*

Whence springs this sudden hope, this warm desire?
To what enjoyment would my soul aspire?
'Tis love! extends my wishes and my care,
Eden was tasteless 'till an Eve was there.

THIS TIME HOLMAN didn't wait for spring. It was still February when he stood on the deck of the Genoa-bound merchant vessel *Providenzia Divina*, feeling the weak breeze that barely filled the sails.

The voyage was inauspicious from the beginning. The ship was sailing without cargo and with only a handful of passengers, since demand for civil transport was drastically waning. In the five months since he'd crossed the border, Italy had become a much more dangerous place. Naples was now at war with Austria. Milan and Piedmont were on the brink of revolution, and the so-called secret societies were openly preparing for insurrection almost everywhere else. Holman hadn't just been discouraged from proceeding further, he'd been told emphatically that such plans were nothing less than insanity. Especially since he himself wore a military uniform—albeit a uniform that he had lately taken to topping with a broad straw hat.

But it was hardly a matter of choice. He couldn't just loiter, and pride would not allow him to retrace his steps, reimposing on the hospitalities of so many. During his naval years battles had proved elusive even when he sought them out. Now, he trusted his former bad luck to remanifest as good fortune. Should he be caught up in hostilities, his best hope was to take refuge in an English ship, and those were no harder to find on the Tyrrhenian Sea than on the Mediterranean.

The *Providenzia* was not an English ship, and would never be mistaken for one. Small, single-masted, and built close to the waterline, she was suited only for short offshore coasting runs, preferably in fair weather. At midnight, when the wind picked up and a light rain began to fall, the captain immediately made for the nearest port and presented his passengers with two options. They could take mules from here into Genoa, or they could stay aboard and take their chances.

Mules were tedious and expensive, but in the end only two passengers chose to continue sailing: Holman and a twenty-five-year-old Italian lady, "whom my imagination might lead me to suppose beautiful as an *houri*." It was a carefully chosen word, one that means "dark-eyed woman" in Persian. In literature, houris are exotic seductresses, yet they're also the voluptuous virgins that the Koran promises to each male true believer, upon the afterlife achievement of Paradise. This one was married but traveling alone, already anxious over the delays and the worsening weather.

The rain remained sparse, but the wind grew colder and churned the sea with greater force each hour. By nightfall the captain again ordered a bearing toward shore. Then there was a sudden wrenching that set gear tumbling and men staggering to the deck. Holman didn't need to translate the urgent cries to know what was happening—the ship was no longer afloat, but aground.

Soon the shouts gave up details: they were on the rocks of a minor, uninhabited island, far from help, in danger not only of sinking but being torn apart by tides. There was nothing to do but lash even more tightly to the rocks with the anchor chain, and keep bailing. The two passengers were hurried into the ship's sole cabin, told to stay there until further notice. Then, in the press of the ordeal, they were all but forgotten for two days.

IN THE WINDOWLESS chamber, Holman and Signora Houri heard the wind strengthen to a gale, the drive of rain crescendo into a storm. At first, he tried to maintain a respectable distance, slinging his mattress on a bench and leaving to her the more spacious floor, but as the hours wore on disaster seemed no less imminent. The woman grew more and more afraid, and at last Holman understood she needed comfort more than propriety. He pulled his mattress next to hers. Each opened their blankets to the other.

"We shut ourselves up close, to keep out the wind and rain," was how he delicately documented the situation. "I must have had indeed a heart of rock, had I not poured in all possible consolation."

They lay together, side by side, for a night, a day, and then another night. Outside they heard nothing but the unabating storm. Holman's sense of time began to slip and fade. He perceived the nights only when Signora Houri drifted off into fitful sleep, too often awakening in terror when fresh creaks rose from the hull.

"Monsieur! Monsieur! We're against the rocks!" she'd cry. This couldn't be disputed, only answered with another reassuring touch.

The weather, in time, seemed to lessen slightly. Shortly after daybreak on the second day, the signora looked through a hole in the cabin's canvas screening and let loose another cry, this one a shout summoning the captain. She'd been watching the mast relative to the island they'd run up against: either the island's trees were moving, or the anchoring had slipped and set them adrift. The captain, not expecting a distraught, confined woman to be more perceptive than his crew, first dismissed her observation, then confirmed it—the anchor had indeed failed. They had no choice but to haul it in, raise a reefed sail to the still-considerable winds, and hope to steer clear of obstacles.

The *Providenzia* never delivered her passengers to Genoa. She made landfall without further incident, but the spooked captain resumed the passage only at a cautious pace, putting into port on the slightest pretext: *this town is good for provisions, this one sells cheap sails.* On the sixth day of what should have been a two-day voyage, Holman and the signora gave up and resorted to the roads, but not before buying wine for the entire crew as a gesture of gratitude. They boarded a carriage together, but by the time Holman reached Genoa, he was again alone.

•   •   •

DAYS LATER HE was floating in the Gulf of Spezia on yet another felucca, this time working up a sweat as a temporary member of the crew. For days, the ship had been becalmed, and with dwindling supplies the decision had been made to start rowing southward. Holman, happy for the exercise, insisted on taking regular shifts at the oars.

He was, unwittingly, traveling in a private pocket of peace. Behind him, revolutions were breaking out in Nice and Genoa. Before him lay the Neapolitan States, which the Austrians were now invading. When he finally made land and caught up on current events, he wisely decided to proceed in the general direction of Rome, where the pope's presence offered at least a short-term degree of safety from the political stormfronts.

But first he endured a personal crisis, a private drama that quietly unfolded before a stagefront in Florence.

Holman wasn't much for opera. Music itself was a constant and profound joy throughout his life, but when it intersected with drama he found his powers of listening too finely attuned. Inevitably, at least one performer would prove a fine voice but an insufferable ham, or a passable actor but an indifferent singer. Others in the audience might be distracted from this disparity by the spectacle of the sets and the pomp of the staging, yet for him it remained a grating dissonance.

That evening's performance at the Teatro del Cocomero—Rossini's recent opera *The Barber of Seville*—was a revelation to Holman. For once, no one on stage was jarringly out of step. The music and the drama fused seamlessly, and he was soon caught up in the experience. A baritone delivered the title character's cheerfully pompous self-announcing solo—*Figaro Figaro Fi-ga-ro!*—then fell to helping the noble Count (tenor) triumph over the conniving Doctor (bass) for the love of the music student Rosina (mezzosoprano). Complications furiously ensued: shaving cream became a weapon, ladders strategically disappeared, and everyone kept singing, wittily and vigorously. And Holman himself became more and more enamored with Rosina, or rather with the *prima donna* who played her.

"I would have given the world to have seen her pretty face and figure," he would remember, quite certain of her beauty.

In a strange fashion, his desire was immediately granted. "The tones and expression of her voice . . . appeared to connect themselves in my mind, by pure sympathy, with exact delineation of her person and attitudes," he noted.

The flood of sensation had begun to mingle and fuse, transforming into something entirely new. This was no mind's-eye mental image—it seemed tantamount to sight. "I heard, I felt, I saw, or *imagined I saw*, everything which words, gestures, and actions could convey," was how he described it, judiciously resorting to italics.

He rose from his seat, ignoring the audience around him, transfixed on the images that seemed certainly before him. He leaned forward; his greatest impulse was to bound up on the stage. It would halt the performance and almost certainly get him arrested, but it seemed the only possible way to dispel the condition. These could only be illusions, but illusions so vivid that he felt compelled to shatter them, "to convince myself that I could not see." Instead he fought himself, standing still until the impulse passed. Then he resumed his seat. Soon the images themselves diminished and departed.

A PERSON DOES not need eyes to experience sight. So long as the visual cortex remains functional, impulses introduced into its pathways will be processed as visual data, even if the input is randomly generated or mischanneled from another sense—hearing, smell, taste, touch. In fact, every portion of the brain devoted to a particular sense can experience the phenomenon of synesthesia, a sort of neurological crosswiring that floods it with nonsensory stimuli. The condition is congenital in some, induced in others by disease or hallucinogenic drugs. It's common for someone under-going synesthesia to speak of "tasting colors" or "the shape of sounds." It's also not uncommon for the blind, particularly those blinded in adulthood, to develop a susceptibility to visual synesthe-sia in the absence of other cortical input.

Holman's incident in the theater was his first such episode, but not his last. He would, from time to time, be visited by simi-lar flashes: a stranger would speak and suddenly, "if my powers of sight could admit of a use of the pencil, I could at this instant depict his portrait, as correctly as if I had actually seen him." These phantom images were exquisite to experience, but they left in their wake an equally profound sadness. Nothing else quite so acutely awakened the memory of what he had lost.

IT WAS EASY to tell where the glorious but cash-strapped domin-ion of His Holiness Pope Pius VII began. The roads were suddenly a slogging tumult of mud and furrows, and Holman resumed his habit of walking in concert with the carriage. This time all his fellow passengers joined him. The combination of fine weather and amiable conversation fueled the spirit of a pedestrian party, marred only by the need to step past the rotting corpse of an exe-cuted criminal, presumably a robber. Such bodies were a common presence on the roadsteads of the Roman States, doubly warning both the abundant *banditti* and their potential victims.

Holman carried the momentum of physical exertion into the city itself, bounding up Trajan's Pillar, the Palatine Hill, the Tar-peian Rock, and even Monte Testaccio (not a mountain but an ancient trash heap), all on a single day, much to the exhaustion of his hired guide. He'd been indifferent to Paris, largely because the sights there were just that—sights, meant to be gazed upon. But much of Rome's grandeur was more to be evoked than seen, especially since many monuments (since reconstructed) were, at the time, little more than piles of stone in neglected fields. He was as well equipped as anyone to run his hand across a section of long-scattered column and mentally reassemble it whole, or to pace a battered, weedy foundation and imagine when the ground was not the Campo Vaccino, cow pasture, but the Forum Romanum.

Some tactile pleasures had to be taken furtively. The Vatican sculpture collection was off-limits to the touch and thickly guarded by soldiers. He made confederates of fellow art lovers, who kindly cued him when the soldiers' backs were turned. There were also auditory pleasures. The onset of Easter may have dulled the night-life in Florence, but here it prompted a profusion of sound—cannon salutes and open-air bands and concerts of sacred song. He found the *a cappella* concerts especially rapturous.

Holman knew no one in Rome, but he did have a letter of introduction to Dr. James Clark, an expatriate Scotsman who quickly became a friend, and whose friendship would be a crucial asset in years to come. They had much to talk about. In fact, it's surprising they hadn't met sooner, as their lives had long run in parallel.

Clark, slightly younger than Holman, had interrupted his Edinburgh medical studies to join the Royal Navy. When Holman was struggling to keep his commission on the *Guerriere*, Clark was assistant surgeon of the *Thistle*, stationed out of the same harbor. Idled on half-pay after the peace, he'd resumed his long-deferred medical education and graduated from Edinburgh in the same year as Holman. He'd even made a leisurely trip through the south of France a year in advance of Holman, sampling and analyzing the same mineral waters the latter had found so therapeutic.

Now he was writing a book about those mineral waters, and establishing a practice tending to English-speaking invalids in Rome for their health. Like Holman, he was an advocate of fresh air and physical exercise, and a literary gentleman, not a poet himself but an admirer of the art. The two hit it off so well that Holman soon shifted from his hotel to a boarding establishment only a few steps away from Clark's house in the Piazza di Spagna, a move suggested and arranged by the doctor himself.

Clark perhaps neglected to mention how he knew of the vacancy. These lodgings were the recent scene of the drawn-out, agonizing death of one of his patients—another young Englishman, this one so poor that his friends had taken up a collection to send him here. His British doctors were unanimous in their opinion that he was dying of tuberculosis and should stay abed, but Clark had made a maverick diagnosis of stomach trouble and prescribed not rest, but exercise. Unfortunately the patient proved the doctor wrong by collapsing and coughing up copious quantities of blood. He sank into a months-long decline so torturous that toward the end he'd wake up, discover he was still alive, and start crying.

When the end arrived at last, Clark sentimentally commissioned a death mask of the young man, who'd shown some promise as a poet. Holman moved in a few weeks later, by all accounts unaware of his predecessor at this address. If anyone mentioned the name to him, he probably didn't recognize it: only the poet's last volume had gathered even modest attention, and it was published after Holman had departed for the continent. Number 26 Piazza di Spagna has since become a popular pilgrimage, a meticulously preserved shrine to the memory of John Keats.

TIME WOULD NOT permit even a beginning familiarity with the whole of Rome, so Holman picked three grand edifices—St. Peter's, the Capitol and the Pantheon—and began to haptically construct them in his mind, visiting them again and again, "by which repetitions I imagine that I gained almost as correct ideas, as if I had actually seen these objects."

He was frustrated in these inspections exactly once, after laboring up a miscellany of stairs and ladders to the very top of St. Peter's. Not just the roof of the dome or the cupola surmounting it, but the ball, the small hollow copper sphere that perches like a landed satellite atop them both. It would be, he thought, a simple matter to crawl through the last portal to the open sky, then clamber up the cross that comprised the very pinnacle of the largest church in the world.

He was unafraid, even eager. Blindness had rendered him immune to vertigo, as he was happy to demonstrate. But this final ascension was barred to him—not out of concern for his condition, but his nationality. The last man to attempt it was also an Englishman, and he'd irreverently left a Union Jack fluttering from the cross at the highest point.

No matter. A greater challenge awaited beyond the city, in the southern lands skirting the Bay of Naples. Holman knew that in the days before the war, "the experimental citizen who brought away a snuff box from the lava of Vesuvius, was then considered a sort of miracle of a man." And that was when the volcano was docile, almost dormant. Now it was transforming, dangerously thundering and bellowing anew—it was, in fact, building up to what would be its greatest eruption in the century.

Holman was ready to continue his own transformation. He'd started this journey as a frail invalid, a bit of human baggage. He'd bloomed into an expatriate, a tourist, then an active, questing, and questioning traveler. Now he was ready to become an adventurer.

THERE WAS ANOTHER purpose drawing him toward Naples. He'd heard a familiar name arise in connection with that region, the name of an old naval shipmate and "a most intimate friend of my own some years before." The fellow Englishman was indeed his old companion, and the reunion was joyous, although marked with a strange balance of pathos. While the man was saddened to see his old friend now blind, Holman was equally dismayed to learn that *his* friend was now deaf.

The two fell into constant company—they had a lot of catching up to do. "Perhaps few had experienced more vicissitudes of fortune than this gentleman," Holman enthused, "or been exposed to a greater variety of dangers and adventures, many of which bordered not a little on the romantic."

With typical maddening reserve, he recorded the man's exploits but not his name, instead labeling him Mr. C——. Only once, in a careless variation, did this expand to "Mr. C—l—b—k." That slip makes an exact identification no less impossible, but it does allow the exasperated biographer to substitute a slightly more humanizing pseudonym. In these pages C—l—b—k shall be Colebrook— an arbitrary filling-in of those blanks, but a liberty to be viewed in light of the possibility that it was an assumed name in the first place. Those "dangers and adventures," as related to Holman, have a distinctly covert cast to them.

In 1815, Colebrook had been caught in Napoleon's encampment outside Paris, traveling under an American passport. The French were marching him to prison as a spy when an argument broke out among two groups of soldiers, over which would have the honor of carrying out his execution. The conflict escalated to inter-rank gunfire, until one contingent—perhaps out of spite—allowed him to get away. He then appears to have been attached to the staff of the Irish general-turned-mercenary Sir Richard Church, who (with King George IV's blessing) was serving as commander-in-chief of the Neapolitan troops in Sicily. For reasons that are murky at best, some of the general's own soldiers ransacked Colebrook's hotel room as he looked on, leaving him with nothing but a greatcoat and a single pair of pantaloons.

He was also, in Holman's words, "well acquainted with almost every European language," but that skill had sadly waned with the onset of his deafness, the cause of which Holman never bothered to explain.

Communication was a challenge but soon the two were closer than ever, both thankful for a friend whose own affliction rendered him immune to the practice of pity. And neither could deny the compatibility of those afflictions. Holman's Noctograph could transcribe the unheard, while Colebrook offered a guiding arm and a watchful eye.

Together they visited the royal palace at nearby Caserta, and enjoyed strolling about the grounds so much that they imprudently stayed past nightfall, ignoring the warnings of their driver. He had good reason to be nervous. Occupying Austrians kept the peace in Naples, but outside the city cashiered soldiers competed with the local *banditti* in perpetrating highway crimes. The roads were lawless in the dark.

They were rolling toward the outskirts when shadowy forms emerged in the wake of their carriage. Not on the road but at an angle of interception: three men, striding fast and purposefully over the heath. A few minutes later, they were in step close behind, clearly sizing up the passengers. A minute later, and one was grasping on to the rear, hidden from the driver's sight, looking for a foothold to spring himself onboard.

Colebrook, seeing this, wasn't about to cower and hide. Instead he shouted out—not a cry of alarm, but a rattling stream of colloquial if not obscene Italian, aimed straight at the attacker's ears. Whatever he said, it was sufficient to instantly dislodge and disperse the robbers.

Holman was impressed by his friend's aplomb, and further impressed the next morning. He'd gone straight to bed after the incident, but Colebrook hadn't let deafness keep him from arguing, laboriously, over the fare for two hours straight (the coachman had tried to extract extra for hazardous duty). Clearly, here was a man temperamentally incapable of being victimized.

The deaf man stayed behind when Holman took Robert Madden in tow and tackled Mount Vesuvius. But when he returned, bright with triumph and primed for further adventures, Colebrook made known his intention to close up quarters and undertake a journey of his own. He would be heading northward, passing not only out of Italy but out of Europe altogether. It was only logical that they consider traveling together.

Holman had made many friends in his travels, yet it was a point of pride that the travel itself remained a solitary undertaking. But now there were other considerations. His southerly progress was effectively ended, as there wasn't sufficient time remaining on his leave to venture much further down the Italian peninsula. So he and Colebrook would be going in the same direction. And it was clear that Colebrook's company would allow him to move faster. Not that he wanted to hurry back. He wanted to cover as much territory as possible.

Then there was the thought of deaf Colebrook on his own, wearing himself out trying to understand, and be understood, every time a bill needed disputation. But ultimately there was the sense that a joint journey would, in its way, be more of an adventure than Vesuvius. Not in the sense of risk, but in an off-kilter, lurching and laughing way.

"It may be regarded as a curious incident in our traveling connexion—that I should want sight, and he hearing," Holman admitted. "The circumstance is somewhat droll, and afforded considerable amusement to those whom we traveled with. We were not infrequently exposed to a jest on the subject, which we generally participated in, and sometimes contributed to improve."

It was the first time Holman ever took on a traveling companion. It would also be the last.

COLEBROOK LEARNED THE pleasures of abandoning a cramped carriage for a stride alongside in the open air, and the two walked arm-in-arm through the Pontine marshes. Back in Rome, Holman dragged him to sculpture galleries he'd missed the first time through, taking full advantage of his new private lookout. One morning, assured of the all-clear, he joyfully flew his fingers over a cluster of celebrity busts—Lord Byron, the prince and princess of Denmark—then moved on to the next exhibit. His hand sailed out into confusion: surely, that was a leg he was touching—an *actual* leg. Attached to a very real, very male torso.

He heard the snickering close behind, then ringing around the room. Colebrook had deliberately steered him toward a model in the posture of a statue—attendants were getting ready to make a plaster cast from life, and everyone was in on the joke. Holman, of course, joined in the laughter.

They remained in high spirits as they barreled through the countryside. Traveling with Colebrook had a double advantage: not only did he describe the scenery, he understood his friend's notions of scenic. Now Holman knew when they passed "a beautiful female on horseback, riding after the fashion of men." Or when their supper was served by a "neat, interesting young female." One fellow passenger was "a languishing beauty, with a pair of such bewitching black eyes" that Colebrook, something of a ladies' man himself, could hardly meet their gaze.

Other small but telling details of the journey entered into vicarious notice. Holman could now record that the natives of the Susa region were "ludicrously dressed, wearing cocked-hats, very long tails, and black breeches, and frequently without either shoes or stockings." A traveler to Turin spoke grandly of a rich wife and a thriving horse-trading business, but Colebrook quietly confirmed that his clothes were sadly shabby.

There were additional benefits. Colebrook was readily capable of steering them clear of political hotspots, and easing them through the checkpoints, which were numerous; each region had their own customs inspections and diplomatic apparatus. By the time they swept through Florence, Holman was obliged to get a new passport. The old one, all but blank at the beginning of his trip, was now "filled up at every point with signs and countersigns, until the original writing was nearly lost in the midst of marginal additions."

But the greatest advantage was the absence of others taking advantage. The cost of traveling was a fluid quality, usually based on a quick assessment of the traveler's worth, gullibility or simple need; tickets, rate cards, and menus with fixed prices were scarce.

Each day brought a brace of fresh arrangements to make—for a carriage, a room, a meal—and so, they worked out a routine.

Colebrook inspected, then signaled his approval. Holman conducted the negotiations and asked that the terms be conveyed to his deaf friend on a scrap of paper. When items were switched or prices retroactively increased (all-too-common occurrences), the two produced the scrap, which, written in the proprietor's own hand, was enforceable as a contract. This wasn't just a guard against unscrupulous businessmen. They caught at least one fellow traveler, a friendly and seemingly benign Frenchman, trying to strike bargains at their expense: *charge them double, and charge me nothing*.

The only failure of their routine came when they were crossing from Savoy into Switzerland. The inn was full of unruly Sardinian soldiers. They clawed covetously at the baggage of the new arrivals, whipping off the cord from Colebrook's trunk as soon as he put it down. The two needed a private, lockable room, and quickly. But the young woman waiting upon them not only declined to put anything in writing, she seemed unable to comprehend their request. Holman ran through his rudimentary Italian, his passable French, his native tongue. Then Colebrook pitched in, tonelessly shouting out phrases in each of the several languages he knew. Still nothing.

The soldiers crowded, waiting and watching. It took a stretch of charged silence and a procession of tentative gestures, then touches, but soon Holman understood why the militia were running roughshod in the inn. The young woman was both deaf and mute.

The soldiers' attitude changed from ominous to amused as the three launched a mutual search for common ground, beating the air with a flurry of improvised signs, the woman taking care to press those signs into Holman's skin. At length they each succeeded in making themselves understood. She not only found them a secure room, she fed them dinner and saw them safely off in the next day's coach.

• • •

THE RENOWNED NATURALIST François Huber had the unmistakable presence of a Great Man. There was both a vitality and a dignity to him, qualities underscored by a perpetually contemplative manner and a slight resemblance to George Washington. In movement he seemed younger than his seventy-one years; in the stillness of listening he seemed as ancient as a rock formation. When Holman and Colebrook's carriage pulled up to his country home outside of Geneva he was walking alone in the garden, lost in thought. But not physically lost. His fingers idly traced a string, permanently threaded past the flowerbeds and hedges.

Huber was the most famous blind man in the world.

He'd started to lose his vision at the age of fifteen after a case of scarlet fever, just as he was finding his vocation in science. When he realized the disease would inevitably claim his sight, he didn't abandon his studies; instead, he accelerated them, reading as much as he could, while he still could. Then, as the darkness closed in, he centered his attention on a matter that seemed outside the realm of human sight: the mystery of the beehive.

For thousands of years, no one could rightfully claim to know what happened inside a beehive. You could tear one open, but whatever the bees were doing, they'd stop it and start attacking you. The obvious solution, once the technology became available, was to build a hive with a glass wall or viewing port. But it didn't work—the bees shrank from the light and immediately began to honeycomb over the opening. Whatever their life was like apart from flowers and flight, it was conducted in darkness.

Huber solved the problem by freeing it from conventional notions of observation. He built a beehive that folded open and closed, like a book. Both halves had glass walls on the inside, but the hive was tightly shut and sealed from sunlight. By now he was completely blind, so he recruited François Burnens, a servant whose powers of observation he could trust.

He instructed Burnens to open the hive—just for a few seconds at a time—and read it like a book, committing to memory as much as he could before the bees flew into full defense. Then Burnens would shut the hive, leave the bees to their darkness, and bear witness for his master. *I saw the queen. I counted the wings of those around her, as you requested.*

The glimpses and descriptions continued for decades. Over those years, Huber constructed his own mental maps, until he could summon himself into a hive at will. He began to make observations of his own, which were confirmed by Burnens. These coalesced into discoveries: How bees make wax. The location of their sensory organs. How air circulates in the combs. How insects could construct cells of geographical exactitude. His essays, titled (with a willful irony) *New Observations on the Natural History of Bees*, became the instant foundation of a new apiarian science.

This was a pilgrimage for Holman but a pleasure for Huber, who'd heard tales of the blind medical student through mutual friends at Edinburgh. He was more than willing to offer praise and encouragement, but that was the awkwardness at the core of their conversation: Holman needed no encouragement, as he had no ambition. The idea of a life's work seemed to belong to his previous, sighted life; wasn't it enough of an achievement that he regained his mobility and retained his independence?

In the august presence of the Great Man, Holman couldn't help but feel, for the first time, slightly on the defensive. He found himself fixating not on Huber but "the respect and affection of all around him," particularly the constant attentions of Madame Huber. Their courtship had begun when both were seventeen—when Huber was still sighted—and as his vision failed, he'd engaged in elaborate stratagems to keep her from learning the truth. The deceptions were inevitably discovered but Maria Aimeé remained constant, even when her father forbade the match. She waited until she reached her majority, then marched to the altar on her own. Their marriage was, by all reports, one of mutual devotion, even after forty years.

"He has been particularly fortunate in the companion of

his domestic happiness," Holman recorded. The words have an almost palpable greenish tinge of jealousy, particularly since he was nursing a grumbling attitude toward the perceived general neglect of females in Geneva, where all men seemed "members of some learned society or other." Soon he was resorting to his standard means of sublimation—breaking out into poetry, this time by Thomas Otway:

Oh, woman! Lovely woman! Nature made ye to temper man—
We had been brutes without you.

THE JOURNEY HAD been a gradual ascension from the sea to the Alps, but now they were declining into Austria and the flood plain of the Rhine. This was an enjoyable enough passage—the local carriages were *chars*, little more than couches on wheels—but Holman began to lapse into a pensive passivity, for the most part simply recording the sights as reported by Colebrook.

The peasant women of Berne, wearing intriguingly short black petticoats, not even reaching to the knee. Their ill-dressed driver, stopping outside of Lausanne to change into an ostentatious red coat. The balloon in Strasbourg, built in the shape of a cask of wine and saddled with a Bacchus.

These were peaceful lands and orderly people. The flood of a new language in his ears offered some distraction, but there was little need for him to puzzle it out. Colebrook understood written German quite well, and could shout it out sufficiently. If they were subjecting themselves to any risks at all, it was the risk of being rushed through their dinner.

The final complaisant comfort was a switch from carriages to the *coche d'eau*, "water coach." Now they were floating tranquilly down the Rhine, and all Holman could do was listen to descriptions of the scenery drifting by. There was nothing to touch, no sounds but the chatter of passengers. Scents drifted in only faintly from the shore.

Still, there was little need for Holman to express his discontent to Colebrook. When they landed in Cologne, it was clear that their traveling connection would soon be coming to an end. There they found newspapers with weeks-old news from home: Queen Caroline was ill. Queen Caroline was dead.

She was the estranged wife of George IV, and also his cousin. Their marriage was an act of dynastic statecraft, and it quickly collapsed when they discovered that each profoundly loathed the other. They lived apart for twenty-six years, and for most of that time the then-prince regent did not go to the bother of seeking a divorce. By the time he did get around to setting the proceedings in motion, it was too late—the old king died, and Caroline was suddenly eager to claim her place as the rightful queen of England.

A royal soap opera ensued. He accused her of immorality, conveniently overlooking his own parade of mistresses. She showed up at Westminster Abbey on coronation day, prepared to be crowned alongside her estranged husband. The Knights of Windsor were among the attendants ordered to forcibly block her from entering. Just weeks after her public humiliation, her sudden death from a stomach ailment converted her into a martyr for the forces already coalescing in opposition to the new king, who had been a profligate prince too long. The funeral procession of the "injured queen of England" turned into a deadly riot.

This was not a time to stretch out an absence already overstayed. After missing out on two royal funerals and one coronation, Holman could no longer postpone his return.

THEY TOOK TO the roads again, making only necessary stops on their way to Utrecht, then Amsterdam. There, they knew, they'd need to part company. Relying only on each other, they'd made their way across more than 1,400 miles of continent. But now Holman was heading west to Haarlem, the North Sea, and England, while Colebrook was plunging back into Germany and resuming his northward course.

In the flower-laden neighborhoods of Amsterdam, they locked arms and embarked on a last leisurely walk. Colebrook was happy to guide his old friend's touch across one final bit of statuary— this time a topiary sculpture, a cluster of hedges trimmed into the shape of a table and chairs. Both touched the portals of the close-set buildings, knowing that local tradition kept one in each house permanently closed except for funerals and weddings. They were fortunate to find one such door opened, and a newlywed couple heading to their wedding feast. The bride, they were told, had a handsome dowry of windmills.

When it finally came, the parting was thankfully sudden. "We fortunately had little time to spend in useless regrets," Holman recalled, "for the boat, when we reached the canal, was on the point of setting off, and they make it a rule to wait for no one." There was just time for the most curtailed of farewells as he clambered up the gangplank, not entirely unhappy to be once more on his own.

The miles had strengthened, not strained, their friendship, and both hoped ardently that their paths would cross again. Nevertheless, Holman would never again seek out a traveling companion, even one who required as well as offered help. The deaf man's assistance had been paid in kind, but interdependence had not quite the taste of independence. Colebrook's "uniform kindness and anxious concern for me" had been a constant comfort. But as Holman was now beginning to realize, comfort was the enemy.

The passage from Belgium to Kent was a ten-hour run, so familiar to the crew of the packet ship that they had no qualms about setting sail from Ostend Harbor in the middle of the night. The voyage that Sunday was thoroughly routine. The wind went lax, then returned with the sunrise. A late-morning fog burned off to reveal the shore, and a few minutes later Holman was prodding his way down a pier at Margate, back in England at last. He'd been gone just over seven hundred days.

Holman in St. Petersburg, acclimating himself to cold in the winter of 1822. His unidentified companion may be Colebrook.

NINE

A Circuit of
the World

THE RETURN TO Windsor was thankfully free of drama. After seeing his evident good health, the Naval Knights grumbled but chose not to formally censure Holman for the small matter of overstaying his leave by almost a year—little realizing the precedent that would be set by their silence. Acquaintances marveled over his walking stick, which bore scorchmarks and a partially melted metal tip from the ascent of Vesuvius. They clamored for as many anecdotes and particulars as possible, and he did his best to oblige them.

He resumed the routines of duty. Up the Hundred Steps. Through the Dean's Cloister, then the Canon's Cloister, then a trodding over the Kings' Bones, past the Sovereign's Stall, and into an empty seat in the Quire. A wash of words, sonorously intoned. The swell and reverberation of the organ, still not quite drowning out the wheeze of its own bellows. The high, fluting voices of the chorister boys, giving flight to the same anthems and motets first sung centuries before. Finally, a benediction and a shuffle back to the Hundred Steps.

Twice a day, morning and evening.

Only his presence was required. It was all too easy to drift from attention into reflection, to cast himself back into the company of

Colebrook, blind Huber, Signora Houri, and the Countess. They crowded memories that did not begin to fade. If anything, the dullness of his days now brought them into more vivid contrast.

He couldn't return, but he could relive. Soon, "as a matter of employment and selfish pleasure," he made a shift that was, to him, imperceptible: oration became dictation. Instead of spinning out his stories to friends, he told them to recruited scribes, quills and ink at the ready. In the long hours between services, he began to compile and organize a written account. "None but those who have traveled," he wrote (or dictated), "can appreciate the delight experienced from recalling in this way the interesting points of an interesting journey, and fighting, as it were, their battles over again."

He had plenty of notes to begin with. The Noctograph had stayed by his side throughout his travels. But he'd needed to conserve his limited supply of carbonated paper, so much of these pages were a hurried compression of details, trivia that might slip even from his magpie mind: the price of cologne in Cologne (eight francs the case), the height of Rome's Tomb of Cestius (120 feet). The whole of his experience was still raw sense memory and haptic knowledge, ready to be fitted out with words and unloosed in a stream of narrative.

There was nothing but time, yet he dictated with a speed approaching urgency. It was just "a plain and faithful statement of a journey," but when others read the growing pile of pages, they gave voice to the notion no doubt already resounding in his own head. His friends' "too kind partiality (for such he fears it has been) induced [me] to think that if published, they might not prove wholly unacceptable to the public."

With the idea of a readership in mind, the stream of dictation became a torrent. The manuscript transmuted into something more than a catalog of private exploits. He larded it with as many travel tips as possible, ranging from general admonishments on bargaining ("Offer only half what they ask, and from thence ascend") to timely specifics ("After staying the third night at Bolsena, it is very necessary to set off early on the following morning"). Then, to leaven the mix, he sprinkled it liberally with appropriate poetic quotations. When he felt his own powers of description were inadequate to evoke a strongly visual scene, he unabashedly borrowed from published accounts by sighted travelers. His ascent of Mount Vesuvius, for instance, includes pages of verbatim passages from John *Moore's View of Society and Manners in Italy* and the Reverend E. Polehampton's *The Gallery of Nature and Art, or a Tour Through Creation and Science.* This practice, common enough at the time, was not strictly plagiarism, as Holman credited the authors and saddled the paragraphs with quotation marks. It constituted a concession to popular tastes, but at the expense of periodically demoting the author to the role of bystander in his own narrative.

Yet despite its padding, omnibus nature and quavers of confidence, the manuscript had little trouble finding a publisher. The long war had simultaneously confined the British populace and expanded their awareness of the world, thanks to the combat's unprecedented international scope. For the first time in decades, English men and women were now notionally free to roam the continent and beyond, although high costs still limited such journeys to those of financial means or spartan wants. As a result, armchair travel was a popular pastime, and travel accounts of almost any stripe were selling briskly—even ones entirely in verse, such as *Memorials of a Tour on the Continent* by William Wordsworth (*Bruge I saw attired in golden light*). As one author of the time frankly admitted:

> *There are few readers who are not fond of the perusal of long voyages; the most trifling event, when it takes place at many thousand leagues distant, acquires a degree of importance; and almost any narrative of that kind is sure to excite curiosity, if for no other reason than that the author has returned from the Antipodes.*

The longstanding London publishers (and secondhand book-sellers) F. C. and J. Rivington were known for staid, safe titles, such as reprints of Shakespeare and religious miscellany like *The Christian Remembrancer*. But they also indulged in the occasional unconventional work, such as *The Memoirs of the Life of Mrs. Elizabeth Carter*—the autobiography of a brilliant linguist, poet, and polymath, who struggled with the twin burdens of being an invalid and a woman. This new manuscript seemed to offer a similar vein of commercial appeal: not a pure novelty item—it was too substantive for that—but with a definite curiosity factor in its favor. It was readily accepted for publication.

Holman added his final touches on the first of May. By June the volume was on bookstore shelves, bearing a title that was relatively terse for the day: *The Narrative of a Journey, Undertaken in the Years 1819, 1820, & 1821, Through France, Italy, Savoy, Switzerland, Parts of Germany Bordering on the Rhine, Holland, and The Netherlands*. Only the small print of the subtitle revealed the work's unique nature:

Comprising
INCIDENTS
That occurred to the author, who has long suffered under
a total deprivation of sight;
With various points of Information collected on his Tour.

By July, the book was successful enough to warrant a seven-page review in the *British Critic*, a leading literary journal. The anonymous reviewer praised it as "a specimen of how much might be done by an active and energetic spirit," and perceptively singled out Holman's couplet-motto (*Some difficulties meet, full many*) as "the key to its author's character." There were some standard-issue critical cavils ("we can scarcely recommend it as a guide-book to the practical tourist"), but the notice ended with a ringing endorsement.

The tone of contentment and good humour, which runs through it, attaches us to the author; and it is with a feeling of much satisfaction, that we deposit him in safety once more on the shores of England.

Such laudatory words would ring gratefully in any writer's ear, but Holman was not around to hear them. He'd already given up the safety of England's shores, embarking on what, if all went as planned, would be one of the greatest journeys of all time.

As a TEN-YEAR-OLD boy departing Exeter, Holman had vowed "not to rest satisfied until I had completed the circumnavigation of the globe." Somewhere between Vesuvius and Windsor, he had begun to contemplate renewing that vow. It was an ambition he kept secret from everyone, even Colebrook, and wisely so. To talk openly of setting out to circle the globe—particularly alone, as was now his preference—was to invite an uproar, if not a diagnosis of insanity.

In the early 1820s there was no such thing as an amateur, independent circumnavigator. There were people whose careers had carried them around the world—sailors, merchants, diplomats, missionaries, and a handful of naturalists—but no one had yet succeeded in doing so solely for the experience, setting their own path and pace (or at least doing so and writing about it). If there was any precedent at all for a gentleman of no particular profession joining the ranks of circumnavigators, it was the recent return of Jacques Arago, a thirty-two-year-old Frenchman and habitual wanderer.

Arago was the slacker in a pack of hyperachieving brothers. The eldest, already one of France's most famous scientists, was Astronomer Royal (and credited with building the first electromagnet). The second was a general in the Army of Mexico, and the youngest a well-known dramatist who collaborated with Balzac. Since the age of twenty, Jacques had been content to travel, ambling through southern Europe and the North African coast with little more than a knapsack and sketchpad. His drawing was strictly a hobby, but with the help of abundant family connections, it landed him a berth as draftsman on a government-funded around-the-world scientific expedition sailing in 1817 under the command of Louis de Freycinet. Returning four years later, Arago surprised everyone by proving not only a capable visual chronicler, but a verbal one as well. His book, *Narrative of a Voyage Round the World in the Uranie and Physcienne Corvettes,* had been published in French during the final year of Holman's sojourn on the continent, and an English translation was in preparation.

The work was groundbreaking in its refreshing lack of solemn self-importance. Arago formatted his book as "a series of letters to a friend" and adopted a decidedly chatty tone, frankly admitting that he was bored by the "profusion of barbarous and tiresome nautical details" found in most books of voyages, filling his pages instead with a grand critique of various cultures. Of South Sea islanders, he wrote, "Almost every body has some taste, and plays tolerably well; but their voice is nasal." Of South American *gauchos*, "I know not why, but the presence of one of these men excites in me a species of veneration." A colonial dance on a tiny Indian Ocean island earned the ultimate compliment: "Almost Paris."

With Gallic panache, Arago made circumnavigation seem like an extension of the European Grand Tour—given, of course, that one traveled in a phalanx of experienced mariners underwritten by a generous government. "I also have made the Tour of the World, but not as a seaman," he wrote. "The vessel carried me, and I wandered with it."

Holman dreamed of doing him one better. Arago's exposure to foreign cultures was necessarily superficial, limited as it was to brief shore leaves in the expedition's ports of call. In contrast, Holman was circumspectly preparing to embark on a journey of equal length, but of unprecedented breadth. Years later, an awestruck journalist would write:

> *We do think that the formation of such a scheme would have argued great boldness in the clearest-sighted mortal that ever lived; in one buried in a "total eclipse" it was altogether marvelous; yet it was formed, arranged, entered upon, and completed in a manner which has already earned for Mr. Holman the respect of his contemporaries, and will command for him the admiration of future ages.*

TO BEST APPRECIATE just how audacious Holman's secret plans were, it's helpful to hypothesize a theoretical Englishman, contemplating a private circumnavigation in 1822. What would be his most logical itinerary? It would begin by heading westward, as Arago's expedition had done, since civilian transportation across the Atlantic was readily obtained (in contrast, eastward voyages, to India and China, were tightly controlled by merchant monopolies, and rarely available to people not on some sort of official business). The first leg of the journey would be the easiest: just book a ticket on a passenger schooner and arrive in North America about a month later. After that, patience and resourcefulness would be required.

Traversing the American continent overland was not an option. The trailblazing of Lewis and Clark still belonged to the recent past (the expedition's journals were not published until 1814), and it would be another decade before wagon trains traveled as far as the Pacific coast. The only way to make progress westward would be to sail south. In New York it was possible to buy a passage to Buenos Aires in the fledgling country of Argentina (whose independence from Spain had been formally recognized one year earlier), but from there one's course became a matter of chance. Most regional sailing traffic confined itself to the Atlantic; the notoriously dangerous passage around Cape Horn into the Pacific was not undertaken lightly. One could eventually find a merchant ship, bound for Mexico or Alta California, willing to take on a passenger as supercargo. But then the enormous expanse of the western ocean presented a formidable challenge.

These waters were plied primarily by American whaling ships, which were not configured to take on passengers, and hardly optimal for transportation. They were either outward bound, on the hunt, not knowing how long they would spend on the open seas, or packed to the gunwales with cargoes of whale oil, hurriedly homeward bound in the wrong direction, toward New England. But if one's luck—and pocketbook—held, one might wrangle a stay on a ship that in due course put in for provisions in the British territory of New South Wales (present-day Australia), then a penal colony with a population of twenty-four thousand, huddling on the edge of a partially explored island continent. From there, passage homeward would be easy enough to obtain: prisoner transport ships, on their return voyage, usually had plenty of room. Their captains typically sailed straight for Rio de Janeiro in Brazil, then doubled back across the Atlantic on a northerly course for England. Our hypothetical traveler, however, might want to choose among the occasional ships that touched port in Cape Town en route to Rio, giving him the right to claim at least a brief exposure to the African continent.

That would be the most straightforward path around the world, a circumnavigation that could be expected to take at least two years. Even a solitary man, traveling light on this streamlined route, would face considerable costs: twenty-five pounds just for a cabin berth on the very first leg, across the Atlantic, an amount roughly equivalent to a generous year's wages for the average servant or laborer. The prices of subsequent passages are harder to calculate—fares were typically not advertised, and negotiated individually—but it's certain they would be more expensive still. From there the expenditures would pile up, particularly if our postulated traveler wished to linger in some of the ports of call. Arago complained that in Rio "the bare walls of a house, consisting of two or three rooms," rented for about fifteen pounds per month. Add to that the costs of supplies, guides, translators, and land-based transportation, and it's clear that even a bankroll of hundreds of pounds would be thinly stretched on such a journey. Which raises yet another obstacle: the challenge of carrying that much money around personally, thereby becoming a magnet for bandits, pilferers, cutpurses, pickpockets, and other assorted criminal types.

A solitary blind man possessing so large a bankroll would be the most tempting of prey. Which for Holman was a moot consideration, as he was incapable of commanding such sums. While he hoped for eventual royalties from his new book, at the moment, his income was still fixed at approximately three-quarters of a lieutenant's salary. How could anyone, sighted or unsighted, aspire to globetrotter status on only eighty-four pounds a year? Holman, no stranger to frugality—he had, after all, managed both Edinburgh and Europe on the same income—thought there was a way.

HE DID NOT presume to think of it as a circumnavigation, since he would, strictly speaking, navigate nothing. When he dared to call it anything at all, he would call his journey "a circuit of the world." The path would be chosen by circumstance, the means improvised, the particulars discovered only in the doing. It was less an expedition than an act of self-abandonment, to faith and fate. There was, however, a strategy.

The key lay in reversing direction, and in clinging to the land. By heading east instead of west, one could, in theory, travel almost one-third of the way around the world not only on solid ground but within the borders of a single country: the empire of Alexander I, tsar of All the Russias. Vast as imperial Russia was, it was also home to an impoverished peasantry, and Holman proposed to get around the same way they did, in simple horse-drawn carts and wheel-less sledges. He would recruit one such peasant as his driver, then plunge directly into Siberia, into the realm where all maps lapsed into a white silence.

He'd keep expenses to a stark minimum, by sleeping in roadside hostels and subsisting on the cheapest of fare. He'd also conserve funds by engaging no guide or translator, trusting himself to pick up the notoriously difficult Russian language in transit—and then to puzzle out regional languages like Tchuktchi and Yakut, since by the time he neared the easternmost province of Kamchatka, native Russian speakers would be very much in the minority. It might take him as long as two years just to reach the Pacific coast, but once he arrived a second ingenuity would come into play.

Whaling ships pursued their prey not haphazardly but by confining their cruise to a specific hunting ground where whales were known to be plentiful. Since this concentration of ships inevitably led to the decimation of whales in the vicinity, new grounds were periodically located and exploited. The played-out Greenland Ground had given way to the Galapagos Ground, and now ships were weaving through the Japan Ground, discovered just two years earlier. This was a region centered around the tiny Bonin Islands in the North Pacific, five hundred miles south of Japan. Since Japan itself was closed to foreigners, whalers bound to and from the new grounds were beginning to put in at Kamchatka for supplies. Holman was confident he could hitch a ride on one of these—at least as far as another newly popular supply station, the Sandwich Islands (present-day Hawaii), themselves opened to the whaling trade only three years earlier.

From there, he could expect to find a berth to go around Cape Horn to the Atlantic easily and cheaply enough. Many ships anchored off Lahaina or Honolulu were short a sailor or two when it came time to depart, thanks to the temptations of the islands. With some prior arrangements, Holman could walk into a bank in Buenos Aires or Boston, withdraw three years or so of accrued back pay awaiting him, and be on his way, already having traversed three-quarters of the globe. He could then make forays into the interiors of South America and Africa, then finally drift back to Europe by way of the Mediterranean.

This sort of circuit of the world would take far longer—five or six years—but would be considerably cheaper, as most of his time would be spent not in expensive port towns and ship's cabins, but among natives, traveling and living in native mode.

The plan had an attraction beyond economy: it was fantastically improbable, and therefore unlikely to be interfered with. Had Holman ventured west, like Arago and most circumnavigators, well-meaning acquaintances would no doubt step in as soon as the scope of his ambition became clear. "My motives for concealing so important a part of these views," he would later write, "will not be difficult to explain: they are attributable to the opposition my kind friends have always been inclined to make against what, under my peculiar deprivation, they are disposed to regard as Quixotic feelings."

An eastward land-based course, on the other hand, could be disguised. His old traveling companion Colebrook had moved to Saint Petersburg, then the capital of Russia. That provided ample cover for the beginning of the journey. He would pay Colebrook a call, then press on toward Moscow and beyond, always pretending to be an eccentric tourist on a jaunt "which I only admitted to be undertaken from fancy." By the time the true nature of his plans was apparent, he'd be in the wilderness of Siberia, out of the reach of well-meaning intervention.

It was a brilliant plan, with only one real drawback: nothing remotely like it had ever been done before. Absolutely no one— no group expedition, much less an individual—had ever combined a transit of the planet with the traverse of its largest landmass. The first leg of such a journey would be an achievement in itself. While a Russian-sponsored "secret geographical and astronomic expedition" to Siberia in 1785 had included a few Englishmen in the employ of then-empress Catherine the Great, no foreigner had ever traveled independently across the full width of Russia, at least as far as Holman knew (although coincidentally, the Royal Society in London had just received a letter from an Englishman claiming to have done so). Reaching the Pacific this way meant crossing some of the world's coldest, harshest, and least-charted terrain, lands so bleak that even the more hospitable parts had been serving as a much-dreaded penal colony for almost two centuries.

How, exactly, might a solitary gentleman make his way across a trackless wasteland, without freezing or starving? Just how would a foreigner proceed to, and directly through, the tsar's prison landscape without attracting official attention—much less the malicious attentions of the criminal population—all on the slenderest of purses? Finding answers would be difficult, and Holman had the additional burden of concealing his questions under the guise of a casual visitor's idle interest. Preparing for an unprecedented journey around the world was challenge enough. Doing so without anyone noticing would be a tour de force.

Holman was eager to try. On July 19, 1822, as his book was being delivered to bookstores, he delivered himself to the London docks and climbed onboard a merchant vessel, the schooner *Saunders-Hill*, bound for the Russian harbor of Cronstadt in the Gulf of Finland, not far from Saint Petersburg. This time, he didn't bother to obtain medical sanction, leave of absence, or any other form of permission. As he blithely and disingenuously explained to one and all, this was by no means another adventure. He was simply going to visit a friend.

True Sentiments and Powers

T HE CRUISE OF the *Saunders-Hill* almost ended in disaster, even before the ship had left English waters. The collision at midnight on July 21 was the fault of a coal ship, clumsy, burdened with cargo, too eagerly taking advantage of a favorable wind to plow up the Thames. The crashing sounds—wood splitting, seams popping, ropes plucked like violin strings—were violent enough that Holman quit his berth and raced to the deck in his nightgown. He fully expected to find the ship splitting in two.

Confusion was universal. A few hand lanterns could scarcely cast enough light to assess the damage, and Holman knew better than to inject himself into the hurry and shouting. But he could lay a hand on the rail and sense a new freedom in the pitch and yaw of the ship: the shock of the impact had knocked them off anchor. They might sink, but a more immediate danger was the prospect of drifting into the path of other ships. He made his way to the ship's wheel. Surely the helmsman—who by necessity would be staying put, rather than scurrying about—would not object to keeping him apprised of their bearings.

There was no helmsman. The ship's wheel spun free.

For the first time in twelve years, Lieutenant Holman took control of a ship. He grabbed two spokes and set the rudder at an

John Dundas Cochrane, the Pedestrian Traveler.

angle to the wind, rapidly weighing his options. Standard naval procedure under such circumstances was to heave-to, which meant canceling forward momentum by swinging directly into the prevailing breeze. But such a sudden stop would put further strain on the damaged ship—and how would he know if he wasn't steering them into a second disaster?

Thankfully, a shout arose from the general din of alarm. "Starboard!"

He recognized the voice. It was Captain Courtney, some ways off, no doubt wanting to stay forward to get a better look at the damage. Holman spun the wheel counterclockwise.

"Port!"

He eased the bow over.

The distant prompting continued, and Holman kept the course. His one puzzlement was why the captain used only the most rudimentary commands, just "Starboard!" and "Port!"—never "Starboard rudder ten degrees!" or "Port handsomely!"

The captain completed his survey. The colliding boat hadn't just loosened their anchor, it had snapped the chain entirely and carried away part of their rigging. It had hit hard enough to shake loose the figurehead, but not hard enough to put them in immediate danger of sinking. They hoisted fresh sail and made for shore. Only then did the captain come aft to the wheel. The last shock of the crisis was discovering his blind helmsman.

He'd shouted simple commands because he thought the figure at the wheel was his wife. In the darkness, he'd mistaken Holman's white, flowing nightshirt for Mrs. Courtney's dress.

Holman was happy to laugh at the mistake. And Captain Courtney was happy to let him stay at the wheel, steering them toward the docks at Gravesend, his nightshirt flapping in the fresh breeze.

HARD WEATHER PLAGUED the rest of the voyage. A squall on the tenth day carried away the top third of the foremost mast. On the twenty-first day, a gale was blowing them breakneck into the Gulf of Finland. They had hopes of making the shelter of Cronstadt Harbor when a cannon fired, aimed wide of their bow but a warning nonetheless. It was a guardship of the Russian Navy, forcing them to halt for immediate inspection. There was no choice but to anchor in sight of the harbor, in open, furious water. Captain Courtney sent down two anchors, just in case the first one snapped. It did.

It was early morning, but when the customs officers lurched onboard, they were obviously drunk. Each incoming ship was, by tradition, expected to greet them with liquor at the ready, and they'd already refreshed themselves in the course of several inspections. Holman could tell that Captain Courtney was "unwilling to increase their exhilaration," but their first demand was for brandy—not just for the inspectors but for their entire crew. Then the wheedling began. Not theft or extortion, really, just the pointed appreciation of items, bursts of rapturous effusion intended to get the admired object handed over as a gift. They were known to covet things as petty as needles and thread, as personally precious as the doll in the arms of a crying child.

This time the wheedling stopped suddenly: they'd finally taken notice of Holman's uniform. It was an unexpected development, finding a British naval officer, much less one that outranked them, on a merchant ship. The inspectors took on a new air of dignity if not sobriety, and actual business was quickly transacted. They departed in a flurry of salutes, but not before invoking one last tradition. The shot they'd fired over the bow, to force the ship to stop? Ah yes, that will be an extra charge. To compensate for the waste of a perfectly good cannonball.

Holman knew there had been no cannonball. He could tell from the sound that the firing was just a noisy bit of wadding, not a genuine shot. But it wasn't his place to protest. *Dobro pozhalovat v Rossiyu*. Welcome to Russia.

In the evening twilight two days later a droshky, a horse-drawn transport halfway between a carriage and a cart, pulled up to a door in Saint Petersburg. Holman climbed out and knocked, no doubt with an extra fillip of vigor. This was the new home of his "old and particular friend," who could not be summoned quietly.

The door opened, and gentle hands were placed against his. Colebrook, his former traveling companion, was expecting him.

AFTER LESS THAN a year of residence in the Imperial City, the deaf man of mysterious profession was sufficiently connected to sweep Holman into the social whirl of the British diplomatic community. They dined with the consul general, with a multitude of embassy members, and finally with the ambassador himself, Sir Charles Bagot, an elegant fellow just five years older than Holman, married to a niece of the Duke of Wellington, and nicknamed "Beauty" Bagot for his dark, patrician good looks. Thus anointed, Holman found almost all doors open in the expatriate community, which was substantial. At least three thousand British subjects lived and worked in Saint Petersburg, most clustered into a district hard by the River Neva. There was a similar German enclave, and a French one, all populated by merchants and "projectors," seeking their fortunes through the favors of the tsar. "St. Petersburg . . . may be regarded as a city of strangers," Holman concluded. "It will be difficult to derive from it anything like a correct picture of the manners and customs of the Russian nation."

He met a man who drank only saltwater in commemoration of his grand scheme, which was a shipping canal from Lake Lagoda to the sea. He met the members of the English Club, where "I was vain enough to attempt a participation in their amusement." The club members staved off homesickness by maintaining a bowling green to London standards, and Holman, pacing off the distance to the pins, was as surprised as anyone to find himself capable of bowling a respectable game.

His most fateful encounter among the expatriates of Saint Petersburg was with Sir James Wylie, a medical adventurer of the highest order. The son of a Scottish porter, Wylie had been a bright but somewhat roguish youth, making it through only two years of medical school in Edinburgh before departing under somewhat murky circumstances (by some accounts, he was caught stealing sheep). A few years, later he resurfaced in Russia, working as a regimental surgeon in the tsar's army. His star rose quickly, thanks to an emergency tracheotomy that saved the life of a choking nobleman. He liked to joke that he "owed his promotion to cutting Count Kutaisof's throat." By the age of thirty he was personal physician to the paranoiac Tsar Paul I, son of Catherine the Great.

There was still something of the old rogue in him, as he was not immune to palace intrigues. Tsar Paul was nowhere near as competent a ruler as his mother, and in the fifth year of his reign, he fell victim to an assassination conspiracy—ironically, just forty days after moving into a palace he'd had specially built, with secret passageways designed for safe flight from assassins. Despite these precautions, three of his own officers had little trouble stabbing him while he slept. When Wylie was called upon to perform the postmortem examination, he prudently overlooked the abundance of knife wounds and certified the death as due to natural causes.

The true cause was soon an open secret, but instead of prosecution the doctor was rewarded with still more honors and influence. That was because his lapse of ethics had been prompted by knowledge he was savvy enough to keep to himself: the assassination had been sanctioned by the victim's son and successor, Tsar Alexander I. *A silent man*, as the Russian proverb goes, *is not a conquered man.*

TWO DECADES LATER, Tsar Alexander was now an august and secure ruler, growing increasingly religious and concerned with an eventual celestial accounting. The eminently respectable Wylie, still physician to the royal family, was overseeing dozens of projects, from hospitals to medical schools to new malaria treatments. He may not have been a paragon of virtue, but the doctor was unquestionably transforming the quality of medicine in his adopted country.

Holman soon became both a friend and another project. Wylie was impressed by the blind man's spirit and intellect—after all, Holman had lasted longer at Edinburgh than he had—and quickly threw his considerable influence into a search for a cure. He recruited every physician of notable competence for the medical equivalent of a command performance, and in succession they examined Holman, prodding and squeezing and squinting into unresponding eyes. Their consensus: again, coction. "Until some change took place in the organ, an operation was not likely to prove beneficial."

The colloquium yielded nothing new, but still it served as a milestone. Holman understood that he had now exhausted the resources of modern medicine. If he had any lingering hopes for reclaiming his sight, they were quietly extinguished. Folk remedies would continue to be patiently endured, but there are no further records of him seriously pursuing a cure.

JUST AS ROME was best understood by way of fingertips, Saint Petersburg was comprehended through the tongue. First there was the revelation of fresh caviar, not the salted kind that was all England could offer. Then a steady, gratefully received onrush of delicacies entirely new to Holman's palate: reindeers' tongues, a succulent small fish called *navaga*, a peculiar sort of pancake called *waffle*. The common and double snipe, "the latter of which, in season, is literally fat as butter, and this of the sweetest kind." Of fruits: the *moroshka*, "in appearance intermediate to the raspberry and mulberry," the mountain-ash berry ("It imparts a most agreeable bitter flavor"). Apples, soaked in honey and beer and hawked to passersby. Pea pudding, left to cool and congeal, then sold from carts by the slice.

By now they were a common sight around the city, Colebrook and the thin *angliiski* lieutenant, the deafness of one betrayed only by the fact that they spoke little, the blindness of the other chiefly evident in their habit of strolling arm in arm.

Simply walking the streets was, to Holman, a vivid demonstration of the tsar's absolute power. He smelled a refreshingly small amount of tobacco smoke, and learned that smoking out of doors was banned. He noticed something missing in the soundscape— no one, not even little boys, ever seemed to whistle. It was also a crime, at least in public. The flagstone sidewalks sometimes displayed a slight unevenness, a minor break in elevation, due to the method of their creation. The tsar admired such footpaths on his last visit to England, so on his return he simply decreed that every householder pave the frontage of their property, then connect it to the pavements of their neighbors. A few weeks later, the city had sidewalks.

Yet public obedience seemed to go hand in hand with private hypocrisy, if not outright connivance. Holman was puzzled by the paradox of Russian manufacturing. Wanting to reduce dependence on foreign goods, the tsar imposed steep duties and often banned the import of some items altogether. This was intended to encourage native enterprise, and indeed the shops were flooded with goods bearing Russian labels—but that was all that was Russian about them. Making foreign products expensive to buy was not the same as making native products affordable. It was still cheaper for "manufacturers" to smuggle in contraband inventory from Europe, slap their trademarks on it, and engage everyone in a grand charade.

Holman's attention to the interplay of law and custom was rooted in practicality. In this land of open secrets, he was harboring a secret of his own. He was quietly compiling as much intelligence as possible about the rest of Russia, making personal inquiries and asking friends to read him passages from relevant books: travel memoirs, political treatises—even cheap Russian novels, so long as they were laced with dollops of described landscape. "I was always particularly cautious in divulging my real plans," was how he remembered this juncture. "On the contrary, I rather endeavoured to keep them concealed, by appearing to show a greater interest with respect to parts that I least contemplated visiting."

Although he felt guilty about deceiving his friends, he understood more than ever the need to keep his preparations clandestine "to avoid fruitless argument, and prevent my being accused of wild and chimerical views." If the good doctor Wylie got wind of his plans, Holman would be facing far more than a gauntlet of friendly discouragement. Sir James had the compunction, compassion, and medical authority to hold the traveler against his will, if he considered the man a danger to himself. But there were easier means of dashing dreams or delusions. One word from Wylie to the Imperial Palace, and Holman could find himself forcibly escorted over the nearest border, banned from reentering the country and effectively stalling the attempt before it was properly begun.

"Alas! How little are they able to appreciate my true sentiments and powers," Holman wrote of his friends, old and new. Among his few possessions was a relief map of Russia, useful for acquainting himself with geographical features and distances by touch. In unwatched moments, when he knew himself to be alone, he let his forefinger trace his real intended route: southeast to Moscow, then due east and onward across the Tartar steppe, the Siberian tundra, and beyond.

The finger flew straight off the map.

WINTER'S ARRIVAL WAS announced by sheets of ice floating down the Neva, chasing the last of the ships from the harbor. Then came a clear frost, followed by snow in such quantity and

force that even on the streets of the Imperial City, carts and carriages were abandoned for sledges and sleds. One by one, before
the ice could claim them, the city's bridges were methodically dis-
mantled and stored.

Finally the Neva froze solid, and the police began their usual
task of laying out roads across the river. They constructed grand
boulevards of leveled ice, flanked by transplanted fir trees, and
revelers clambered across them. Winter society was pursued in
something of a hurry, for public amusements and private parties
were, by law, canceled or severely curtailed when the temperature
dropped to sixteen degrees below zero. Too many coachmen had
frozen to death while waiting for their masters and mistresses to
finish celebrating.

The streets were therefore quiet on February 5, 1823, the coldest
day of what everyone agreed was a notably mild winter: twenty-
two degrees below zero. Holman, who maintained a daily account
of thermometer readings, and of the skies (*Snowy. Very dull. Ditto,
with snow. Ditto.*), kept to his exercise with a sense of diligent purpose. He was trying to acclimate himself to subzero temperatures
as much as possible.

Cold and snow are great facilitators of rheumatism—Holman
viewed the Nova Scotian winters as the primary source of his
affliction. Yet, to his gratification, on the frozen streets he seemed
to sustain nothing past the usual inventory of pains. It was a lung-
searing, pore-invading chill, but sometimes that was preferable to
the Stygian fust of Saint Petersburg interiors. Russians, he found,
put great stock in the proverb *Heat breaks no bones.* They donned
their winter furs and woollens early, and kept them on well into
spring. Few strayed from a tight orbit of their stoves, which were
stoked as if they were boilers. Windows were double-paned and
shut for the duration. "In short, the smell of a stable is comparatively odoriferous."

In the open air Holman thrust out his cane and listened for the
dry chuff of new-fallen snow, the thud, not thump, of truly solid

ice. Everything echoed less. It was harder to judge distance and size, but every sound was sharper, unmuddied by reverberations. The soundscape was clarified by cold.

As imposing as the task was before him, at least now he could console himself with the knowledge that it wasn't flatly impossible. Word had arrived that another Englishman—a fellow Royal Navy officer, in fact—had penetrated as far as Kamchatka. This was Captain Cochrane, the gentleman who had dispatched a letter from Okhotsk to the Royal Society in London the previous year, and whose exploits were now trickling back to the expatriate community in Saint Petersburg. Holman greeted the news that he would not be the first solitary traveler to transverse Russia with genuine happiness—the precedent was more valuable to him than any claim of primacy. And to judge from the stories that were circulating, Cochrane seemed a fascinating figure, almost as unlikely an adventurer as himself.

JOHN DUNDAS COCHRANE was the illegitimate son of the black sheep of "the fighting Cochranes," one of Britain's most famous families. His uncle, the earl of Dundonald, was a noted inventor, credited with the method recently adopted by the Royal Navy of protecting against shipworms by coating hulls with tar. Another uncle and three first cousins were career navy men, rising to the rank of admiral. One cousin, now Lord Cochrane, was presently also supreme commander of the fledgling Chilean Navy, and would go on to command the Brazilian and Greek navies in turn. The blot on the family's prestige was the career of Andrew Cochrane-Johnstone, one of the most notorious scoundrels of the age, and John Dundas's father.

Cochrane-Johnstone had served admirably as a colonel in the king's army, but when appointed governor of the island of Dominica in the West Indies, he proved himself corrupt and dissolute on a near-historic scale. He openly profited from the slave trade, kept a harem of women, mismanaged his troops to the point of mutiny, and embezzled, rather sloppily, from the Crown. When the inevitable court-martial came, John Dundas, then ten years old, was quietly extracted from the mess and shipped off to the flagship of his admiral uncle.

That would have been mortifying enough for the boy passingly acknowledged as his son (and given only half of his surname; the "Johnstone" reflected marriage to a woman not John Dundas's mother), but Colonel Cochrane-Johnstone shrugged off the disgrace and went on to an even more ignominious career. Arrested for fraud in Tortola, he escaped and drifted into gun-smuggling, an illegal enterprise made more dangerous by the fact that the guns he collected payment for turned out to be imaginary. He fled back to England, where he took advantage of a false rumor of Napoleon's death to perpetrate a profitable stock-dumping scheme on the London Exchange (conniving members of his own family in the bargain). Tried and convicted, he forfeited bail and scrambled out of the country. Decades later, he was a fugitive still.

Meanwhile John Dundas had done his best to emulate his more noble-minded relations, choosing the navy as profession and rising through the ranks, although not quite so meteorically as his cousins. By 1814, he was a commander, a rank that technically entitled him to the honorific of "captain," despite the fact that the navy had not yet awarded him a ship. Unfortunately for his ambitions, that was the year that peace broke out, and the dismantling of the fleet began. After six more years of waiting for a command that never materialized, Captain Cochrane understood that his career had reached a dead end. He left active duty, learned to subsist on half-pay, and reinvented himself as an explorer.

He began by proposing an Admiralty-sponsored quest into the unknown interior of Africa, to chart the River Niger and fix the location of the legendary city of Timbuktu. The last expedition to attempt this had vanished without a trace in 1805, but Cochrane was confident he'd found a way to avoid their fate. To attract minimal attention from the presumably hostile natives he'd travel alone, disguising himself as a Muslim (not that he knew Arabic, or any language indigenous to Islam), attaching himself to a trade caravan "in some servile capacity," and blending in, "unfettered by the frailties and misconduct of others." He even volunteered to sell himself into slavery "if that miserable alternative were necessary, to accomplish the object I had in view."

Just how a slave might conduct a geographic survey, extricate himself from bondage, and return to England were topics not addressed in his proposal—which was rejected, to his indignation. The Admiralty did, however, offer him a two-year leave of absence on his usual half-pay, and so, since "a young commander like myself was not likely to be employed afloat, much less ashore, I determined to take a journey."

Like Holman, he'd hit upon the idea of a land-based, eastward circumnavigation. But with no Windsor stipend to supplement his naval income (in his case, about fifty pounds a year), he was even poorer than Holman; commercial transportation such as merchant ships to Saint Petersburg seemed well beyond his means. Instead, he bought a cheap ferry ticket across the English Channel to the Normandy region of France. On the morning of February 14, 1820—his fortieth birthday—he laced up his shoes, slung a knapsack over his shoulder, and began to hike northward, following the upstream course of the Seine. The Admiralty had failed to underwrite his solo mission, and so he was launching another, without budget or sanction.

John Dundas Cochrane was setting out to become the first person to walk around the world. And while he was at it, he was going to solve one of the enduring mysteries of geography.

Cochrane suspected that, somewhere in the still-uncharted expanses between Russia and North America, there was a land route from the Old World to the New. Such a passage had proved elusive to at least four sailing expeditions, but Cochrane believed he could find it on foot. Russia was, of course, a long way from

France, but both finances and his sense of the dramatic dictated a purely pedestrian route—he would walk across Europe and Russia, locate the land bridge, and keep going until he hit the Atlantic yet again, a plan which would "enable me to wander through the wilds, deserts, and forests of three quarters of the globe."

It was a destiny he pursued with such strenuous intensity that it scarcely qualified as walking; trotting or jogging were more fitting terms. Despite a sprained ankle, a constant crop of blisters, and the fact that "snow fell in considerable quantities, and everything assumed the most wintry appearance," he managed the fifteen hundred miles from Dieppe to Saint Petersburg in just eighty-three days. By then he was indistinguishable from a vagrant (for which "foot-traveler" was a common euphemism), and the British Embassy had to step in and confirm his identity before he was allowed to proceed.

Although he was already billing himself as the Pedestrian Traveler, the purity of Cochrane's quest soon buckled under the sheer distances involved. There are records of his accepting carriage rides as early as Latvia, and as he bore eastward, he grew less and less scrupulous about his means of transportation, so long as it was free. He served as a Volga boatman, working his passage as an oarhand and cook. The governor of Kazan personally escorted him, in his own combination carriage-sledge, some three hundred miles to Perm. A canoe took him over a thousand miles downstream the River Lena, until it froze solid in the ice two days short of Yakutsk. "The natives felt surprised, and pitied my apparently forlorn and hopeless situation," he wrote of those who helped him along his way. "Not seeming to consider that when the mind and body are in constant motion, the elements can have little effect upon the person."

Although he still looked more like a hobo than an explorer, he had little trouble commanding the respect (and generosity) of provincials, since he carried with him an impressive set of credentials from the tsar himself. According to one account, with the help of well-placed friends in Saint Petersburg,

[H]is proposed exploit obtained higher countenance than could have been anticipated. Not only was he furnished with the customary passport, but also with a secret letter to the governor-general of Siberia, and open instructions to the civil governors and police, "of all the towns and provinces lying in his track, from Saint Petersburg to Kamchatka, to aid him as far as possible to proceed on his journey without interruption; to afford him lawful defense and protection; and in case of necessity, to render him pecuniary assistance."

Why was a shabby, impoverished foreigner given such a mark of imperial favor? This puzzled others but not Cochrane, who accepted it as his due—even when further support suddenly appeared midway through the journey, in the form of a personal Cossack bodyguard dispatched to his side by the tsar. The Cossack brought with him the right to commandeer horses at will. This helped convey the two up into the Arctic Circle, where they progressed via dogsleds, rafts, and even a bone-chilling swim across the Okita River.

Cochrane gave away his snowshoes. Never a large man, after years of lean traveling, he was light enough to scurry across the deep drifts without falling in. At last, they passed the final Russian outpost and entered the semiautonomous realm of the Tchuktchi, nomadic natives similar, and perhaps related, to the Esquimeaux of the American Arctic. By July of 1821 he was on the shores of the East Siberian Sea, ready to begin his search for the intercontinental land bridge in earnest.

Holman did not know all the details of Cochrane's journey—how much the Pedestrian Traveler had departed from his self-appointed title, or the full extent of the tsar's protection. What he'd gleaned was that a fellow officer and countryman had gone a very long distance on very few resources. And that Cochrane, for reasons yet to be explained, had abruptly stopped his circumnavigation and was heading home, retracing his steps. His reported route would bring him through Moscow sometime in the sum-

mer of 1823, and Holman resolved to be there to greet him when
he arrived. He expected the captain to be a ready source of insight
and encouragement, and an instant friend.

THERE WAS A river upon the river. The Neva was still frozen, but
more tenuously so each day. Meanwhile the warming days, north
of zero now, melted the snowfall quickly on the open expanse, and
so a stratum of water began to course over the ice. There were still
tree-lined roads across the river, but by the second week of March
Holman's rented droshky couldn't use them without plunging the
horses belly-deep into the slurry.

Everyone was hurrying to get a summer's worth of ice chopped
up, sprinkled with sawdust, and stowed in their cellars. Soon the true
river would begin to reassert itself, breaking up and carrying away
the frozen floes. The roadsteads were always the last to disappear—
constant usage compacted them until they were the densest part of
the icefield. It was common to watch them wash away as a piece,
landscaping and all, a floating strip-island of melting boulevard.

As springtime arrived, Holman's options seemed limited to a
small circumference of civilization. Russia was enormous, but also
overwhelmingly wild. Even the new Moscow road was not, strictly
speaking, a road to Moscow. Someday it would be, but at present it
only extended for about seventy-five miles before petering out into
an obstacle course of herding paths and unbridged streams.

Three days later Holman was rushing to the coach office, late for
the scheduled time of departure. A party of his friends, assembled
there to see him off, were forcibly detaining the coach. Again there
was time for only a hurried but heartfelt farewell to "my estimable
friend" Colebrook, a parting rendered more poignant by his subterfuge. Colebrook was fully expecting to see him again in a few months'
time. Holman's private intent was to never pass this way again.

He squeezed into a seat, and the cheers of his friends were
lost in a clatter of whipcrack and hoofs. The coach, an ungainly

great-wheeled conveyance called a diligence, set down the still-unfinished road to Moscow.

SEVEN WEEKS LATER, Holman was amusing himself by thrusting his hand into the crack of the Kremlin's great Tsar Bell. This was the largest bell in the world, a hundred and sixty tons of bronze, so massive that the ground sunk beneath it. The official story was that it broke by accident, when a suspension beam caught fire. But he could feel the striations of the fissure, and they were smooth, not jagged. This was glaring evidence to him that the crack was caused by a flaw in casting.

He gave no thought to calling attention to the fact. His explorations in Moscow were already inducing sufficient indignation. When ushered into the Treasury Room, where the thrones of past emperors were preserved, he'd taken the liberty of climbing into the ancient seat of Boris Godunov (1551–1605). When encountering Peter the Great's immense gun, the Tsar Cannon, fifteen feet long, he handed his coat to a nearby sergeant and unhesitatingly stuffed himself down the full length of its interior. Such stunts were a means of kicking against the omnipresent sense of order, and of marking time.

Moscow, both ancient and brand-new, was a place of neat demarcations, everything and everyone bounded and buffered and contained. The city itself, still rebuilding from the fires and decimation in the wake of Napoleon's occupation in 1813, was double-walled, and gardens now filled the belt between inner and outer ramparts. More walls and gates isolated the Kremlin, the spiritual and governmental center, as well as the Chinese Town, where the city's bazaar was confined to a few constantly crowded streets. A simple ditch served to isolate the Tartar Town. Only a blind man could fail to notice where the houses of the nobility began—that was Beloigorod, the White City, where every wall was made of brick sheaved in snow-white stucco, where the roofs were uniformly of a dark-painted iron.

Holman discovered that Moscow society was largely open to him, since as an officer he was himself considered nobility. Adding to his attractiveness was his fluency in French, the language of preference in upper-class households, and a rich stock of recent news from both England and the continent. He was showered with invitations, and could have stayed in the White City indefinitely as a houseguest, but he decided to surround himself with a different sort of elegance. Aware that the road ahead would long deprive him of one particular sensory pleasure, he moved into a boarding-house that catered to professional musicians. The sounds of their constant rehearsals were cacophonous to others but deeply enjoyable to him, a sort of sonic furnishing. He particularly savored the glissando strains of one neighbor, a female harpist.

One went to Saint Petersburg to seek one's fortune, to Moscow to seek survival. Among the city's indigent were crowded delegations of peasants, licensed by the police to beg as a team on behalf of their native village, usually because their village had been destroyed by fire. Many of them never departed, helping to swell the already massive ranks of the serving class and making domestic help absurdly cheap. With such a superabundance of attendants, their employers often strained to find things for them to do. A servant might find himself part of a private comedic troupe, not because of any acting skill but because he simply looked amusing. Domestic orchestras spread out the work by subdividing horn parts: a servant-musician might spend an entire concert playing only a single note of the scale. Overstaffing meant dinner parties were served with breakneck efficiency, which Holman found left little time for conversation; often a plate might be plucked away "while I rested my fork, in the act of addressing some one or other of the party." In his boardinghouse he himself retained a full-time manservant for a salary of five roubles a month—about the cost of two meals—but he soon regretted the hire. The man was clearly supplementing his income by steering his master to more expensive merchants and claiming commissions.

Socializing and idle tourism quickly paled. Holman was anxious to depart, but equally anxious to solicit the advice of Captain Cochrane, who had yet to arrive. By the second month in Moscow Holman was letting off steam by divulging a sanitized, extremely foreshortened version of his travel plans—a test of his cover story's credulity, really. Providing he could find a means of transportation, he would venture across the Volga into Kazan, the heart of Islamic Russia and home to its greatest population of Tartars, the Muslim descendants of Mongolian invaders of the thirteenth century. Then perhaps a few more weeks of ranging eastward, into the vague beginnings of the region called *Sibir*, "the sleeping land."

Siberia! "Everyone made it his business to demonstrate the madness and absurdity of attempting so dangerous, uninteresting and disagreeable a journey," Holman discovered. "The name . . . seemed connected in their minds only with sentiments of horror."

That was by design. The idea of going there voluntarily was almost an affront to the Russian psyche. For centuries, the absolutism of the tsar drew strength from the idea of Siberia as his personal purgatory for criminals, both violent and political, a deterrent much more powerful than decrees of death. An execution merely killed one man. Banishment to Siberia condemned his entire family, including generations yet unborn, to a life of workhouse labor or other subsidence existence, in conditions that even a frost-hardened Muscovite would find intolerable. There were no border guards, nor even a border. Geography alone, distance and the difficulty surmounting it, formed a natural barrier to return.

Holman had no plans to return, but that fact remained unspoken. And besides, he was counting on the counsel of perhaps the greatest expert in surviving Siberia, a man expected to arrive any day now. Finally, on the last day of May, the musical soundscape of his boardinghouse was punctuated by the clump of well-worn boot heels on the stairs. The Pedestrian Traveler had come to meet the Blind Traveler.

·   ·   ·

JOHN DUNDAS COCHRANE was strikingly small—so much
so that when he crammed himself into the Tsar Cannon as Holman had, he had plenty of room to sit upright. But his minuscule
stride was powered by a nimble-nervous, seemingly indefatigable
vitality, and he cut a flamboyant figure. Unlike Holman, who still
wore his Royal Navy uniform, he was now dressing like a romanti-
cized version of a rustic Russian, in gray blouse and yellow trousers
of nankeen cotton, topped off with a broad silken sash. He'd let his
hair grow, and now his sleek features were framed by dirty blond
ringlets. But even more striking was the beautiful young woman
on his arm—the new Mrs. Cochrane. He was forty-four. She was
fourteen.

As he explained to Holman, on the Kamchatkan peninsula, a
regional official named Ushinsky had introduced him to his daughter. In the most remote of hinterlands, almost as far from England
as physically possible, he'd fallen in love. To judge by the surname,
the family was at least partially of Slavic rather than indigenous
stock, and the daughter was demure, delicately featured, and fortunately quite petite. So, with her father's approval, "I was left to the
free enjoyment of a passion that was crowned with marriage—so
much then for my travelership."

Was that why he had abandoned his circumnavigation? Well, not
exactly. Cochrane had another story to tell. According to him, he'd
reached the Arctic coastal region of the indigenous Tchuktchi, and
was on the verge of proving his theory that Russia and America
were contiguous—surely, two great landmasses could not miss each
other by the geographic equivalent of a hairbreadth. But when he
sought a guide to accompany him over the ice, his imperial endorsement, which had opened so many doors and smoothed so many
paths, served to trip him up.

If the tsar is so interested in this man's journey, the Tchuktchi said
through an interpreter, *then the tsar will have no objection to paying for*

his passage. They noticed he was a smoking man; they offered to comply for fifty bags of tobacco, payable in advance. Not modest tobacco pouches, like the one Cochrane carried, but full-weight export lots, in total about five thousand pounds worth. "He could be no great emperor who could not make so small a present," their chieftain concluded, "seeing that he could command the riches of all his people."

Cochrane, who had painstakingly dragged fifty pounds of tobacco through the wilderness, thinking it adequate for just such a bargaining session, was frustrated, if not furious. It does not appear to have occurred to him that the price was impossible because the task was impossible, and that the Tchuktchi were having an elaborate joke at his expense. Still, such a setback meant only that he could not *walk* to America; he encountered several ships provisioning on the far shore, including a Portuguese brig and an American vessel crewed entirely by Sandwich Islanders. Why didn't he seek passage with them?

Cochrane had a third story to tell. While wandering up and down the edge of the continent, he learned that an official Russian naval expedition was presently engaged in surveying the Alaskan coast. He tried to join the expedition, was refused, and therefore bowed out in an altruistic show of professional deference. "I cannot be allowed to act with them," was how he put it, "I will not act against them, and therefore I cannot act at all."

In short, Cochrane's true motives for abandoning his quest were lost in a muddle of anecdotes. Holman did not push the matter, focusing instead on extracting information useful to his own journey. He said nothing of his own circumnavigation, but he did tell Cochrane he was planning to be the first to follow in his footsteps.

IT IS TO Cochrane's credit that he did not greet this news with derision, or open laughter. He was in a foul mood. Instead of a triumphant reception upon his return to Moscow, he'd found an indifferent city with "no hospitality, voracious appetite for gain, innumerable beggars." Instead of invitations to stay among the palaces of the White City, he'd been compelled to pay exorbitantly for a squalid hotel room. The newlyweds had a wait of three weeks until the next diligence to Saint Petersburg, and he was not looking forward to the expense of keeping his Kamchatkan child bride amused in the interim. He'd called upon old friends, only to find them urging a meeting with this recent arrival, already hailed as "among the most conspicuous personages of Moscow . . . Lieutenant Holman of the Royal Navy, a poor blind Knight of Windsor." And now this benighted soul was acting as if Siberia would make a splendid tourist jaunt.

Cochrane had suffered from frostbite, snowblindness, near starvation, bandit attacks, horses dying underneath him, and canoes frozen solid in the ice. He'd been so cold that he'd taken to building a U-shaped fire and crawling inside it to be flanked by flames, sleeping as still as possible to keep from burning to death. It had been an ordeal of heroic proportions, and its uniqueness was his sole asset—aside from selling a book of his adventures, he had no particular prospects back home. There was every reason for him to warn off Holman as vehemently as possible, but he did not. "I passed several pleasant days with him," he recorded of his new friend, "and considered the accomplishment of my design of penetrating through Siberia as nothing when compared to his determination of proceeding also."

Cochrane confirmed one important fact: traveling overland in native fashion was fantastically inexpensive, particularly when augmented by the generosity of the locals. He claimed that his travels within Russia had cost him, in total, slightly more than a single British pound—a trifling amount, no doubt an exaggeration, but encouraging nonetheless. And when it came to the rewards of minimalist travel, he was all but rapturous. As he would write soon after:

"Go," said I, "and wander with the illiterate and almost brutal savage!—go and be the companion of the ferocious beast!—go and contemplate the human being in every element and climate . . . It is only by patience, perseverance, and humility, by reducing thyself to the lowest level of mankind, that thou canst expect to pass through the ordeal with either safety or satisfaction."

Cochrane could not be all encouragement, however. Invoking the full weight of weary experience, he explained that one does not simply wander into Siberia. It was necessary to obtain an official order of special protection from the minister of the interior, and such an order would be exceedingly difficult to obtain. In fact, Holman would have to return to Saint Petersburg in order to apply.

To Cochrane's surprise, Holman politely disagreed. He said that he'd already researched permissions, and determined that no such vouchsafe was required. They agreed to further investigate the matter together, and on the following day, they proceeded with linked arms, first to Major General Verevkin, the commandant of Moscow, then to Governor-General Balk-Polief. Both officials greeted Holman as a dear friend—he had dined in their homes, admired an amateur performance of the governor's eldest daughter, helped the commandant celebrate the birth of a son. Both were forced to admit that Holman was, technically at least, quite correct. Siberia functioned as a prison, but it had the same legal status and administration as every other part of the empire. A Russian citizen might be enjoined from leaving there, but there were no restrictions placed on the movements of a foreign national. If he was planning on using his own conveyance he'd have to take out a post license, but that would apply no matter what the destination.

Horse-drawn travel of any real distance did not rely on a single team of horses. In fact, many travelers owned a cart or carriage but no horses at all. Instead they availed themselves of a system of thousands of post stations, spread throughout Russia and much of Europe. These were depositories and through-stations for the mail, but that was just one of their roles. The "post" might be literally that, a single hitching post, or a large corral. A post license gave those in transit the right to unharness their tired horses, harness up fresh ones, and be on their way. The animals left behind were fed, rested, groomed, and readied for the next exchange, at least if regulations were obeyed. The life of a post horse was hardly enviable, since they belonged to no one in particular, but their interchangeability kept them from being driven to death over the expanses of Europe, and particularly across the largest empire in the world.

Cochrane watched as his new companion inquired after the farthest-reaching post license possible. That would be to Irkutsk, the new capital of Eastern Siberia, both were told. From there a restless traveler could obtain an extension in any direction he pleased. Holman calculated the distance from Moscow to Irkutsk, converting from *versts* into miles in his head. It was 3,567 miles, a distance slightly longer than the entire width of North America. Once there, he'd still be only two-thirds of his way across the continent.

Did he want a license to take his vehicle to Irkutsk? It would cost him slightly more than two hundred rubles, or about nine British pounds. An ebullient Holman, who possessed no cart, carriage, or sledge—much less the ability to use them—said yes.

FINALLY, LAUGHTER.

Cochrane and Holman had been wondering for days—what would it take to evince a genuine emotional response from this stoic child-woman? Both thought that the young Mrs. Cochrane was sure to be beguiled by Moscow, plucked as she was from the Arctic tundra, where the largest city consisted of exactly forty-two dwellings, where the mail arrived only twice a year.

She was certainly beguiling enough herself, "represented as very handsome," a description that Holman was, for once, not permitted to confirm with even his most discreet touch. Her one known portrait shows a complacently serene teenager of porcelain-perfect skin and almost doll-like proportions, improbably swan-necked and small-waisted.

It is perhaps significant that her portrait has survived, but her first name has not. Cochrane would go on to write of his adventures in two exhaustive volumes, but his bride all but disappears from their pages immediately after the wedding day. His narrative remains firmly fixed in the first person (*I entered Moscow's crowded streets*), and even Cochrane family accounts from later years are silent on her Christian name. A charmed Holman found her to be far from a rude, rustic innocent, "by no means unpolished or awkward in her manners . . . Her parents had been conversant with the more civilized parts of the empire, and had educated her according to their customs."

But her polish belied a deeply diffident, almost impassive nature. As hard as they tried, neither Holman nor Cochrane were able to impress her with anything. Together they escorted her to the top of a Kremlin high tower, for the double thrill of sheer height and of seeing the city spread out at her feet. "We naturally expected that she would have expressed her admiration with much warmth; she appeared pleased with what she saw, but not at all surprised," Holman observed. They took her to her very first theatrical event, and, to their joint relief, she burst out laughing during the performance of a vaudeville skit called *The Parrots*. Although "we did not notice that expression of astonishment which we had anticipated."

Cochrane soon moved on to business matters. Now that he had a post license, perhaps Holman would wish to buy the *povozka* that had brought them from Kazan? A *povozka* was an open wagon, built lightly to require a minimum of horses for pulling power, without shelter, padded seats, or even springs for the axles. Of course, he'd need a postillion—a combination driver/rider who guided the vehicle while astride one of the harnessed horses—

and as luck would have it, the native Tartar who had driven the Cochranes all the way from Tobolsk was still in Moscow, available for hire. He was a fierce-looking man with a formidable beard, in girdled caftan and tall boots, but, to Holman, he was a torrent of muttered oaths and a gathered smell of horses, *kvass* (a naturally carbonated, fermented beverage made from rye), and Russian leather (which Holman's nose could distinguish from European leather). If Cochrane knew the postillion's name, he did not record it, and neither would Holman, who was content to call his new companion simply "the Tartar," as the title reflected both his ethnicity and his temperament (in British vernacular, a *tartar* was someone irritable and ungovernable). Happily assuming both ownership and employment, Holman declared, "I was thus at once nearly fitted out for my journey."

Nearly, but not quite. He had a ritual to follow. Retreating to his boardinghouse, he made very sure he was alone, then locked the door. Packing required a great deal of concentration, and "the presence and assistance of a second person would only serve to distract me further, and to make confusion more confused." He needed not only to securely stow possessions and provisions but to memorize them, building a precise three-dimensional mindmap of every last bit of baggage. He could not count on the Tartar to identify items, since they had no language in common, and there were things best left concealed.

Foremost was the money. He placed a stash of banknotes, all of the five-ruble variety, in one location. Then he distributed the coins in a series of five cloth bags, each containing exactly one hundred of a particular denomination, from silver rubles to twenty-kopek pieces. He would use the banknotes only when necessary, and insist on receiving his change in coin, which he could confirm by touch. Financial transactions with him could be disorienting, resembling a sleight of hand; he'd plunge his hands confidently into the depths of his luggage, and sums would appear or disappear.

He packed six bottles of brandy and an equal number of passable French wines, although he would ultimately drink none of them. His preferred libation was tea ("I always find it, when on my travels and overpowered by exertion, the most agreeable and refreshing beverage"). A supply of leaves and sugar, alongside a complete set of kettle and cups, made him "quite independent of the accidental and inadequate entertainment the post-houses could furnish, with the exception of hot water." He laid in a supply of food, but only a little. Canned goods were a rarity, expensive, heavy and bothersome to open (one used a hammer), and dried foods such as jerky and pemmican weren't to his taste. He preferred instead "at each town, to lay in sufficient bread and meat to serve until our arrival at the next."

On this departure's eve, he took special care to memorize the sequence of a series of tightly stoppered glass vials and small jars, all padded to protect from breakage. For the first time, he was traveling with his own private pharmacopoeia. A Moscow physician named Lyall had pressed the drugs on Holman after learning of his medical education, "not only with a view to my own relief, should sickness invade me in a country where medical aid might be sought for in vain, but also to enable me to be instrumental in affording assistance to others." The gravest threat to life in Siberia was not the cold, the doctor explained, but the appalling lack of available medical care. Under the circumstances a blind physician would be better than none at all. Aware that the slightest confusion could have disastrous consequences, Holman fitted the tinctures, salves, and opiates snugly into his trunk.

WITHIN AN HOUR of each other, on an early summer morning, the London-bound Pedestrian Traveler and the Siberia-bound Blind Traveler took up their opposite directions like participants in a long-distance duel. According to Cochrane, his last minutes in Moscow were spent "having seen Mr. Holman safe upon his road."

Holman remembered matters differently: it was he who arrived at the diligence office just in time for a farewell handshake with the captain, a salute to his young bride, and a *bon voyage* to them both. Soon after, he was sitting on the rearmost bench of Cochrane's old *povozka*, listening to the Tartar haranguing the horses in an unknown and interesting tongue. At last, he was on his way.

> *My situation was now one of extreme novelty, and my feelings corresponded with its peculiarity. I was engaged under circumstances of unusual occurrence, in a solitary journey of several thousand miles, through a country, perhaps the wildest on the face of the earth, and whose inhabitants were scarcely yet accounted within the pale of civilization; with no other attendant than a rude Tartar postillion, to whose language my ear was wholly unaccustomed. And yet I was supported by a feeling of happy confidence.*

That confidence was less than entirely warranted. After an hour or so, it was clear that the postillion's unintelligible chatter was no longer directed to the horses. Their first intended stop was the country house of one of Holman's acquaintances, but the Tartar could not find the way. His passenger was powerless to guide him, and both were incapable of asking passersby for directions. The two rode on in their private Babel down one road, then another. By a remarkable coincidence, a horseman rode alongside and began speaking English—the nephew of the very person Holman hoped to visit. "I congratulated myself on being now in the right way, but no! . . . our new guide actually found himself lost, and after leading us from one road to another at length fairly admitted that he knew not where to go." Just a few miles outside the gates of Moscow, they were in the midst of a darkening wood, utterly disoriented. It would be several hours before a peasant would pass by and rescue them.

Holman sighed, and settled into his seat. This was hardly the way to conquer a continent.

ELEVEN

The Sleeping Land

THE VOYAGE ACROSS the Volga began with the clatter-and-tumble sounds of twenty wooden slabs falling heavily to earth. It was the tradition of the boatmen to fling their long oars into the air just before disembarking, as a means of drawing divine attention to the journey. None of the oars broke—a sign that protection was forthcoming—so they removed their hats, made signs of the cross, and took their stations on the barge.

It was the prince of Georgia's private barge, and Holman was the passenger of honor. After weeks of slow, rattling progress over dreadful road, so tortuous in the springless *povozka* that "my brain . . . felt every instant ready to burst out of its tenement," he had arrived in Nizhni Novgorod (only four hundred miles from Moscow) to find his notoriety preceding him. The prince had read about the prodigious Blind Traveler in couriered editions of the *Petersburg Journal*, and he was eager to extend him every courtesy: a stately dinner, fresh provisions, a scenic floating tour. That Holman could not admire the scenery was inconsequential—the prince's son was happy to sit by his side and give a running description in French. They docked at a waterside monastery, where the solemn monks played ninepins as if it were a ceremony, not a game. The abbot, also given to superfluous gestures, presented his distinguished visitor with a gift: a landscape portrait of the monastery.

Holman's forced departure from Siberia,
in the custody of Imperial Feldjager Kolotovin.

Holman could only admire the texture of the engraving, roll it up,
and reboard the barge, just in time for the prince's son to murmur
in his ear an elaborate description of the sunset.

AFTER SUCH DEFERENTIAL treatment, his reception in
Kazan a few weeks later was something of an unsettling shock.
There he warranted no welcome, just a curt notice from the vice
governor that so long as he stayed, a policeman would be detailed
to shadow his movements. "I felt myself treated by this gentleman with much less respect than I had been accustomed to," Holman observed of the vice governor, who did not even offer him a
seat during their brief interview. "I could not avoid entertaining a
suspicion that this behavior had its motive, the more particularly
as my letter [of introduction] was from no less a person than the
governor-general of Moscow." He ascribed the ill-concealed hos-

tility to rivalries of power, and amused himself with another letter, one he'd found awaiting his arrival. In it, a Moscow friend spoke frankly: Holman's acquaintances were divided into two camps, those who expected him to turn back at Kazan ("sickened by experience") and those who believed he'd keep going a little while longer. Holman smiled and pressed on.

By now he was traveling mostly at night, which had a multitude of advantages. Rested horses were easier to come by, and the postillion was compelled by the darkness to navigate the ruts, paths, and other approximations of roadstead a shade more slowly, softening slightly the bruising, bone-rattling ordeal of simply remaining seated. The stress, indeed violence, of traveling in this fashion has no modern equivalent. While Holman only cracked jokes about his brain exploding from his head, subsequent travelers would be more explicit in describing the trials of native transport. An American adventurer, crossing the same terrain in a similar cart almost sixty years later, wrote.

> *A bad, rough road . . . will simply jolt a man's soul out in less than twenty-four hours. Before we had traveled sixty miles . . . I was so exhausted that I could hardly sit upright; my head and spine ached so violently, and had become so sensitive to shock, that every jolt was as painful as a blow from a club.*

HOLMAN'S NIGHT JOURNEYS also kept to a minimum "the obstinacy and sulkiness of my Tartar," who was proving progressively lackadaisical in his duties, not the least because they were now passing through his homeland, where Cochrane had recruited him in the first place. Once they crossed the Urals, the mountains separating Europe from Asia and the threshold of Siberia, they would both be strangers to the land.

Kazan was the first in an increasingly puzzling series of suspicion-tinged receptions. One evening, in minuscule Malmyche, the post stationmaster delayed him, insisting on an interview. Since no

English speakers were on hand to translate, he sent for a French-speaking townsman. After some hours the townsman appeared, ebullient, teetering, laughing and pouring out a torrent of a language incomprehensible to Holman. The man, he learned, ran the local brandy distillery; he was indeed fluent in French, but only in the relative sobriety of the morning, before the fumes and sampling duties reduced him to a convivial muddle. Shaking hands all around, Holman departed, only to later learn that the station-master "took it into his head that I was a spy, and although he was informed that I was blind, observed that it was impossible a blind man could be traveling in the way I appeared to travel."

To be fair, it was an excursionary party that grew increasingly improbable in appearance as the miles wore on. Both Holman and the Tartar were looking drawn—Holman's decision to carry no stocks of preserved food and instead eat what they could, when they could, had translated into a severely sparse diet—sometimes bread alone, for days at a time. The *povozka,* thoroughly used long before he purchased it, broke down with depressing regularity; it had already torn through two axles since Moscow, and Holman had sacrificed much of the cargo space to carrying a third as a spare. The iron wheels were bright with recent blacksmith strikes, the mark of improvised repairs. And when the Tartar began to complain of feeling poorly, Holman permitted him to move from the usual postillion stance, astride one of the horses, to the more comfortable seat at his side. A casual observer could easily conclude that the equipage had lost its driver, and that the sullen, muttering man who slackly held the reins was the less alert of the two passengers.

BY MIDSUMMER THEY were past the Urals and on the threshold of Siberia, a milestone that rendered Holman practically intoxicated with achievement. "I almost imagined that a supernatural power was imparted to me, and that I had only to wave my wand, and will it, and every obstacle, every difficulty, would give way before me." But such exuberance was quickly dampened by a sobering first encounter with his involuntary fellow travelers, newly condemned exiles making the same journey under even greater privation. He was in Ekaterinburg, waiting for still further repairs to the *povozka*, when he witnessed them being driven through town on the usual schedule. Males, about a hundred at a time, on Tuesday. Females, about twenty or so, on Friday.

Both groups were on a forced march, compelled to keep a pace that seemed calculated to cripple, if not kill, by exhaustion. If a transportee could walk no further, a passing peasant might be compelled to temporarily offer up a cart. Otherwise, Holman observed, "They are left behind on the road, and not unfrequently relieved by the friendly hand of death from future misery." It struck him as a gratuitous cruelty, especially since "the females who survive the journey are generally so far broken down by its hardships or disease, as to be incapable afterward of bearing children." Most of the women were innocent of any crime. They were simply following their husbands into exile.

NOW HIS JOURNEY was becoming a race. Even in the wane of summer, the air was beginning to chill. Fall would be a stub of a season, bringing frost and snowstorms long before the official onset of winter. They needed to cover as much ground as possible while weather still permitted, and that meant a continuous day-and-night dash to Tomsk, a thousand miles distant. Holman hired another man to take shifts with his postillion, but soon the reins had to be handed over entirely, to a succession of haphazardly recruited drivers. The Tartar was no longer sluggish and out of sorts; he was genuinely ill, groaning with stomach pain. Holman touched, prodded, and palpated, diagnosed food poisoning, and administered the treatment himself, hand-feeding morsels of stale bread to the Tartar until he slumped alongside on the bench, asleep. The *povozka* pitched, yawed, and rattled eastward.

This was the most fearful part of the journey, the passage through the path-swallowing marshlands known as the Baraba Steppe. Just as Russians dreaded Siberia, Siberians blanched at Baraba: hundreds of miles of bog and stagnant waters and pestilential bleakness, terrain so malevolent that almost no one emerged unscathed. Holman, used to shrugging off well-meaning admonitions, took to heart the warnings about this region, that "in addition to the risk of ague, fever, of being poisoned, or stung to death, there was no little chance of being robbed and murdered."

Only desperados and the desperately poor lived in these miasmic wilds, clinging to the perimeter of insect-dispelling greenwood smoke, their faces permanently scarred from innumerable stings and bites just the same. Outside of the smoke, the air darkened and quivered with tiny wings: gnats and flies and mosquitoes in such profusion the prudent traveler wore not only a horsehair mask, but chain mail to protect the neck and shoulders. Even then they hurried, lest their horses be driven mad by infestation. The water was lethal to drink, the land often submerged into a soggy morass, passable only on planks so wobbly they frequently induced a nausea similar to sea-sickness.

Holman and the Tartar had no masks or chain mail. Instead, they wrapped their faces in gauze and hoped that the torrential rain, inundating the open-air *povozka,* would keep at bay the worst of the insects, as well as airborne illness. Malaria and typhus were not the only unwelcome souvenirs of transit; there was also "a disease peculiar to this horrid Steppe . . . a tumour, that commencing on some part of the head, but more commonly on the cheek, continues to enlarge until it bursts and frequently proves fatal." The tossing and tedium was punctuated by anxious self-examinations under the soggy gauze, which produced no ominous lumps, just fresh arrays of welts that itched infernally.

Holman emerged from the Baraba Steppe exhausted, bone-chilled, and obsessed with improvising a proper cup of tea, but otherwise in sound health. The Tartar was not so fortunate. Unlike his employer, who could wrap gauze around his head abundantly, without regard to seeing, he could only veil his sight with a few translucent layers. Irritation began to well up. By the time they arrived on the outskirts of Tomsk his vision was impaired, his eyes painfully inflamed.

It was pointless to seek out a doctor. No one in a radius of thousands of miles was better equipped to diagnose severe ophthalmia than Holman, or more familiar with every possible treatment. Ignoring the class boundaries between servant and gentleman, he found a single room and made the Tartar as comfortable as possible on the floor. Then he began to methodically unpack his portable pharmacy.

After a few days of rest and his master's ministrations, the danger of permanent blindness seemed to pass. The Tartar was restored to functional vision in one eye; the other was healing behind bandages, still painfully sensitive to light. One serviceable eye between them was deemed sufficient by Holman, and they resumed their journey.

The *povozka*, of course, broke down again. The Tartar attempted repairs on his own, further aggravating his injured eye in the process. Their progress reduced to a torturously slow pace by the rickety vehicle and the rough hills, Holman tried to convince his postillion to join him in his usual fitness routine. His exhortations were declined with an unintelligible grumble, so he fished in his pocket for his handy tether and jumped over the side.

They were halfway across Siberia, approaching the borderlands of Mongolia. Holman was thrilled to cross paths with a trade caravan wending in from China, a long train of carts, each pulled by a single horse, each laden with a cargo of tea. He stood transfixed by the timeless, peaceful air of the procession, the unhurried clatter of hooves, the exotic aromatics of the tea chests wafting by. He gave little thought to the spectacle confronting the merchants as they passed: a ludicrously ramshackle three-horse cart, hardly fit to wobble a peasant to market, driven by a fierce-looking but obviously miserable one-eyed Muslim, towing an Englishman on a string.

SIX MORE WEEKS brought them to Irkutsk, and astonishment. It was one thing to hear of the world's most isolated city, but another to experience it. Further east than Singapore, Irkutsk was a study in incongruity, if not improbability, nestled in a bend of river near the border of Chinese Mongolia. After crossing thousands of miles of isolate terrain, passing through few villages larger than a cluster of huts, it was jarring to encounter a metropolis of fifteen thousand souls, the size of Holman's native Exeter, complete with a cathedral, a theater, an orchestra, an art museum, and an imposing array of mansions. It was bustling with voluntary exiles, merchants who had moved there to rack up fortunes in furs and the Chinese border trade. Some would take their money and return to Moscow as soon as possible, but most of the newly wealthy found it hard to abandon the source of their wealth. They remained, and indulged in a collective orgy of ostentation. Not only did they build mansions, it was a point of pride to construct them with as many windows as possible—more windows, Holman learned, than could be found anywhere else in the empire. Glass was both costly to import and lacking in insulation, making the structures prestigiously expensive to heat. Winters were so cold that the chill would break many of the windows, allowing the cycle of spending to begin anew.

Holman's reception here was the strangest of all. At the first mansion he stopped to visit, the answering manservant shouted and slammed the door in their faces. Further knocking produced no response, and the Tartar could only shrug and lead his confused, reeling master back to the *povozka*. Of the Russian language "I had now collected sufficient knowledge to be occasionally serviceable," Holman assessed, and he understood the gist of the servant's dismissal: *You are intoxicated. Go away.*

It was a puzzling response to an innocent social call, but Holman shook off the rejection and proceeded to the "White Palace," the grandest mansion of all. It was home to Aleksandr Stepanovich Lavinski, governor general of Eastern Siberia, the ultimate authority over a region twice as large as all of Europe. This time, Holman was greeted with such cordiality it seemed his celebrity had once again preceded him. Brisk officials whisked him into the presence of the governor general himself, who shook his hand with eagerness and genuine warmth. This was curious, as it soon became clear that Lavinski didn't have the slightest idea who Holman was.

Nevertheless, the governor general had been looking forward to meeting the new arrival for quite some time. As he communicated (in French, the language they had in common), mail addressed to Holman had begun to arrive some weeks previously, and since one of the envelopes contained money it became a matter for government investigation. Lavinski had personally ordered an inquiry into the entire exile population, to see if a prisoner with a name approximating "Holman" could be found. When none was accounted for, his curiosity was piqued. And now that the addressee was before him, clearly a gentleman, he was anxious for his company. Holman emerged with "a very particular and general invitation from his excellency, both to his public and private dinners," and the beginnings of an important friendship.

This was gratifying, as it suited his private plans. It was late September, and the nights were already freezing, but instead of hurrying on, covering as much ground as possible before the onset of winter, he intended to linger in Irkutsk for a while. Mongolian China lay on the other side of Lake Baikal, a passage that was long, storm-ridden, and dangerous even in the mildest weather, and impossible this time of year. All boats capable of the journey had already been hauled out of the water. But in midwinter, when its surface froze solid, Lake Baikal could be crossed by sledge in a few frigid, windy hours.

The borders of China were not officially open to foreigners, but he might slip through. If so, he could repeat the strategy he'd been pursuing in Russia, dashing to the point where being expelled would simply speed him on his way. If unable to penetrate the border, his next recourse would be to set out for Kamchatka and the Pacific coast, where Cochrane had found his princess and where Holman could hope to find a berth on a whaling ship bound eastward. But forging toward Kamchatka meant skirting the Arctic Circle, at latitudes where there were only two seasons: the time of snow or the time of snowmelt muck. The snow was easier to traverse.

Holman paid off the Tartar, wished him well, and settled in. Not to wait out the winter, but to wait for its greatest height.

GOVERNOR GENERAL LAVINSKI proved to have "an intelligent, polished mind, with the strictest integrity," as well as a passion for fresh air that rivaled his own. Long, conversation-filled walks together became the keystone of their friendship. Holman took great pleasure in these excursions, even as the daytime temperatures began to plummet. But afterward, he would find his way to the house of another new and particular friend. Someone whose companionship could not be quite so public.

She lived in the mansion he'd first visited, the one with the shouting servant and slamming door. Intrigued by that rude reception, he'd paid a return visit—and found himself showered with abject apologies. The doorman, he learned, had turned him away because he thought the English accent was phony, that Holman was a con man attempting to prey on the lady of the house. She was renowned not only for her great wealth but for her exoticness, being an Englishwoman herself. "The incident, the recollection of which often amused us, rather contributed to increase our future friendship," Holman wrote.

He would commemorate her only as Mrs. B.—but for once it is possible to loosen his veil of discretion. She was Mrs. Bentham, the former child bride of a British adventurer. She'd been fourteen when she married Mr. Bentham, willfully giving up London for Siberia for what was, by all accounts, a true love match. The years since had been prosperous. Beginning as a simple horse trader, her much older husband had compiled a mercantile fortune, then won a land grant and rank of nobility from the tsar. John Dundas Cochrane had enjoyed the Benthams' hospitality when passing through two years earlier. In a backhanded fashion, he found them a fascinating pair:

> *Of all the methodical people, preserving their originality of manners, customs, and opinions, this couple are certainly the most extraordinary I have ever seen moving on their own axis or in their own orbit: they appear to exist between light and darkness, unconscious and careless of what passes around them. Mr. Bentham has been forty years in Siberia, in the full enjoyment of the same proverbial reputation that his honesty would have entitled him to had he forever remained a citizen of London . . . As to Mrs. Bentham, she has just been long enough in Siberia to forget her own native language; but not long enough to learn that of her adopted country.*

The "forget her own native language" remark was a not-so-subtle dig. She had, of course, not lost her English; it had been the couple's intimate language for fifteen years. Cochrane was alluding to the softening of her accent, in which he could still detect her origin in the poorest parts of London. Mrs. Bentham had been born a Cockney.

Now she was barely in her thirties, "very young and handsome," in the opinion of Holman, who noted that her beauty and youth had long caused suspicion. "Many imagined that she had been carried off from England contrary to the consent of her friends," he wrote, "and she was often interrogated by some of the Russian nobility to that effect." Mr. Bentham had died ten months earlier, which was why her servants had been especially protective: she was a rich widow, nearing the end of her formal year of mourning. In two months' time, she could put away her somber clothes, the black wardrobe known as widow's weeds, and resume a social life. Until then, she was supposed to maintain the semiseclusion of the bereaved—which means she had to mute her delight at the presence of an English gentleman with a thorough stock of stories from home.

"Her attentions to me were assiduously kind," Holman would remember. But those attentions had to be paid privately, and with decorum.

THE APPROACH OF winter began to curtail the length of their conversational walks, but Holman's friendship with Governor General Lavinski continued to deepen. By now, they were on a first-name basis, a rare informality for them both. Yet the most profound sign of their growing closeness came in the first week of October, after a particularly relaxing Sunday dinner. Concluding that Lavinski was an entirely sympathetic soul, who could see "more or less deeply into the various shades of my character," Holman at last took the plunge. The persona of whimsical eccentricity was getting harder to maintain by the day, and he at last felt comfortable entrusting his secret plan "to complete the tour of the world."

He fully expected Aleksandr to joyfully applaud this revelation, and offer his enthusiastic support. His confidant had a decidedly different reaction.

They were seated in one of the White Palace's drawing rooms, presumably before a roaring fire, but the atmosphere was suddenly more frigid inside than out. Summoning a stiff formality, Lavinski spoke not as a friend but as His Excellency the Governor General. He informed Holman that although he was free to roam around Siberia at will, he had no such liberty in leaving it. Should he survive a journey to Kamchatka, that would necessarily be the end of the line. He would not be permitted to board any ship of any nationality, bound in any direction, at least not without the express written permission of the tsar himself.

Holman struggled to find a suitable response. No one—not Cochrane, nor the powers-that-be in Moscow—had mentioned such a prohibition. But then again, why would they have? He'd presented his expedition as a casual incursion, not a passage through and beyond. He listened with patience as Lavinski proceeded to soften somewhat, following his formal notice with a heartfelt plea to give up notions of venturing further.

"I assured him that my determination was the result of very serious deliberation," Holman would recall, "and that I felt it was not to be shaken." If written permission from the tsar was required, could the governor general request it through official channels? Lavinski agreed to do so, and the matter was dropped there.

THE REST OF Irkutsk society fell over itself to entertain the *angliiskiy gentleman*. There were invitations to formal dances, state dinners, horseback riding parties, even an elaborate costume ball, to which local color was added by inviting Tunguskan nomads and Mongol tribesmen to attend in their native garb. Holman was bundled off to kiss the mummified hand of Saint Innokenti, a supposed surefire cure for blindness. He was escorted through round after round of ceremonial "inspection tours"—missionary schools, foundling homes, the hospital for prisoners.

Holman and Mrs. Bentham spent a private Christmas with each other. The Russians observed the holiday on January 6, and the young widow was elated to share in a second, earlier celebration in the British fashion, on December 25. The temperature was a dozen degrees below zero, and dropping still. "The cold was so intensely biting that we could not put our noses out the door," he wrote, "without the risk of losing a part of them." Holman continued to inquire of the governor general: what was the status of his official permission to proceed? The tsar, he was assured, was still contemplating the request.

ON THE DAY after New Year's Day, in weather skirting twenty degrees below zero, a solitary sledge entered Irkutsk and skidded to a stop outside the White Palace. A bundle of frost-hardened furs rose from the passenger seat and shambled stiffly into the vestibule. Servants swarmed to peel back the pelts, revealing a dauntingly upright man in an impressive military uniform. The new arrival offered brisk regards to the governor general and introduced himself. He was Alexey Kolovin, a feldjager of His Imperial Majesty's service, here to quietly resolve a delicate matter.

Most Russians reacted to the word *"feldjager"*—a German term, meaning literally "country hunter"—with a mixture of awe and dread. They were the tsar's personal corps, limited to a hyperelite of 115, trusted as his bodyguards and dispatch runners of his most confidential messages. Feldjagers had superlegal status—they did not need to obey speed limits, nor were they liable for damages caused by their furious transits. A feldjager delivering an imperial edict was an intimidating sight, but an even more fearsome presence was one who arrived with no documents at all. A feldjager without papers was understood to be carrying out the tsar's will through unofficial channels. His actions were therefore beyond appeal.

This feldjager presented no papers. He informed Lavinski that his was a confidential mission, announced to no one, and that it would need to remain covert. Then he got down to business.

Kolovin's words were couched in the language of courtesy and sympathy. His Imperial Majesty had learned of Holman's plight, and expressed the greatest concern for his well-being. It was unthinkable that such an esteemed personage as the Blind Traveler should wander alone through the bleakest parts of the empire. The tsar had personally dispatched his trusted aide across four thousand miles to act as a personal escort. The Englishman was doubtless weary of Siberia, if not of all Russia, by now, and would be anxious to return to Europe immediately.

In theory, Governor General Lavinski wildly outranked this glorified messenger—Feldjager Kolovin was not even technically an officer. In practice, he knew he would have to obey the young man's bidding.

LAVINSKI TRIED TO break the news gently. He discreetly informed his friend of the new secret arrival, pointing out that the feldjager had brought with him no documents authorizing Holman's further progress eastward. Holman chose to deliberately miss the point, speculating that the tsar only wished for him to wait for warmer weather, or to contemplate an alternate route out of the empire—perhaps down to Odessa, then Constantinople. He could sense that the governor general wasn't telling him the whole truth "Something still remained undivulged," he noted, "which a feeling of delicacy restrained him from communicating." He didn't want to go anywhere until Lake Baikal froze over, until he could attempt to slip through the Chinese border. But as he was finally made to understand, he would be leaving in the feldjager's protective custody, and soon.

It was time to abandon his dream of a circumnavigation, and make his farewells.

The hardest parting was with Mrs. Bentham, because he knew that she would gladly go with him, if only it were possible. Her dearest wish was to return to England, but she had a ten-year-old son being schooled in how to be a perfect Russian gentleman (Cochrane described the boy as "spoilt"), and she was firmly hemmed in by her late husband's success. Under Russian law, she inherited his substantial estate but had no right to sell it off—she was, in effect, expected to tend it for a future husband, or her son. Abandoning Siberia would mean abandoning her family or becoming penniless, or both.

Holman, as usual, drowned his romantic impulses in poetry.

The stranger is gone—Oh, he will not forget,
When at home he shall talk of the toil he has known,
To tell with a sigh what endearments he met,
As he stray'd on the banks of Angara alone.

He took his place on the sledge. In addition to the feldjager and a driver, there was another passenger, a young Mongolian serf being returned to his master (Russia would not abolish serfdom for another thirty-nine years), and enough baggage to tax the pulling strength of a four-horse team. Then they were off, at a speed that only a feldjager could choose. Despite the snow and subzero temperature he kept the horses at a constant gallop for fifty miles, until one of them collapsed and died. The driver unhitched the corpse, already beginning to freeze solid, and resumed a pace only slightly diminished. Holman was informed that, as the transportee, "it was my place to pay for all dead horses."

The feldjager proved as cruel to men as to animals. Their haste and the condition of the roads made it inevitable that the sledge would overturn at least once each day, setting the stores and passengers tumbling. Kolovin would unsheath his sword and mercilessly beat the driver with the flat of the blade, shouting at his carelessness. But he would not, under any circumstances, allow the driver to proceed at anything slower than top speed. What was the overwhelming hurry? Holman was finally able to wrest an explanation: Kolovin wanted to impress his superiors with the swiftness of his mission, of course, but more importantly he knew a posting to Paris was coming open soon. He had reason to believe it would be his—but only if he was around to accept the appointment. Since he was exempt from the consequences of his actions, he saw no reason not to attempt a land speed record across the frozen steppe.

Holman no longer knew how cold it was getting. The mercury in his portable thermometer was almost always frozen solid. He was dressed to near-immobility, adding to his normal clothing two pairs of woolen stockings, inner boots (of wild goatskin), outer boots (leather, fur-lined), a thick fur cloak for his legs, and "a thickly wadded great-coat," over which was thrown an immense shroud of wolf-skin. Still, "I could never, with all my clothing and precautions, keep the extremities warm." As touch was the primary sense by which he comprehended the world, numbness was a sort of second blindness. The threat of frostbite held special terrors.

They found shelter late each night—usually well past midnight—and Holman was forced to admit that there was one advantage to traveling with a feldjager: the terrified peasantry fell over themselves to provide the best meals and accommodations they could offer, meager as they were. But the pace was still brutal, and after a week Holman found himself "considerably indisposed" and severely weakened. That morning, he refused to go any further, demanding a rest. Fuming, Kolovin allowed him a single day. The ordeal resumed the following day and continued across another thousand miles and then another, settling into a grim routine. The horses would be overdriven to the point of mishap, the feldjager would beat the driver, and the frost-shrouded sledge, "heavily laden and in a very crazy state," would shudder back into motion. Kolovin experimented with various punishments and found he could torture the driver by merely forcing him to remove his hat, exposing his head to the elements.

There was one moment of respite. While taking on supplies in Omsk, Holman was allowed to wander over to a nearby tent settlement of nomadic Kirghizs, where he feasted on sour cheese, huddled thankfully around the communal fire, and flirted with a Kirghiz maiden. "The young woman, however, who I understood was very pretty and very reserved, hung down her head with at least the affectation of modesty, and it was only with some difficulty that I succeeded in securing a half stolen kiss."

He also met another stranded English traveler, a Royal Army officer on half-pay whom he recorded as Lieutenant L——. The lieutenant had attached himself to a group of Persian diplomats returning to their native land, getting as far as Astrakhan on the Caspian Sea, where he took a brief walk and returned to find himself abandoned. Since then he'd been drifting, destitute, up the Volga, only recently finding a modicum of respectability as a tutor but still without the means to get back home. His countryman, who knew the feldjager would not permit another passenger, could only wish him well.

By now Holman was realizing, with some dismay, that Kolovin did not particularly care if his charges lived or died. The Mongol slave boy was already limping from frostbite, and Holman himself knew "I was seriously unwell; indeed I felt myself every day grow sensibly weaker." Yet the feldjager's urgency only increased as they approached Moscow. This callousness was all the more surprising, since Holman had recently saved the man's life. One night they'd slept in a heated but poorly ventilated room, unaware they were being poisoned by carbon dioxide gas. "I fortunately awoke in the middle of the night, found myself suffering from a dreadful headache, and with some difficulty succeeded in reaching and opening the door," he noted. "Otherwise it is probable that neither of us would have been alive in the morning."

HE MADE HIS final stand in Moscow. Kolovin sequestered his charge in a hotel, but allowed Holman one escorted outing to withdraw funds from Gillibrand & Holidays, an English banker. There Mr. Gillibrand, startled, rushed to greet him. As he explained, in casual but rapid English (to confound the watching feldjager), the city was buzzing with rumors of the Blind Traveler's fate. One story was that he had already passed through, bound in chains. Another was that he was in Moscow, but a prisoner.

As Holman discovered immediately thereafter, the latter was more or less true. Once back in the hotel he was informed that no other excursions would be permitted, and that he would remain in the room indefinitely until the minister of police arrived for a private interview. He was, in effect, under house arrest. He was also forbidden to correspond with anyone, or indeed to write anything at all.

But a blind man can take full advantage of the night. That evening, he waited until Kolovin had doused all the lights and gone to sleep. In the darkness he stealthly unpacked his Noctograph and wrote a message:

CIRCULAR.

The prisoner Holman begs leave to acquaint his friends in Moscow, that he has just arrived from Siberia, under charge of a feld-jager. As his keeper does not allow him to visit his friends, he begs to inform them that he may be seen at the Hotel de l'Europe, in the Twerskoi, for three days only. Should it be necessary for him to remain in Moscow any longer, no person will be allowed to visit him after that time, with the exception of his physician and banker.

P.S. He has just learnt that a tailor will be included in the exception, which precludes the risk of his being exposed on the frontiers sans culotte.

He smuggled out the note the next day with Mr. Gillibrand, who had contrived to deliver funds to him. Friends did arrive soon after, and they were begrudgingly allowed brief visitations, always under close supervision, and under the condition that the conversation was in Russian or French, not English. But the visitors only expressed relief that Holman was alive, and hopes that he would recuperate—he was clearly feverish and exhausted. Despite the jocular tone of his message, Holman had secretly hoped that proof of his captivity would spark a diplomatic uproar. Where were the emissaries of "Beauty" Bagot, the British Ambassador, demanding his immediate release?

They did not appear. The British Embassy had no offices in Moscow. But there was a new, mysterious presence in the room.

In whispers from his visiting friends he learned details: there was a hovering, silent man, dressed in black and wearing spectacles, following the conversation and recording their names. Later, he could hear the same person pawing through his belongings and searching his papers, and simply loitering in the bedchamber. More than anything Holman needed rest, but the dark-clad man ("I could not fancy his interior as dark as his exterior") was clearly laboring under a common misconception about the blind—that in their presence, silence equaled invisibility. This annoyed Holman no end, as he was perfectly aware of the man, and could have hit him with a tossed pillow were he so inclined.

Two mornings later, Holman was still too ill to be moved. There was a physician at his bedside, confirming that he needed "to remain perfectly quiet within doors." Nonetheless he was told to get packed; they'd be back on the road in a matter of hours. He ignored the ultimatum, which prompted the summoning of the minister of police. The scene that followed struck Holman as so like a farcical play that he was moved to transcribe it in that format, complete with a Dramatis Personae (he was "Prisoner") and stage directions.

Enter the various Characters.

M. of Police. (To the Doctor.) Is it not possible for this gentleman to proceed on his journey?

Doctor. It is possible, but I do not recommend it.

M. of Police. Why surely, if he is well wrapped up, and carries medicine with him, he cannot suffer *much.*

Doctor. He is very feverish, and otherwise unwell, and therefore I cannot think it prudent for him to proceed in his present state.

Feld-jager. The weather is so fine that it is impossible it can hurt him.

Doctor. He is so much shaken by his late journey, that repose is necessary for him.

Feld-jager. He will not experience much fatigue in the sledge, and we can stop whenever he feels worse.

Prisoner. Yes, I can stop, if it happens to accord with your plea-sure or convenience; but what comfort, what medical assistance, can I receive at the stations on the road? . . . I cannot go to-day, but, if I feel better, will certainly leave to-morrow, as I can have no com-fort in being detained a prisoner at Moscow.

M. of Police. (*To the Prisoner.*) I do not see what is to prevent your leaving to-day; for, if you are well clothed, and rub your hands and face with spirits, there will be little fear of your taking cold.

Prisoner. You may prescribe, sir, what you please, but you will not induce me, voluntarily, to leave this hotel to-day, where I can have every comfort, to expose myself to the risk of being laid up at a miserable post-station on the road.

M. of Police. But the governor will not let you remain.

Prisoner. Then he must *compel* me to go.

THE GOVERNOR HAD no qualms about doing exactly that. The following day Holman was forcibly led down to the sledge, and onto a mattress that now occupied most of the cargo hold. In that horizontal state he was trundled westward for another week, until the snow roads disappeared and the feldjager traded their sledge for a dilapidated peasant's carriage.

This took them as far as the Russian border. There Kolovin propped up his prisoner, returned his passport, and "we parted, with mutual congratulations on our respective liberations."

There was a tiny cart, woven of wicker, with room for only one passenger, waiting just over the border. Holman weakly climbed aboard and curled up, finding its dimensions and construction very like a cradle. Overcome by exhaustion, he let the sway of the horses rock him. He entered Poland fast asleep.

Holman's 1825 author's portrait. Note the visual joke of the blank globe.

TWELVE

A Salvo Upon
All Defects

AFTER RECUPERATING FOR several weeks in "a comfortless room" in Cracow, Holman was at last strong enough to face the crisis posed by his expulsion. Almost all of Poland's polite society was closed to him. Given the suspicious circumstances of his arrival he was considered no longer a gentleman; if not a criminal, then at least a rogue. Few believed he had gone to Siberia voluntarily—the tsar must have put him there, then plucked him out.

There was nothing to do but press homeward, but even that proved complicated. He tried to obtain a visa to cross the next border, into Austria, but the Austrian consul refused to give it, on the grounds that such arrangements should have been made in Saint Petersburg. Holman, who had been whisked through Saint Petersburg flat on his back, could only sigh and send off a salvo of letters of protest. It was a month before he was finally allowed to proceed to Vienna.

Vienna was not, he discovered, a city that welcomed strangers, particularly those wearing wild wolfskin coats and tapping walls with a cane. He was escorted immediately to the police station and given a three-day pass. At the end of those three days, he would have to reappear with evidence of respectability—either a citizen to vouch for him or proof of sufficient funds.

This was problematic. He was almost out of money, and the letter of credit he had asked Gillibrand & Holidays to send ahead of him was nowhere to be found. Worse still, his single letter of introduction applicable to Austrian society was addressed to someone who had just died—the day before his arrival, in fact. Such letters were not just social niceties; they were vouchsafes that established him as a gentleman of leisure, giving him the freedom to open lines of credit and avoid charges of vagrancy. Holman kept a meticulous collection of introductions (organized geographically, since he could not read them himself), and usu-ally did not depart from a city without replenishing his stock for the next. But the black cloud that hung over him in Cracow had closed off that methodology, and for the first time he faced the prospect of becoming genuinely destitute.

He faced it with a shrug. He was, he admitted, "the most anxious of mortals" when agitated by uncertainty, "[B]ut let the excitement cease, no matter whether in an agreeable man-ner or the reverse, and my mind at once regains its tranquility." He ignored the three-day deadline and spent his dwindling funds enjoying the opera and visiting the monuments of the city, cal-culating correctly that largesse and visibility, rather than frugality and lying low, would keep the police at bay. The letter of credit arrived at last a week later, and he was off—but not before seek-ing an audience with Sir Henry Wellesley, the British ambassador (and brother of Lord Wellington). Holman wanted to report on his curious treatment in Russia, and ascertain if it perhaps had a larger diplomatic meaning. There seemed no other explanation as to why "a single humble and afflicted individual . . . against whom no offence, either political or moral, had been proved, or even so much as brought to the threshold of accusation" should be subjected to "an incessant journey of nearly five thousand miles, at this inclement season, through the wildest country in the world."

Sir Henry Wellesley could not speculate —at least not publicly, or even privately to Holman. But the episode appeared to reinforce a suspicion that British and American diplomatic circles had harbored for quite some time. In the lands beyond Irkutsk, Russia had something to hide.

ON JUNE 20, 1824, two years and one day from the date of his departure, Holman landed in Hull, overjoyed to be back in his native country. "Happy England! land of liberty, of virtue, and of beauty," he enthused. "In thy favored clime none of those arbitrary proceedings, which it has been my fate to experience." But while unpacking at Windsor, he was surprised to learn of two developments, one gratifying and one unsettling.

The happy news: *Narrative of a Journey*, his debut book, had sold briskly, well enough to warrant a second printing, and the critics had been kind. "Few things would appear more absurd or improbable, prima facie, than that a person wholly blind should undertake the grand tour," one wrote. "Mr. Holman, nevertheless, has performed this feat with additional wonders." The unhappy news: there was another, better-selling book, containing a vicious verbal attack against him.

John Dundas Cochrane, landing in London with his child bride the previous year, had published his *Narrative of a Pedestrian Journey Through Russia and Siberian Tartary*. Among the self-referential tales of privation and bravado, there was a haughtily dismissive portait of the Blind Traveler. To make his point even more loudly, Cochrane excerpted this section in a preview published in the *Monthly Magazine*, a popular periodical of the day.

What object he can have, without a servant, of going to Siberia, I know not. He, indeed, may go there as well as anywhere else, for he

*will see just as much; but there is so little to be seen by those who
have even the use of their eyes, that I cannot divine what interest he
can have to attempt it.*

Having painted Holman in shades of delusion, Cochrane moved
on to a pre-emptive strike against the man's future writings:

*If his journal, which may be made interesting, be composed of hear-
say, as it certainly cannot be of ocular evidence, he will indeed have
enough to do to record the information he may receive, and which
can only proceed from exiles or criminals, and consequently not to
be relied upon.*

In increasingly screed-like language, Cochrane lofted a barrage
of objections. Holman's notes, being voluminous, could not help
but fall into official hands, and be censored. His rudimentary command of the Russian language would deafen him to insincerities
and outright lies. As a crowning fillip, he leveled the charge that
would haunt Holman for the rest of his life:

*Who will then say that Siberia is a wild, inhospitable, or impassible
country, when even the blind can traverse it with safety?*

This was a cruel assertion. The wilderness had not been tamed
in the months between his expedition and Holman's. But it was an
effective way to encapsulate contempt for the Blind Traveler: to
view him not as a risk-taker, but as a sort of harbinger marking the
end of risk. Holman's further adventures would put the lie to this
time and time again, yet his critics would consistently adhere to
the line first hewn by Cochrane. *It's not impressive that this was done
by a blind man—it's unimpressive precisely because he's blind.*

Holman was stunned to see his friendship betrayed so vocifer-
ously and publicly. "I cannot divine the state of feeling by which
Captain C. was actuated by writing the passage in question," he

wrote, "which appears to be composed of compliment and sarcasm, mixed up with an affectation of pity."

There was no confronting Cochrane directly. He'd left England a few months before Holman's return, departing for his next pedestrian feat: a transit of South America. Instead, Holman chose to reply in the same forum where the attack was first mounted, the pages of the *Monthly Magazine*.

> *Great as my affliction may be, Mr. Editor, I beg to assure you, that I neither seek for nor require the pity of any man; and although I by no means reject the sympathy of my friends, yet I feel that if it were not expressed with greater delicacy than Captain C. appears to possess, it would be more chilling to my heart than the freezing blasts of a Siberian winter.*

Where Cochrane had deployed scorn, Holman used gentle humor. "As Captain C. admits there is little to be seen [in Siberia]," he wrote, "I think my prospects were likely to be nearly as good as his own." Concerning the notion that his journals would be bulky and censored, "I effect upon a principle which might not have entered into his contemplation—that of depositing them, in a portable and invisible form, within the cavity of my cranium." His Noctograph notes were merely scraps; the bulk of his reporting was done entirely from memory, and his facts were yet to be faulted. As to the remainder of the charges:

> *Captain C. asserts, for instance, that my information must be hearsay, when he has just accused me of not knowing the language in which this hearsay information is to be communicated; surely this is paradoxical!*

The gracious wit of this retort, coupled with the fast-spreading rumors about his captivity and expulsion, made Holman's next book one of the most eagerly awaited titles of 1825. Hastened to the printers that April, the two-volume *Travels Through Russia, Siberia, Poland, Austria, Saxony, Prussia, Hanover, &c &c* was an easy-reading travel narrative, gripping at times, at other times overlaced with minutiae. As if to prove his powers of observation, Holman threw in a chart of temperature readings, instructions on how to use a Russian abacus, and even some poems transcribed from the prayer book of Mary, Queen of Scots, which he'd found in the tsar's imperial library. There was also room for one last dig at Cochrane: "Physically blind as the Author is, he cannot but be sensible of the mental obscurity of Captain C."

To underscore his unique blend of irreverence and implacability, a visual joke was worked into the frontispiece portrait. It was clearly endorsed, if not concocted, by Holman—had it been perpetrated against him, his sighted friends would have noticed and taken exception. It shows him in full naval uniform, gazing blankly but benignly into the distance. Through a window, a ship is glimpsed, presumably the *Guerriere*, rounding an iceberg in an arctic storm. His left hand rests on a stylus and his Noctograph writing machine. His right hand drapes comfortably over a globe that is handsomely mounted but entirely blank.

But the addition that practically guaranteed the book bestseller status was on the page following the frontispiece. A single sentence: *To The King's Most Excellent Majesty.*

The dedication of a book to a public figure was not done lightly or easily. Since the tradition stemmed from thanking nobility for underwriting a text (the King James Bible is dedicated not to God but King James), such dedications still carried at least a hint of endorsement from their subject. Permission to dedicate a work to a member of the royal family was strictly regulated, and the degree of royalty invoked was seen as analogous to the rise of the author's star. In the public's eye, the crowning praise of Jane Austen's *Emma* was the fact that she'd been allowed to dedicate it to the prince regent. In contrast, Holman's first book had warranted only a dedication to Princess Augusta, the wife of George III's tenth child.

Cochrane did not submit his book at all, choosing to dedicate it instead to a Siberian ex-governor of his acquaintance.

Holman's *Travels* received a rare honor: its author was permitted to dedicate it to the king himself. Such a dedication was usually occasion for effusive swoops of royal flattery, but Holman's was heartfelt and direct. "My powers of personal exertion have been too much curtailed to allow me to offer your Majesty, in return, more than a heart replete with loyalty and gratitude."

The critics rushed to add their approbation. "Notwithstanding his blindness," wrote the *British Critic*, "his readers will not fail to derive gratification from accompanying him." The *Literary Chronicle* labeled it "of intense interest" and "a delightful work." The *Literary Gazette* enthused for pages, concluding anxiously with "we hope we have said enough to recommend this extraordinary production to the public." Apparently so. The public not only snapped up the book, there was sufficient demand to bring the earlier *Narrative of a Journey* back into print for a third edition, then a fourth. Instead of undermining his rival's exploits, Cochrane's attack had been the best promotion possible. Holman was now a celebrity.

DESPITE THE ATTENTION now given to his Russian captivity, there was still no official explanation forthcoming, which gave rise to numerous theories. It was possible to conclude that Holman's high-profile friendship with the deaf Colebrook in Saint Petersburg, a man with vague but real ties to British intelligence, made him suspect from the start. Another supposition was that Holman had inadvertently paid for Cochrane's transgressions—that the Pedestrian Traveler had committed some nameless offense and the tsar's men had mistaken his fellow unlikely traveler for a confederate. Holman took pains to disavow this, stating in his book "we were not, as has been intimated, acting in concert."

But Holman suspected professional sabotage, perpetrated by the man who'd taken such pains to attack him in print: John Dundas

Cochrane. He hinted broadly at this in his book, when he insisted that the tsar, "magnanimous and benevolent," would never "have sanctioned the harsh measures, to which I was afterwards sub-jected, unless his feelings had been influenced, or his confidence abused, by misrepresentation!" He rounded out this accusation with a choice quote from Act IV of *Othello*:

> *I will be hang'd if some eternal villain,*
> *Some busy and insinuating rogue,*
> *Some cogging, cozening slave, to get some office,*
> *Hath not devised a slander.*

One thing is clear from Cochrane's writings. He had, or at least wanted people to think he had, a surprising amount of pull with Russia's power elite. He'd begun his tramp in France as a nearly impoverished private citizen. But by the time of his departure from Saint Petersburg, the government was entrusting him with "a secret letter to the governor-general of Siberia," presumably dictating that he should be received with all courtesies. Out in Kamchatka, the tsar dispatched a Cossack guard to his side—in his case, not to retrieve him but to help him on his way. The tsar had also granted him the extraordinary privilege of appropriating horses as he pleased, and on repeated occasions, "his Imperial Majesty did afterwards request of Sir Charles Bagot to be informed whether I really needed money, accompanied with an intima-tion that in such case I should be supplied from the imperial treasury." These signs of royal favor, combined with the fact that his last stop in Russia was to give "my official reports at the court of Saint Petersburg," give credence to the notion that Cochrane at least imagined himself important to the tsar. If so, his final report would have been a perfect opportunity to ask one last favor.

But the tsar had far deeper motives than the petty rivalries of wandering Englishmen. The reality was that Russia did have something to hide: its growing presence in North America. Other nations knew the empire maintained fur-trading settlements on the far Pacific shore, but exactly how much this constituted a colonial claim, the establishment of a Russian America, had yet to be asserted. There were *promyshlenniki*, fur hunters, ranging east as far as the Snake River in Idaho, and living permanently as far south as Fort Ross, a two days' northerly ride from Yerba Buena (present-day San Francisco). Less well known were Russian efforts to establish similar footholds in the Hawaiian Islands. Or to encourage intermarriage between Russian hunters and Aleut natives in the vicinity of Kodiak, Alaska, a trend that could only buttress a claim of sovereignty. This was all in the name of private enterprise—the Russian-American Company, granted a monopoly by the tsar—but, collectively, it was making established North American powers nervous. Spain had forbidden its Alta California colonists to trade with the Russians. The British had dispatched two survey tours of the Pacific Northwest (Captain Cook in 1778 and George Vancouver in 1793), largely to send the message that the territory was being scrutinized.

In response, Russia had quietly pursued a policy of keeping other nationals out of Russian America, by forbidding them to cross from Kamchatka into Alaska. The cases of both Holman and Cochrane bear a strong resemblance to the fate of John Ledyard, an American who had sailed with Captain Cook on his final voyage (and who had given the only eyewitness account of Cook's death). Like Cochrane, Ledyard had dreamed of being the first man to walk around the earth (his friend Thomas Jefferson is credited with giving him the idea). Accompanied only by two dogs, he'd departed from Stockholm in 1784, heading east. When he showed up in Irkutsk three years later he, just like Holman, had been summarily arrested, trundled back across the entire length of the empire, and expelled into Poland.

The Russians were not concerned with foreigners wandering around Siberia. They simply didn't want them moving on, across continents, to report on the de facto statecraft of the Russian-American Company.

In this context, Cochrane's confusing, conflicting reasons for giving up his circumnavigation can be read as attempts to save face. In all likelihood, his tsar-issued Cossack companion was a guard to ensure that his quest ended in Kamchatka. That the tsar had let him venture farther east than any other foreign national may have been a mark of favor, but there would be no going farther. As to his rival's captivity and expulsion, the particulars of that incident do seem custom-tailored to Cochrane's benefit. Holman's progress was, after all, arrested at the very point of his final push to shatter Cochrane's record for solo eastward travel. And great pains had been taken not to just kick him out of the country but to pointedly return him to his starting point, as if Russia were a board of chutes and ladders and Holman had just lost the game.

YET THE RIVALRY'S true contest was waged not in Siberia, but in the salons of the London intelligentsia. Of the adventurers' two books, which one made the most substantial contributions to the collective body of knowledge? On that score, Cochrane came up short. His work was, in the words of one critic, an "ever-rolling stream of information, *fait divers* [various facts], statistics and proposals for the betterment of everyone," but it is ultimately Cochrane's soliloquy on himself. As rarely as he mentions his young wife, at least she *is* mentioned; most everyone else is huddled in a collective noun. There are numerous references to "the Kamtchatdales," but none are described physically, as individuals. In contrast, Cochrane sketches himself in loving detail, enthusing on his long golden locks, stylish coat, and silken sash, declaring, "Indeed so great a buck had I become of late, that I hardly knew myself."

When his gaze turns elsewhere, he deploys almost no powers of description at all. Kamchatkan villages are declared to appear exactly like all other Russian villages. The Kirghiz and Kalmyc may be two separate cultures, with homelands thousands of miles apart, but according to Cochrane, "their respective characters do not so much vary, for in their laziness, filth, and abject state, they are indeed as one people."

The blind man's book was, paradoxically, a far more detailed, well-observed, and vivid read, brimming with genuine fascination for native people and their ways. Holman documents a card game with a name he translated as "Nosey," in which "the forfeiture was paid by a smart blow on the loser's carbuncled nose, after which a glass of brandy was administered, to comfort his battered proboscis." He removes his shoes and plunges eagerly into a service at an Islamic mosque, declaring "the Tartars, generally, are a more civilized people than their Russian masters." He describes poignantly his encounter with a snowstorm-engulfed "string of convicts on their march . . . These poor wretches were handcuffed in pairs, with a long light chain carrried through the whole length of the party; this chain used to be very oppressive, until the directions of the present emperor diminished its weight."

The book was received not only as an engrossing adventure but as a valid work of scientific exploration, one substantive enough to earn its author some of the highest honors of the day. First Holman was voted into the Linnean Society, the natural history organization that coordinated the international system of taxonomy, cataloging all life in terms of order, phylum, genus, and species. This was prestigious enough, but the following year came an even greater accolade: induction into the Royal Society of London for Improving Natural Knowledge.

Founded by Christopher Wren, presided over for many years by Isaac Newton, the exclusive Royal Society was the nation's foremost organization devoted to natural philosophy (the term *science* was not yet in general use). It was, in its way, an aristocracy of the mind. Membership did not just impart the right to add to one's name the prestigious initials F.R.S., Fellow of the Royal Society, it

ushered one into the regular company of men like Sir Humphry
Davy (discoverer of potassium and iodine, and the first to isolate
sodium from salt) and Sir John Herschel (discoverer of thousands
of stars, and the man who coined the term *photography*).

If news of Holman's elevation managed to reach Cochrane
in South America, it no doubt infuriated him—for all his rancor
directed toward the Blind Traveler, his grudge against the Royal
Society was stronger still. For years, Cochrane had been dispatch-
ing to them what he imagined to be formal scientific papers,
expecting publication, praise, and membership as his due. Since
these were mostly muddled speculations on geography, the Society
had ignored them, thus earning his public wrath. When his *Narrative of a Pedestrian Journey* went to a second edition he added a
long, bitter appendix devoted to the matter, complete with tran-
scripts of his submissions condemning the Society's "ignorance of
the forms of good breeding," and musing darkly on whether "my
ideas have been pirated and made use of by some Fellow or Fellows of the same learned body."

DID COCHRANE EVER come to regret his vociferous, high-
profile attack on Holman, which had backfired so spectacularly?
His correspondence is silent on the subject, and soon silent altogether. On his way to South America, he'd announced his intent to
march, alone, over the Andes. But that was before he fully comprehended the difference between navigating tundra and rainforest
jungle. If the march materialized at all, it did not take him far.

The last reports of him come from Venezuela, where he was
waxing entrepreneurial, embroiled in mining speculation, brokering
mineral leases from the sister of Simon Bolívar. But the man who had
bragged of being "roasted in some of the worst corners of the West
Indies, during a period of nearly ten years' [naval] service, without,
I might say, a head-ache," was more susceptible to a tropical climate
than he imagined. Inexhaustible as he may have been, he was no

match for malaria; he died of fever in August of 1825, at the age of forty-five. Back in London his notoriously blasé Kamchatkan wife, still a teenager, departed to Russia. There, according to Cochrane's publishers, "by her beauty and accomplishments, no less than by the interest attached to her situation, she soon met with admirers." She thereafter disappears from Cochrane family chronicles, neglecting to leave behind so much as a record of her first name.

THE PEDESTRIAN TRAVELER'S attempts to discredit the Blind Traveler were not, however, entirely unsuccessful. Outside of London cultural circles his aspersions had their effect, and would continue to do so for years to come. Thomas Giordani Wright, a nineteen-year-old surgeon's assistant in Newcastle, read Holman's book and shrugged. In his private journal for 1825, he recorded his dissatisfaction:

> *Holman's Journey through Siberia has occupied my attention for the last hour, and which I find a very amusing volume as the production of a blind traveler. Still there is something incongruous and approaching the absurd in supposing the scenes described by a journalist so imperfectly fitted to conceive them; to read of views and ceremonies and galas with even lithographic illustrations while at the same time the writer's misfortune is constantly in your mind, has to me an unpleasant indescribable, incredulous feeling . . . the circumstances, anecdotes, and all his memoranda being noted from mere hear-say cannot have authenticity enough to warrant their obtrusion on the public. These volumes are dedicated to his Majesty which of course puts a Salvo upon all defects.*

Young Wright had clearly read, and unconsciously parroted, Cochrane's condemnation. But coming from his pen, this sort of dismissal was not a sign of personal condescension to Holman, or toward the blind in general. It accorded perfectly with the dominant aesthetic philosophy of the time, which dictated how the world should be properly comprehended by ladies and gentlemen of culture. For generations, polite society had been instructed that there were three positive qualities to be discerned in nature: the Beautiful, the Sublime, and the Picturesque.

The first was easy enough to identify: The Beautiful was graceful symmetry and harmonious proportion of forms, as defined in antiquity. "As far as human observation and selection can fix a standard for beauty, it had been fixed by the Grecian sculptors," wrote the popular aesthetitian Uvedale Price in 1797. "That standard is acknowledged in all the most civilized parts of Europe." Of the three qualities, the Beautiful was the most connected to touch (or a desire to touch), and necessarily on the personal scale, for "as the size of any beautiful object is increased; and as it approaches toward grandeur and magnificence, it recedes from loveliness."

Grandeur and Magnificence were the realm of the Sublime. As Price explained, this was the humbling, if not frightening, sense of grand forces at work on a grand scale: "The nearer any grand or terrible objects in nature press upon the mind (provided the mind is able to contemplate them with awe, but without abject fear) the more sublime will be their effects." The ocean was "at all times a grand object." Rocks and precipices were "more sublime when the tide dashes at the foot of them, forbidding all access, or cutting off all retreat." Attempting to capture the Sublime was a common pursuit among artists, which is why many paintings of the era featured scenes of natural violence set on huge canvases, with titles like *The Shipwreck*, *Avalanche in the Alps*, and *Woodcutters Defending Themselves Against Wolves*. Contemplating these was supposed to be uplifting, a means of "grasping at infinity."

The third quality filled the gap between the intimacy of the Beautiful and the enormity of the Sublime. The Picturesque was derived from variety, from how nature expresses uniqueness by departing from the ideal—the differences wrought by chance and time. "Beauty and picturesqueness are indeed evidently founded

on very opposite qualities," Price wrote. "The one on smooth-
ness, the other on roughness; the one on gradual, the other on
sudden variation; the one on ideas of youth and freshness, the
other on those of age, and even of decay." *Picturesque* was the
proper label for all scenes and objects not classically beautiful, but
nevertheless visually pleasant: an edge of moss on an oak stump,
a dappled horse. The products of a non-European aesthetic (a
native hut or headdress) also typically belonged to this category.

Parsing the world into this triad of visual qualities was not
an academic abstraction. It was a common pastime, particularly
among those who wished to impress with their well-developed
sensibilities. When Henry and Catherine go for a walk in Jane
Austen's *Northanger Abbey*, "a lecture on the picturesque immediately followed, in which his instructions were so clear that she
soon began to see beauty in everything admired by him."

Nonvisual senses were acknowledged to play a part in the perception of beauty—one can sniff a flower, touch a statue, hear a
birdsong—but that was considered only a minor portion of the
experiential palate. As Edmund Burke wrote in his 1756 essay *On
the Sublime and Beautiful*:

> *Smells and Tastes have some share too in ideas of greatness; but it*
> *is a small one, weak in its nature, and confined in its operations. I*
> *shall only observe, that no smells or tastes can produce a grand sen-*
> *sation, except excessive bitters, and intolerable stenches.*

When Thomas Giordani Wright, a young man of gentlemanly
aspirations, noted the "unpleasant, indescribable, incredulous feeling" Holman's writing inspired, he was giving voice to the sentiment that blindness constituted an emotional as well as physical
deficiency. Holman might be able to discern certain particulars,
but his comprehending and appreciating a place as a whole was
patently impossible. This attitude was pervasive enough to compel
Holman to defend himself in his next book:

*I am constantly asked, and I may as well answer the question here
once for all, what is the use of traveling to one who cannot see? . . .
The picturesque in nature, it is true, is shut out from me, and works
of art are to me mere outlines of beauty, accessible only to one sense;
but perhaps this very circumstance affords a stronger zest to curiosity, which is thus impelled to a more close and searching examination of details than would be considered necessary to a traveler who
might satisfy himself by the superficial view.*

But *Travels Through Russia* marked the end of his writing forth-
rightly and consistently about his blindness. His future work
would be notable for a scarcity of references to his condition, but
also for the defiantly liberal use of visual terms—including *picturesque* and *sublime*. He would also hint that there was one advantage to reading his accounts: he was immune to those overly
romanticizing, purplish fits of descriptive prose all too common
in the writings of sighted travelers, since "I cannot make panoramas to amuse and gratify."

*The luxurious atmosphere of the East, tinting the clouds and trees
with its own delicious hues—romantic defiles and lofty mountains—the surging lake and the virgin river, over which a vessel
never yet sailed—the gloomy forest and the arid desert—these mag-
nificent sights do not make pages of pictures in my work.*

HOLMAN'S NEW FAME had the frustrating effect of both freeing and shackling him. Royalties would eventually be forthcoming
(although a full accounting might be years away), and he could
look forward to accruing a nest egg of several hundred pounds or
more. Not enough to permanently underwrite a more upscale lifestyle in England, but enough to fuel dreams of again launching a
circuit of the world.

It was gratifying to ride the Windsor coach into London and mingle with esteemed company at the Royal Society's head-quarters on the Strand (a building he was familiar with, since it also housed the Navy Board), but with each visit his restlessness increased. With regular member briefings, a collection of maps, and an exhibition room displaying artifacts from Society-sponsored expeditions, there was no better place to keep up to date on the latest geographic, ethnographic, and technological discoveries. As he learned, the world was opening up in new and interesting ways.

In North America, a twenty-five-year-old named Jedediah Smith, inspired to adventure after reading Lewis and Clark's journals, had recently traversed the great Continental Divide, discovering a pas-sage through the Rocky Mountains broad enough for teams of horses. For the first time, "it appears that a journey across the con-tinent of North America might be performed with a wagon," as the *Missouri Gazette* put it. In South America a series of new sov-ereign nations were rapidly emerging—Guatemala, Chile, Colom-bia, Honduras—all territories expected to be more open to foreign exploration than they'd been in the colonial era, when Spain had jealously safeguarded knowledge of its possessions. In Africa, John Dundas Cochrane's old dream—of becoming the first European to locate Timbuktu—was now the goal of a formal race. The French Geographical Society was offering a handsome cash prize of two thousand francs for proof of such an achievement, and several travelers had already launched their attempts (a Scotsman named Alexander Gordon Laing would win the honor but not live to col-lect the prize, dying on the return trip in 1826).

In his book, Holman had admitted that his trip to Russia had been one of false pretenses. It was not an idle visit to Saint Peters-burg, followed by an impulsive excursion to Siberia, but a journey planned from the beginning as the first step of a trip around the world. This confession was necessary for the narrative; otherwise, his reluctance to leave Irkutsk made no sense. But it did not sit well with the Visitors of Travers College, the trustees of the Naval Knights. They were beginning to regret the choice of Holman.

A Naval Knight was, by definition, "aged or infirm," but a young man mustering the strength to gallivant across a third of the globe seemed to meet neither criteria. On the face of it, Holman seemed to be abusing the privileges of the order, pursuing the same sort of absenteeism that had turned the Military Knights into a hollow vault of patronage—the sort of corruption the Naval Knights were intended to counteract. He was far from the first Naval Knight to stray from the prescribed life of cloistered devotion, but he was the first to do so in so public a fashion.

Summoning a brusque formality, the Visitors reminded him that his appointment held obligations, and that he was "under restrictions, both as to time and space." He should henceforth embrace only one profession, that of offering up prayers in Saint George's Chapel. There would be no further leaves of absence, except those issued on medical grounds.

Holman contemplated disputing the decision, but abandoned it as futile. By the terms of Samuel Travers's will, the Naval Knights were totally subservient to the Visitors, a board consisting of whomever happened to occupy two other positions of prominence in Windsor: the chief cleric, or dean, of Windsor Castle, and the provost of adjacent Eton College. There were no mechanisms of appeal.

If Holman was going to launch another circuit of the world, it would have to be undertaken even more surreptitiously than the first. And this time he would need at least one willing coconspirator, someone capable of providing a suitable pretext for his departure.

Fortunately, his new renown had recently made him part of a newly formed circle of men ready and capable to play such a role— men both powerful and completely sympathetic to the pangs of wanderlust. It was an institution that appeared to be only a casual dining club, but in reality had a far more rarefied membership than the Royal Society. It was, in fact, one of the most exclusive clubs in the entire world.

• • •

CAPTAIN SIR ARTHUR de Capell Broke was twenty-three years old, with an aristocratic heritage and dreams of exploration. He took great pride in his extensive travels in Scandinavia, and was writing *A Winter in Lapland* when "he conceived the idea of forming an agreeable dining club, composed entirely of travelers."

> *The world was to be mapped out into so many divisions, correspond-*
> *ing with the number of members, each division being represented by*
> *at least one member, as far as it was practicable, so that the club col-*
> *lectively should have visited nearly every part of the known globe.*

This parliament of explorers was dubbed the Raleigh Club, in honor of Sir Walter Raleigh. De Capell Broke, who had been one of Holman's sponsors in the Royal Society, was anxious that the Blind Traveler be one of the charter members (presumably, representing Siberia). They met each fortnight in a tavern called the Thatched House, and a tradition of exotic dining quickly arose, each meal being an occasion "to present any scarce foreign game, fish, fruits, wines, etc., as a means of adding greatly to the interest of the dinners, not merely from the objects of luxury thus afforded, but also for the observations they will be the means of giving rise to." De Capell Broke served up a menu he personally delivered from the distant North: reindeer venison, Swedish brandy, cloudberries from Lapland. Subsequent dinners featured bread made from wheat retrieved from the Dead Sea, and a ham transported from Mexico.

"Thus the most eminent travelers in London were brought together," wrote the earl of Albermarle, himself "the sole member for Babylon." The concept caught on, and the Thatched House was soon host to a daunting array of the adventurous and famous. There was Admiral Thomas Cochrane—John Dundas's cousin, the one who had headed up Bolívar's navy (and would later be the inspiration for fictional naval heroes Horatio Hornblower and Captain Jack Aubrey). There was the Arctic explorer Sir John Franklin, who would perish on his last expedition twenty years later. There was Francis Beaufort, chief hydrographer of the Royal Navy and inventor of the Beaufort scale, the standard measurement of wind intensity. There was the orientalist Henry Collebrooke, one of the Western world's foremost scholars of Sanskrit and Hindu culture, as well as Baron Broughton, an intimate friend of Lord Byron, who had traveled with him through Greece and Turkey. Holman was gratified to renew one old acquaintance: another member of the Raleigh was Basil Hall, his old fellow midshipman on the North American station, now advanced to a captaincy and well known as one of the first Westerners to visit Korea.

But more fateful was a new friendship, one that Holman struck up at the Thatched House table in 1825. Captain William Fitzwilliam Owen was a man described as "authoritative and generous, humorous and ceremonious, disputatious and frank, a lover of women more than of wine." Although he was far from being the most famous member of the Raleigh Club, Captain Owen was unquestionably among the most respected. He was, in fact, the greatest discoverer of the age.

AT THE TIME, the map of the world owed more to Captain Owen than to any other living individual. But acknowledgment of that achievement was limited to a modest cadre of scientists and sailors, because his discoveries were not in broad strokes. They were in precise calibrations, in exhaustive measurements of landmass and soundings of the sea. Owen was England's master of the new science of hydrography, the charting of shorelines and navigable waters.

Despite the fact that the Royal Navy was now defending a growing empire and enforcing a global *Pax Britannica*, most ships outside of the English Channel had only a vague idea of where they were, and an even more vague idea of where they were heading.

Part of the problem was reliance on inadequate navigational tools (the chronometer, vital for calculating longitude, was not yet in general use), but even an accurate calculation of position became meaningless when plotted onto a chart that was itself far from accurate. As late as 1814, the Admiralty's chief chartmaker admitted "the great deficiency in our Nautical knowledge in almost every part of the world, but more particularly on the coast line of our own Dominions." He compiled a blunt inventory of all the planetary waters delineated poorly, if at all: Most of the Mediterranean. Almost all of Africa. All eastern Pacific shores from Kamchatka to Van Diemen's Land (modern-day Tasmania), including the entire coast of China. Most of eastern South America. Even the coasts of Ireland and Scotland were documented in charts that bordered on the fictional, and a distressing number of shipwrecks were the result.

Peacetime, at last, freed up the resources for more accurate maritime surveys. Captains, eager to keep their commands in the era of postwar decommissioning, avidly took up hydrography. Chief among them was Captain Owen, who quickly dominated the field, thanks to his most unusual temperament, in which boldness and meticulousness held equal share.

William Fitzwilliam Owen was a profoundly unorthodox individual, and had been so from the moment of his birth, in Manchester, England, in 1774. He was an illegitimate child, but strangely enough it was his mother's identity that was a mystery, not his father's. As an infant he'd been spirited off to India, probably because his mother had followed an officer there.

He was four years old, growing up destitute in Madras, when a Royal Navy captain chanced to notice him at play. He recognized the boy at once as the offspring of one Lieutenant William Owen, a friend and fellow officer, now deceased. The captain, it developed, was adept at recognizing the Owen gene pool, because he was already raising another of his late friend's out-of-wedlock sons.

The mother confirmed this, pressed the child on the captain, then disappeared into the crowded streets. The next day the boy was sailing aboard the HMS *Cormorant*, entered in the books as a captain's servant. Both he and his newfound half-brother Edward would eventually become admirals. Owen would return to Madras many times, but never see his mother again. He could not even remember her name.

Young Owen proved impressively intelligent, with a gift for mathematics and languages. But he did not assimilate well. His illegitimacy and street-urchin past were strong stigmas, and a further alienating factor was the eruption of a chronic skin disease. It was probably eczema, but those familiar with his father's ne'er-do-well ways suspected that he had inherited a case of congenital syphilis. Mildly disfigured, with a thin build and goatlike features (which he would later accentuate with side whiskers), Owen was shunned in a succession of private boarding schools, and in midshipman's quarters when he returned to sea.

Yet his unpopularity did not embitter him. It made him a resolute individualist, socially fearless and unafraid to move in the face of conventional wisdom. "The distinguishing feature of this eccentric man," a naval historian would write of Owen, "was total commitment to the task in hand: whatever he did, he did with all his might."

Nowhere was this more evident than in his hydrographic expeditions. Assigned to survey the stretch of Canada's St. Lawrence River known as the Thousand Islands (later of salad dressing fame), he emerged just four months later with an exhaustively detailed chart, accurately tracing the shoreline of every single island—he counted 1,768—even those scarcely an acre in size. One of the perks of surveyors was the bestowal of names on hitherto-unidentified places, and Owen took great pleasure in naming things, bringing a near-poetic sensibility to the task. The Thousand Islands was now adorned with the Old Friends Isles, the Amateur Isles, and, of course, the Hydrographer Isles. The Old Friends Isles bore the names not of companions (he had few of those) but of his previous ships.

Despite his growing idiosyncrasies—he was now firing rockets from the deck of his ship, testing his theories of longitude—Owen was the logical choice for tackling the greatest single project in hydrographic history. In 1821, the Admiralty appointed him commander of a squadron devoted to "the great African survey," the first attempt to systematically chart the shores and seaways of the Dark Continent. It was a task so dauntingly huge the Admiralty resorted to deception to set it into motion. They issued Owen orders to survey only the eastern coast, fully intending to command him, upon his return to England, to turn around and survey the western coast.

They never needed to follow through on the subterfuge. Word of their plans reached Owen while he was still in Africa, and after mapping the eastern coast (and southern Arabia, and the islands of the Indian Ocean to boot), he moved the squadron westward without complaint.

The work, both tedious and dangerous, could not be performed simply by hugging the shore. Likely harbors had to be tested as anchorages, risking shipwreck and demanding improvised diplomacy with inquisitive natives. The ships carried guns, but Owen resolved to never fire them, for fear the shockwaves might damage their delicate survey instruments. River mouths were the riskiest of all—they called for the dispatch of exploratory teams upstream into the interior, to see if the rivers themselves might be navigable. Owen's newly coined place names reflected what they found, in terms both colorful (Hippopotamus Point, Elephant Island) and tragic (Thieves River, Murderers Bay, Coffin Island, Grave Island). Hostile attacks, meager rations, and especially malaria began to take their tolls. Soon the map in progress was sadly populated with places named in memory of those who had died compiling it.

The survey took four and a half years, and exactly half the lives of Owen's corps of forty-four officers, a toll that prompted one hydrographer to observe that the charts "may be said to have been drawn and coloured with drops of blood." But the results—over twenty thousand miles of coastline, reliably rendered for navigation—changed trade routes, opened up new markets, and made a hero of Captain Owen, who, not with false modesty but characteristic indifference to praise, sought to distribute the credit. "The African survey stands," he wrote, "due to the officers who served under me, unparalleled in the Annals of the World."

BACK IN LONDON at last, Captain Owen was pleased to meet and befriend Lieutenant Holman, the intrepid author and celebrity of the hour. Owen was working on a manuscript of his own adventures, but it had to be set aside in January of 1827. He'd received orders to prepare a second expedition to Africa—this time not to survey it but to settle it.

Parliament had authorized a new permanent presence in the strategically significant Gulf of Guinea on the western coast, close to the equator and not far from where the Congo flows into the sea. This self-contained settlement was to be built from scratch, intentionally at a distance from any other European presence, and in fact removed from the African continent itself. It would be on an island twenty miles offshore, a location so isolated that even the coastal-dwelling Pygmy and Bantu tribes, who could see it rising out of the sea, knew almost nothing about its inhabitants.

Westerners had named the island Fernando Po, after the Portuguese sailor who had chanced upon it in 1471 while searching for a route to India. While claimed as a possession of Spain, it remained an unexamined speck on the charts for centuries. The Spaniards' occasional attempts to take up even temporary residence had been a memorable failure; they'd last abandoned it forty-six years previously. They did not relinquish their claim, but were happy to lease the entire territory to England on a long-term basis.

Owen was ordered to lead the expedition to Fernando Po, to oversee the carving of a settlement out of raw jungle, then to serve as its first governor. It was a huge responsibility, and not one he wished for. He had seen his fill of Africa, and was enjoying the

work on his memoir. But he recognized himself as uniquely qualified for the task, and was also passionately devoted to the politics
behind the project. His surveys of the continent had meant years
of firsthand exposure to the slave trade. That familiarity had converted him into an ardent abolitionist.

Fernando Po was intended as the headquarters for a pitched battle against slavery. Owen would command not only the colony but
a small fleet, devoted to hunting down slaving ships, taking them
into custody, and liberating their cargo. England had ended slavery
on its own shores in 1807 (although it would hypocritically tolerate
it in British possessions until 1833), and was trying to choke out the
institution in the Americas and elsewhere by cutting off the supply
at the source.

At the time, an estimated one out of every five slaves were being
shipped out of the Gulf of Guinea, and years of antislaving patrols
in the mid-Atlantic had demonstrated the need to intercept them
much sooner in their journey. It was heartbreaking to capture a
slave ship a thousand miles at sea, knowing that there was little to
be done to alleviate the inhuman conditions until the ship returned
to Africa—a slow journey against the tradewinds and prevailing
currents, which almost inevitably killed more of them than if the
voyage had not been interrupted.

Almost nothing was known about Fernando Po, but in 1821 a
British geographer had declared it "the only proper station on the
African coast, for our cruisers to watch and cut up the slave trade."
That same year, the Royal Navy gave Parliament the opinion that
settling there would be simple, "a very trifling establishment."

O WEN WASTED NO time putting his own iconoclastic stamp
on the mission. For his new flagship, the frigate HMS *Eden*, he
insisted on a stock of marine chronometers, an instrument still
only rarely used for calculating longitude. He fitted out the ship
with another newfangled gadget, a flexible pump that supposedly

conveyed water from the shore (it would prove impractical). And there was a personal eccentricity. The ship's complement of 135 men included his friend Lieutenant James Holman, R.N., K.W., F.R.S., aboard in no official capacity but expected to serve as a chronicler of the mission.

How did Holman, so recently all but chained to the grounds of Travers College, win leave to journey to equatorial Africa? In what must have been an inspired flight of rhetoric, he'd managed to convince the Visitors that "strange and paradoxical" as it might seem, it was necessary to his health. Paradoxical because Fernando Po lay dead-center in the portion of the African coastline known colloquially as the White Man's Grave.

Westerners dropped dead from dysentery and malaria just about everywhere on the continent, but northwestern Africa was known to be especially lethal. Admiralty studies show that at the time, sailors stationed there were five times more likely to die of disease than those on stations closer to home. Europeans in Freetown, Liberia, the nearest antislavery settlement, were dying at the staggering rate of forty percent per year. Holman was flying in the face of centuries of conventional wisdom when he claimed that a visit to the Gulf of Guinea would actually be therapeutic, stating optimistically that "I anticipated an improvement in my general health from a short residence." Fortunately, his argument had been bolstered by a recent article in the *Quarterly Review*, describing Fernando Po as a benign near-paradise:

> In the present state of the island, the savage natives produce the finest yams in the world, and appear to possess abundance of fowls. A refreshing breeze constantly blows over the island from the Atlantic; it has plenty of good anchorage in more places than one, and abundance of clear running water.

IT WAS THE report of the "refreshing breeze" that had convinced Parliament to launch the Owen expedition in the first place.

Malaria means, literally, "bad air," reflecting the dominant belief that it arose from atmospheric conditions, particularly the miasmic gases emanating from swamplands and jungles. Since Fernando Po was twenty miles offshore, it was presumed to be naturally inoculated from the mainland's hazardous air. The expectation was that Owen's men would quickly convert it into a sort of hospital island, where after "liberating them from their dungeons of disease and death," recaptured slaves could recuperate from their captivity before being repatriated to their native land. Holman had won a leave of absence from Windsor by volunteering to be the first patient.

If the Visitors of Travers College were suspicious of his motives, they were reassured by geography. Few ships ventured into the White Man's Grave unless they absolutely had to, and the only ships to visit the isolated island would be confiscated slavers, bound for Admiralty court. As the launching point for a circumnavigation, Fernando Po seemed even less practical than Siberia.

THE HMS *EDEN*, as idiosyncratic as her commander, was not a berth for superstitious sailors. For one, she had begun her career at the bottom of the sea. Back in 1816, the Admiralty had moored the newly built ship among the prison ships in Plymouth Harbor and deliberately sunk her "to test the effect of seawater on dry rot." After four months underwater, she was refloated and deemed eminently seaworthy, although her subsequent years in service are noteworthy for their unusual number of non-battle-related fatalities. In Bombay a wave of cholera infected much of the crew. Off the Oman Sultanate there was a rash of unusual sudden deaths, attributed to heatstroke although the victims were hearty deckhands used to the tropical heat. In Trincomalee one lieutenant succumbed to the bite of a jackal.

But this was a cruise for optimists. Accompanied by the cargo vessel *Diadem*, the *Eden* sailed away on August 1, 1827, fully loaded with everything imagined necessary to create an instant colony. Sixteen complete houses, prefabricated and disassembled. A team of British carpenters to erect them, then supervise the building of still more structures from native wood (it was presumed the liberated slaves would be more than happy to assist). Tons of seed for planting crops. Herds of sheep and cattle ruminated on the open deck; the rolling of open sea made them docile. The horses and donkeys, on the other hand, were slung up in heavy weather in canvas restraints, hoisted and swaying in the salt air.

The three-month cruise took them by Madeira, where they laid in a generous stock of that island's famed red wine. They stopped at Freetown, capital of the newly created Liberia, to take on even more settlers: a hundred laborers, and over a hundred and fifty artisans of various disciplines. They traced the shore southward as far as the Niger Delta, then made west for their new home, eagerly anticipating the historic role that awaited them.

They would indeed make history, but not of the sort they intended. The *Quarterly Review*'s description of Fernando Po had been a fabrication, a manifestation of abolitionist wishful thinking. There was no constant cleansing breeze. The island was not immune to malaria—if anything, it existed there in greater concentration than on the mainland. In the annals of the Royal Navy, the *Eden* mission would be recorded as the deadliest expedition of all time.

THIRTEEN

White Man's Grave

F ERNANDO PO CERTAINLY looked the part of paradise.
It was even more beautiful than anyone onboard the *Eden* had
imagined. The crew and passengers were awed by an island so dramatic in its contours it seemed to belong more to mythology than
geography. Its most arresting feature was a central volcanic peak
rising ten thousand feet out of the sea, a height to match some of
Hawaii's most majestic volcanoes but more abruptly pitched, compressed into a base a few miles across. On approach, one saw the
effect of islands within islands: thick clouds ringed the mountain
almost continuously around its base, clouds which were in turn
ringed by a sloping band of dense jungle canopy that extended to
the island's edge, meeting the water in a series of sharp green cliffs.
It was at once appealingly lush and forbiddingly self-secluded, a
world apart from the African continent.

Holman took extensive notes of his companions' first impressions. "Luxuriant foliage of various tints and hues," he wrote,
"blending with the scarcely ruffled bosom of the ocean, and the
retiring clouds . . . formed such a variegated picture of natural
beauty, that we unanimously hailed it as the land of promise." He
could add to that his own sensory impressions: the uniquely complex smells of truly primeval forest, well populated with parrots,
cuckoos, the African Green Pigeon, and numerous species unique
to the island, awaiting discovery. The land was richly scented, and
alive with birdsong.

Cut Throat, the fierce Fernandian warrior befriended by Holman.

The expedition did not hurry ashore. They remained off the coast for a full week, while Captain Owen sent out survey parties to find an optimal site for the colony. In the meantime, they attempted to establish friendly relations with the natives, whom they promptly dubbed Fernandians. It was not necessary to seek them out—the *Eden* was surrounded by canoes within a few minutes of dropping anchor—but getting them to interact was another matter. The Fernandian men were happy to stand in their prows and barter bits of scrap iron for yams, fish, monkey skins, and calabashes of palm wine. But they adamantly refused to come aboard the British ships. They were not particularly curious about white men; their great-grandparents had watched the Spaniards die, and depart. And, being in the middle of slaving routes, they had developed a natural guardedness about all visitors.

Even at a wary distance, the Fernandians were every bit as striking as the island itself. It was almost impossible to gauge the original color of their skin, as every visible inch seemed daubed in ochre clay (with the exception of the abdomen, which was covered in tattoos). They wore very little clothing, but even a man clad only in a rough-woven loincloth was never seen without an elaborate hat.

Made of plaited palm-leaf, these hats were clearly the culture's chief display of individuality. No two were alike in size, shape, or construction, but all sported at least a pound or two of festooning—beads, turtle shells, parrot feathers, and animal skulls. Beards and mustaches were complementary decorations, braided and trained into topiary-like shapes with thick pomades of palm oil. They carried the simplest of weapons, slings and fire-sharpened sticks, but were fearsome-looking enough nonetheless. The crew began to assign them names: Bottlenose, Chameleon, Thieving Dick.

By the third day, a Fernandian was finally persuaded to board the *Eden*, a young boy fascinated by a looking glass and the tinkling of a bell. That broke the floodgates, and thereafter climb-

ing onto the deck had to be gently discouraged, not encouraged.
At the same time, Captain Owen reached the conclusion that the
best possible site for the settlement just happened to be exactly
where they were anchored. Auspiciously enough, they'd chanced
into one of the best natural anchorages in western Africa. A fresh-
water spring was just ashore.

They planted a flag. Hundreds of machete-wielding men began
to claim ground from the jungle, under cover of armed patrols.
Relations with the Fernandians had gotten off to a friendly start,
but Captain Owen was eager to stave off any incidents of misun-
derstanding that might squander that goodwill. As he was acutely
aware, the natives did not just need to be appeased, they needed to
be converted into active collaborators in sustaining the settlement.
The *Eden's* foodstocks would run out long before crops could be
planted and harvested. If the Fernandians chose not to feed them
in the interim, they would starve.

Holman was not an official part of the mission. His secret understanding with Captain Owen was that *Eden* had provided his escape
from England. He was free to wander away as soon as the opportunity presented itself, perhaps during a supply run to the mainland.
But diplomacy was paramount, and Owen, for all his eccentricity,
was a shrewd judge of character. He was well acquainted with the
Blind Traveler's almost uncanny ability to strike an instant rapport
with people, even people with whom he had no language in common.

He gave Holman and one of his lieutenants the delicate joint
task of making first contact with "the king of the island"—actually
(as they would later learn), the nearest of several regional chiefs
but nonetheless a personage crucial to their survival. Accompanied
by the mission's only translator, Holman and Lieutenant Morrison
paddled to a distant cove and waded ashore.

Their reception went immediately, ominously awry. When he
could not even glean the king's name, Holman realized the interpreter, a native African soldier named Anderson, was no interpreter

at all. "His Fernandian vocabulary was scarcely more copious than a sensible parrot might acquire in a month: his knowledge of the English, at all events, was so exceedingly defective as to make another interpreter necessary to explain what he meant to express, in our language."

Improvising with gestures, Holman managed to convey to the chief an invitation to dine aboard the *Eden* the following day. Then he hastily retreated, leaving Anderson behind to spend the night in the royal enclosure, in the hopes that he might acquire another word or two of the native language. Instead of establishing harmonious relations, the diplomatic party had inadvertently exposed what would become the mission's fatal weakness.

THE CLEARING AND building continued. Owen, the master of filling in blank maps, once again indulged his propensity for bestowing place names. The mountain towering over all would be called Mount Clarence, in honor of the duke of Clarence, the brother of the king and first lord of the Admiralty (and the future King William IV). The settlement was also dubbed Clarence, and its streets awarded the names of other naval men: Nicholas, Burk, John. The steps leading down the cliffs to the landing were named, poetically, Jacob's Ladder, since recaptured slaves would joyously ascend them on their way to freedom.

The most commanding site of all was that of Governor's House, overlooking the anchorage on a bluff above what was now Clarence Cove. It was to be an isolated structure, surrounded by a large level ground that Owen intended to become a public park. He was particularly pleased to immortalize a little jest in his naming: the park, now just an expanse of dirt, was already listed on the surveys as Paradise, "it being the garden of *Eden*."

Still, the lack of a competent translator plagued the men. The Fernandians seemed friendly and cooperative, especially after Owen formally purchased the land underneath Clarence with a

generous supply of axe heads, fish hooks, and straightened bar-
rel hoops, which were quickly honed into knives. Iron was the
chief commodity coveted by the natives, and soon a trade economy evolved in a central marketplace: three inches of iron hoop
would purchase four chickens, twelve yams, or a gallon of palm
wine. But piecemeal, gesture-driven communications fed a growing sense of uncertainty and, in at least one instance, sheer terror.
One afternoon the *Eden*'s master-at-arms discovered a Fernandian
attempting to steal an axe head. Caught in the act, the man rushed
overboard and made for his own canoe, only to be captured and
held by his own people, who began to club him with canoe paddles. Then, "with blood streaming from his various parts, he was
compelled to leap into the sea, in order to wash it away, before
they would allow him to re-enter his own boat."

The ordeal did not end there. Once ashore, the man was dragged
to the vicinity of the marketplace and surrounded by a rapidly
growing angry crowd. One of the *Eden*'s men, a Briton named
Jeffery, had the misfortune of being nearby. He pushed his way
through the natives, hoping to discover the cause of the uproar,
"when, to his surprise, he was immediately laid hold of, and tied
hand to hand with the bleeding prisoner," Holman recorded. "This
proceeding excited considerable alarm in Mr. Jeffery, who was led
to infer that the wounds of the prisoner had been inflicted by our
people, and that the natives were about to retaliate upon himself."

As Jeffery struggled to free his hand, it was all too clear an execution was about to take place. Surprisingly, the Fernandians did
not react as he slipped loose his bonds. Instead, they focused their
attention on the thief, now bound hand-and-foot to a tree. The
crowd fell to their knees in a single moment, leaving one man
standing: a particularly fierce-looking warrior, who produced a
knife and commenced to slowly and ceremonially cut the prisoner's throat. Courageously, Jeffery stepped forward and stayed the
executioner's arm. The ensuing confusion lasted long enough for

Captain Owen to arrive and convey, by signs, that he wished to suffer the man to live.

The thief disappeared into the forest. The imposing knife-wielding warrior was known thereafter as Cut Throat. And Owen and Holman were left to puzzle at the true meaning of the incident. Why, exactly, had Jeffery been taken captive as well? Was he intended to share the thief's fate, or only to witness it? Clearly, the settlement's grasp of the local language needed to proceed past the rudimentary. Attempts to learn from the coastal natives had been unproductive, to the point that their reticence seemed deliberate.

Perhaps the residents of the interior would be more generous with their vocabulary. Owen turned to a low-ranking crewman, "an active and intelligent young man" named Matthew Ellwood, who volunteered to venture alone up the mountainside, seeking out hospitality and instruction. He returned a week later, unharmed but also unenlightened—the language remained elusive. In his absence the uneasily civility had eroded still further. Fernandians were now overcrowding the marketplace, importuning for iron with growing boldness. Soldiers were stationed to stand guard, but the natives grew daring enough to sneak up on one, snatching his bayonet from its scabbard and flinging it into the river. The soldiers responded with musket fire—warning shots in the air, but real violence seemed the inevitable next step.

Ellwood volunteered to return to the mountain and try again. Two days after he disappeared into the forest, Holman decided to join him. As his sole companion he chose the African called Anderson, the man who had posed as a translator. In the clearing past the marketplace, the Fernandians clustered around them. Holman took an arm at random and let himself be led into the interior.

IN CLARENCE, HE had observed how easy it was to lead around a Fernandian, even a fierce warrior. All you had to do was take hold of a hand, or even a finger, and they would submit to your guidance, like small children. Now the process was reversed.

It wasn't as graceful an experience as he had hoped. The man he had chosen took his touch as a sign of status, and became quite proud in his deportment, loudly proclaiming his charge. A cluster of natives, mostly women, began to form and circle, and that made the man prouder still. Their numbers grew as the party progressed, leaving behind the level country for rising ground.

The crowd grew even as they crossed two streams, even as the path became not just rugged and steep but slippery with the damp. Holman sensed that there were hundreds of them, chattering out what must have been broad jokes at his expense, loudly laughing each time he took a false step.

The land was dense-grown even on the hillside, and the recent rains had concentrated a matrix of scent—black pepper, cloves, nutmeg, rubber tree, palm tree. But to Holman, that day, the overwhelming smell was an almost stifling compound of earth and sweat, rancid and rank and redolent of human life. The paste in which Fernandians encased their hair and skin, entirely and perpetually, turned out to be not just clay but an admixture of palm oil and mineral pigments. Unlike the mostly ochre people of the shore, the hillside people were liberal with their coloration. Anderson kept Holman apprised of the tones of the people swirling around them: brown, dark red, a bright almost rose red, ashen gray. When skins appeared yellow, the color of the ruling class, they would be approaching the presence of the king. Indeed, as Anderson had never succeeded in learning the king's name, Holman had been compelled to dub him, simply, His Yellow Majesty.

Even in darkness the voices surrounded, thinning and dispersing only when they arrived in the village, at an hour so late that only Matthew Ellwood stirred in welcome. As Holman lay exhausted in a hut, drinking something that could be considered tea, Ellwood began to explain. Things were not going as planned. The king had treated Ellwood not as a guest but as a sort of victim, or perhaps a hostage. He had been forced to surrender all but one of the bits of iron he had brought for bartering. They'd given him no food in return.

In the closeness of the hut Holman listened, and calculated. He could hear extreme youth in the voice. Ellwood was, in fact, only eighteen. He could hear the rough streets of London outskirts in the broad Essex accent. Ellwood was from the poor parish of West Ham, enlisted as a Supernumerary Boy of the Second Class.

Young Ellwood was eager to be useful, but hardly worldly. Perhaps he had swaggered when he should have bowed, or otherwise neglected to strike a proper note of decorum. At any rate, the crisis was now Holman's to defuse.

At daybreak a delegation of chieftains arrived, to provide company or perhaps underscore the sense of custody. They did nothing, and nothing could be clarified except by the presence of the king. An hour passed, and then another. The delay may have made Ellwood and Anderson nervous, but Holman took courage from it. He understood that the king was preparing himself for his audience, a sign that he wished to stand on ceremony.

At last the king made his entrance, hair resplendent in the glisten of new oil, skin fresh-daubed in clay as brightly yellow as could be managed. Holman rose to the occasion. With all the gravity and dignity perfected during years at Windsor Castle, he reached into his bag and pulled out two knives. Pairing them, making them a symbol both of equality and friendship, he solemnly presented them to the monarch.

ONE WEEK LATER, Holman and his companions were retrieved floating in Clarence Harbor, adrift in a canoe. The natives charged with returning them from the mountain had escorted them to the small craft and paddled into the shadow of the *Eden*. Then, at the moment the canoe touched the ship, the guides inexplicably jumped overboard, taking their paddles with them.

Holman's improvised ritual of the gift of knives had changed the tenor of their time in the King's village. Thereafter they had been treated well, even honorably, and given a cordial sendoff; the intimations of captivity had simply disappeared. But their linguistic progress was made in spite of their hosts' deliberate opacity. To Holman's finely tuned ear, it was clear that the Fernandians didn't want their language understood. They were, in fact, making a conscious effort to convolute their syntax, to use as many different words as possible for any given item. They had cannily grasped the advantages of learning English instead, and were doing so at a rapid pace.

Nonetheless, Holman had experienced enough of native life to compile the first written Fernandian-English vocabulary. Not only did he recognize that "there are distinct dialects, or idioms, among the different tribes," but in a crucial distinction that proved invaluable in future negotiations, he comprehended that "peculiar modes of counting are made use of—for instance, one tribe, after counting five in the usual way, proceeds to ten and twenty; while another, after going on progressively to ten, starts at once to twenty." He also concluded that some attempts to find linguistic equivalents were wrongheaded—for instance, the European notion of a "king of the island" was best abandoned. Even His Yellow Majesty was more correctly a *kokalako*, or regional headman, and such offices were only part of the equation of power. It would also be prudent to pay respects to de facto leaders such as Cut Throat, who was, Holman observed, "the only native we have, as yet, been conversant with who never begged for anything."

Captain (now also Governor) Owen expressed his thanks to his trusted friend in his own unique fashion. A few weeks later, when tensions had dissipated sufficiently, he asked Holman to join him in circumnavigating the island, on a journey to survey the uncharted portions of the shore. They boarded their smallest vessel, a combination sail- and steam-driven launch called the *African*, and made a leisurely clockwise loop, pausing to give rides to astonished Fernandians, chasing after a suspected slave ship (which proved to be an innocuous freighter), and generally enjoying themselves. The hitherto-unexplored southern portion of the island proved to be "possessed of a very considerable degree of sublimity, the shore being bold and rocky, with various picturesque cataracts descending from the mountains."

On one particularly tranquil morning the *African* drifted past an estuary plain, where what was clearly one of the island's larger rivers met the sea. The estuary had an unusual feature: "a remarkably large stone lay on the beach near its mouth." Struck by the way the waters flowed gracefully past this massive obstruction, as if it were no impediment at all, Owen was reminded of his companion. He declared it the Holman River, and its landmark Holman's Rock.

MATTHEW ELLWOOD, THE bright and brave supernumerary boy, was the first to die. "His complaint was a remittent fever, taken on our short journey to the interior," Holman sadly noted. "On the third day after our return he took to his bed, from which he never rose again, excepting on the day previous to his death." The fever was monitored closely by Doctor Burn, the *Eden*'s surgeon, who soon had no doubt that it was malaria. That was the question that now gripped the settlement: how virulent a strain?

Malaria is a notably dramatic disease. After an incubation period of days or weeks, it begins to cycle through a series of stages. The Cold stage resembles a person dying of exposure in the Arctic: the teeth chatter, the limbs shake uncontrollably. The Fever stage is mercifully brief, usually lasting no more than a single day, but with temperatures that can themselves be life-threatening. Brain-baking heights of 107 degrees Fahrenheit are not unusual. Then the much-awaited Wet stage, where the body begins to sweat profusely, rapidly plunging the temperature back to normal range and leaving the sufferer almost motionless with exhaustion, but otherwise seemingly normal. Until the cycle begins anew.

The timing of the cycle is key to identifying the malarial strain. If the Fever stage strikes every third day, it is "Benign tertian" malaria; if every fourth day, "Benign quartan." In both cases, if the patient can survive the systemic shocks and strains, he or she can hope to make a full recovery, although they may be plagued by a lifetime of recurrences. But if the cycle is blurred—if the Cold stage is not quite so chilling, if the fever chooses not to make a grand exit, but remains a continuous, intermittent presence—then there is cause for grave concern. If the Wet stage never arrives at all, the malaria is "malignant tertian," the most persistently lethal strain of all.

Ellwood's malaria never manifested a Wet stage. They confined him to a berth onboard the *Eden*, and in his final delirium he sought to snuff out the seeming fires beneath his skin. It was Holman's task to write the young man's obituary:

> *Under a state of mental aberration, he secretly took off his shirt, and threw himself from out of the port-hole near his bed into the sea; he was soon taken up, but his delirium continued until he expired. At five this afternoon he was buried in Paradise.*

Ellwood's death converted the garden of *Eden* into a graveyard, and sent a shockwave of fear through the more than two hundred Europeans now living on the island. The comforting assumption—that Fernando Po was somehow isolated from the malarial zone that surrounded it—now had to be abandoned.

Many took to a regimen considered the latest, most scientific means of avoiding malaria: keeping the "bad air" at bay by creating a personal smoke screen (i.e., constantly smoking cigars) and keeping the body purified and inhospitable to foreign elements (by drinking large and regular quantities of brandy). Holman, who hated tobacco smoke and rarely touched spirits, had his own theories on prevention, but for now he kept them to himself.

There was little time to dwell on the matter. While the peace with the Fernandians held, the building crews made rapid progress. Patrols began in earnest, and, as 1827 drew to a close, five captured slaving ships were swinging, empty, on their anchors in Clarence Bay.

On Christmas Day, the entire populace of Clarence assembled to mark the formal annexation of the island. Bugles, fifes, and drums sounded as Owen headed the procession, with Holman marching in the position of honor—behind him, to his immediate right. With Cut Throat and his followers looking on as invited guests, they raised and saluted the British colors, then Owen read aloud the proclamation he'd written. It was a remarkably unimperialistic document, asserting ownership of the settlement lands but guaranteeing the Fernandians "perfect security and unmolested possession," should they choose to store their yams within town limits. Then came a salute of cannon fire, a final rendition of "Rule Britannia," and a massive feast where all were welcome.

In a grand egalitarian gesture, Owen insisted that everyone present sign the proclamation. Which is why the original, now kept at the National Maritime Museum in Greenwich, bears not only the signatures of Owen and Holman but the marks of over one hundred liberated slaves. Their scrawled crosses nest neatly in the transcriptions of their Westernized names: Tom X Longpipe, Pea X Soup, Never X Fear.

HIS ONSHORE DUTIES fulfilled, Holman decided to participate in the settlement's main task: the active hunting for slave ships. While he had never been an active abolitionist like Owen, he was constitutionally opposed to systematic servitude of any kind, and thought that "the sight of the poor African, taken from their homes by force, condemned to banishment and exposed for sale, like herds of cattle, in the market-place of a foreign country, is dismal and humiliating." With Owen's blessing, he joined a patrol crew setting sail for the coast of the Bight of Biafra, between Cape

Formosa and the Cameroon River, "where we might have reason to believe that the inhuman traffic was pursued."

They ghosted along as unobtrusively as they could, peering into the numerous river mouths where slavers could easily hide. When on a windless day they at last spied a suspicious vessel they made hot pursuit, breaking out the sweeps and strenuously rowing on an interception course. It was a disappointment to discover the prey was the HMS *Clinker*, a brig also on antislaver duty, and equally suspicious of Holman's ship. Both had come close to firing upon the other.

Further patrolling brought them to the Old Calabar River (in what is now Nigeria), notorious as one of the main arteries for transporting slaves from the interior. To disguise the ship, they obscured its distinctive yellow sides by painting it with "a not very safe pigment"—a mixture of gunpowder and water, giving it a piratically black appearance but also making it vulnerable to the slightest spark.

The masquerade was pointless. As soon as they sailed into view of the nearest village, "we observed the greatest confusion. Armed men, of different colors and nations, were running about in all directions, preparing, as we imagined, to oppose our landing," Holman wrote. "The slave-vessels, afraid of being seized, had disappeared from before the town, and gone farther up the river."

The next tactic was to send scouting canoes up the Old Calabar. The report they brought back was unpromising: three slave schooners and a brig were indeed afloat upstream, but they were not hiding. They were lying in wait, heavily armed, and flanked on both river banks with equally well-equipped reinforcements. Furthermore, none of the four ships had a single slave onboard, as "it is not customary to put them on board until they are on the point of sailing."

Holman and his companions were not only outnumbered and outgunned, they had no legal basis for seizing the ships.

The crew reluctantly gave up any notion of pursuit. They anchored off Duke's Town, so named because it was the headquarters of the chieftain of the Efik people, a semi-Westernized leader named Ephraim, who spoke English well and used the titles Duke and King interchangeably. There they were immediately embroiled in a dispute involving yet another British anti-slaving ship, the HMS *Kent*. The day before, a slave-vessel captain, a Frenchman named Fernard, hadn't bothered to retreat his ship into the interior—he'd simply pulled a gun and shot the *Kent*'s second mate. Now the captain of the *Kent* was demanding that Fernard, who'd taken refuge among the Efik, be turned over to British authorities.

Holman was recruited as a negotiator, and hurried into the presence of Ephraim himself. The duke-king wore only a plain cotton waistcloth on his body, but adorned his head with a white beaver hat dripping with gold lace. He proved to be a most gracious host, serving an excellent vintage of champagne, and conducting a proud tour of his compound, which included sixty wives and an "English house" complete with chandelier—a wooden building imported frame-by-frame from Liverpool, along with carpenters to assemble it.

But for all his cordiality, "it was clear enough that he wished to protect the assassin, as indeed it was his policy to shield the slavers, whose trade was more lucrative to him, than that of any other class of persons." Even when Holman made it clear that Governor Owen would probably "send a frigate to blockade the port, stop all the trade of the river, and perhaps come and burn the town," Captain Fernard was not given over to justice. The threat made Ephraim clearly nervous, but it did not overcome his allegiance to the slavers, who had given him the imported house and stuffed it to the rafters with ostentatious gifts. He did not offer up so much as the name of the Frenchman's ship.

The patrol ship, its hull still streaked with volatile gunpowder paste, headed back to Fernando Po, carrying a dispirited Holman. Their foray had demonstrated to him the near-futile nature of fighting slavery so close to the source, at least under present conditions. Royal Navy ships, it seemed, could only discover each other, as large and slow-moving as they were. The slavers were swifter, more devious, unencumbered by regulation, and abetted by thoroughly corrupted regional leaders. He concluded his adventure by observing wistfully that "the affair gave the slavers an opportunity of exulting over our failure, and their own good fortune; which, I think, was to be regretted."

HE RETURNED TO find Clarence inundated by strange weather. On the Calabar coast it had been consistently, blazingly hot, but Fernando Po was careening through several different climatic conditions in a single day. One moment, it could be balmy, with temperatures a relatively moderate ninety-one degrees Fahrenheit in the shade. But then winds would rise and air pressure drop precipitously, announcing an imminent rainstorm invariably well spiked with lightning. Within an hour the downpour would reach hurricane force and whip up vortexes—tornados and waterspouts—which quickly flared and died. An hour later, all could be calm and still, basking in sunshine.

One waterspout veered dangerously close to Holman's ship, but soon he found graver matters to worry about. Food was growing increasingly scarce, and malaria was beginning to sap the workforce.

The hospital, one of the first substantial buildings in Clarence, was still unfinished, but already rapidly filling with those suffering from the same "intermittent fever" that had claimed Ellwood. There was nothing Owen could do to stave off sickness, and precious little he could do to keep starvation at bay. His nemesis was the bottleneck of bureaucracy—once he had recaptured them from the slavers, he could not simply return the slaves to Africa. He had to wait to bring both the ships and their human cargo before the international Court of Mixed Commission, headquartered in Sierra Leone, to properly adjudicate each seizure. In between the irregular sessions of the court, he was responsible for the care, feeding and sheltering of those he sought to liberate, often for months at a time.

By now the nonnative population, white settlers, hired Africans and rescued slaves alike, had grown to about seven hundred, well beyond the numbers the Fernandians could support with their yams and poultry. Crops of cabbages, pumpkins, turnips, and custard apples were still struggling to take root.

Owen immediately dispatched Holman to return to Duke-King Ephraim's kingdom of Old Calabar. Not to burn it down in pursuit of the rogue French slaver-assassin, but to buy as much food as possible, as well as livestock and harness animals. Holman revisited Ephraim several times, and even slept in his English house. The chieftain himself preferred a traditional thatched hut, erected right next door.

By now, he understood that Ephraim was not only paid off by the slave trade, he was actively complicit in it. The slavers placed orders with him for a certain number of bodies. He passed the orders on to his own villages, who were forced to yield up slaves from among their own population. The first to be chained were convicts, then those even suspected of any crime or misdemeanor. If that did not fulfill the quota, servants were handed over, followed by anyone insufficiently popular or powerful. Under the circumstances, Ephraim could be counted on only to provide a veneer of support to Fernando Po, offering little food for sale, and at exorbitant prices to boot. It was sobering to experience just how deeply Africans were implicit in enslaving other Africans, "that the slavery he endures in his own country, where all things conspire to oppress him, is of a worse character than that which he suffers under a different rule."

Returning two weeks later with a modest cargo of sickly cattle, Holman was startled by a cannonball sailing across the bow, then another. His ship was being pursued, and fired upon. Soon a hostile vessel "was ranging up alongside, with the intention of pouring in a heavy fire and boarding us in the smoke." The smoke cleared, revealing the attacker to be yet another English patroller. In the distance, they'd mistaken the cattle for slaves.

• • •

MEANWHILE, FERNANDO PO was fulfilling its role as a "hospital island," but not in the sense originally intended. Fatal fevers were quickly becoming commonplace, so much so the laborers were grimly joking they had standing orders: *Gang No. 1 to be employed in digging graves as usual. Gang No. 2 making coffins until further notice.* Anderson, the erstwhile translator, disappeared into the forest, one of the many deserting African soldiers choosing to live among Fernandians rather than the sickly Westerners who succumbed at a far greater rate than those of non-European descent. The malaria was not uniformly lethal, but nearly so. When Mr. Glover, the chief carpenter, died, one of his "stoutest and healthiest men" burst out crying—not in mourning, but out of certainty that he was next. "Oh my wife! My children!" he wailed. "I shall never see you again!" He joined his supervisor in the ground of Paradise within the week.

Holman was convinced such self-predicted deaths were from panic or despondency, both "more fatal than the disease itself," and that a healthy attitude and the sheer will to live could trump the affliction. He was in a position to know: for two weeks he'd been battling, and hiding, the symptoms himself.

Others took refuge in their clouds of cigar smoke and flasks of brandy. Holman made an unusual request of Owen, who still lived aboard the *Eden*: could he sleep on the skylight directly above the captain's quarters? It might be a tad disturbing for Owen to look up and see the form of his friend prone on the glass, but Holman's desire was to spend as much time in the fresh air as possible. That particular patch of deck was "tolerably protected" by a sloped awning, which might provide at least partial shelter from the minihurricanes that still swept through Clarence Cove at least once a day.

The death rate climbed, as did the temperature. It was the *Eden*'s sailmaker's task to sew up the dead in their hammocks. He had to hurry his work, as the bodies began to notably decompose within minutes of their conversion from sufferer to corpse. Holman helped where he could, but otherwise kept his outdoors vigil, ate as little as possible, occupied his mind with amusing thoughts, and complained not at all.

"On the top of the Captain's skylight I weathered out many a tornado," he would recall. "Although so many persons were dying around me, I still maintained my cheerful spirits, to which circumstance I attribute the restoration of my health, which was now daily improving."

Soon he felt strong enough to accompany Owen on his next appearance before the Court of Mixed Commission, where, over the course of several days, three captured ships and 365 intercepted slaves were adjudicated. Owen then reversed direction several hundred miles, steering the ship below the equator and toward tiny Ascension Island in the South Atlantic. This was a dry and mostly barren patch of rock, used primarily as a provisioning station for ships whose captains wished to avoid touching port in Africa.

While Owen scrounged what supplies he could, Holman explored the island and made a few quiet inquiries. Unspoken between them was Holman's motive for tagging along on this particular voyage. He was hoping to encounter a ship bound elsewhere, one that might at last launch him on his circuit of the world.

It was a testament to their friendship that the famously restless Blind Traveler had remained by Owen's side, helping as he might, for more than a year. Holman was now more of a valuable presence than ever, since he seemed to be one of the few Westerners building up an immunity to the fevers of Fernando Po. But the fiercely independent captain knew better than anyone the merits of being allowed to go one's own way.

They sailed from Ascension, heading north by northeast. Three days later, between three and four o'clock in the afternoon, the ship crossed the equator. Holman, prompted by "the novelty of the circumstance," thought this an auspicious moment to make his final arrangements. He stepped into the captain's quarters and respectfully presented him with an affidavit for his naval salary: one year's worth of half-pay. Owen was not required to pay it immediately—such requests were subject to his discretion—but he did so straight away.

The following day, "there was a great change in the weather . . . the wind was more unsettled, the clouds were heavy, and there was a general haze around the horizon." All signs, Holman knew, that they were approaching the African mainland. If he was going to move on, he would have to do so soon. That sunset the *Eden* overtook the *Young Nicholas*, a Dutch ship bound for Brazil with only a half-cargo of salt. Holman struck a rapid bargain with the freighter's captain and gathered his few belongings. There was time for one last salute to his "kind and respected friend." Then he was over the side.

CAPTAIN OWEN KEPT his ship pointed toward Fernando Po, the island now acknowledged as the very epicenter of the White Man's Grave. He would remain at this post until 1829, dutifully fighting valiant but losing battles against both slavery and disease. The last and grimmest triumph of his career would be keeping the settlement of Clarence from collapsing in the face of overwhelming mortality. A year after parting company with Holman, he handed over Fernando Po to a civil governor, then made a final desperate bid to save the lives of his men. Gathering up as many as he could, he sailed the *Eden* straight out to sea, hoping to shed the pestilential air. But it was too late. Of the 135 men in the ship's original complement, only 12—Owen and Holman included—would survive.

My Dangerous and Novel Course

I N RETROSPECT, THE *Young Nicholas* was not an ideal choice for the passage to the Americas. The Dutch salt vessel was a galliot, a distinctive Netherlander design in which both ends of the ship arched up sharply, like crescent horns. For Holman, whose berth was a bedless cubby in the hindmost part, this meant weeks of trying to sleep at a ludicrous tilt. "While I was dancing in the air, others in the centre of the concavity were scarcely out of the horizontal line." His mattress was a rolled-up sail, his pillow a bag of clothes. Understandably, he spent as much time as possible in the open air, keeping watch-officers company on the relatively stable mid-deck as the galliot plowed through heavy seas on its course to the Tropic of Capricorn. It was "blowing weather," and frequently wet. By the third week of this routine, he was recording "a sore throat coming on, accompanied with fever, the effect of a severe cold caught by remaining on deck late at night."

By the time they made landfall at Rio de Janeiro, it was clearly something much more serious than a cold. He was too ill to go immediately ashore, and instead waited to disembark until a room ashore could be readied for him. Sick as he was, he was still impatient to begin his acquaintance with Rio. Lying by an open window

The Royal Society portrait of Holman, painted in Canton (modern-day Guangzhou) in 1830.

in the Rua Dirieto, not far from the imperial palace of Emperor Pablo I, he immersed himself in the soundscape of the city.

Each group of porters as they pass along with their heavy loads, chant their peculiar national songs, for the double purpose of timing their steps and concentrating their attention on their employment. To these sounds are added the variety of cries, uttered in

an endless alternation of tones, by the pretty negress fruit venders
. . . These, with the gabbling of foreigners, hurrying on their several
missions of pleasure or of business, the chattering of slaves wait-
ing to be hired, and the occasional expostulations of those who are
unceremoniously jostled from the pavement by the rude encounter
of bales of goods, keep up altogether a din of discordance.

A doctor confirmed the worst: the fever had progressed to pneumonia. Even when helped into a patch of Rio sunlight, Holman was
racked with an all-encompassing chill. "My cough was much worse
to-day," he wrote, "indeed it had become so troublesome that I was
almost exhausted, especially as I dared not partake of any stimulat-
ing food, to support my strength." Sleep was elusive, as "I found the
horizontal position less endurable than any other."

For Holman, the gravity of his illness was all the more reason to
conceal it. He was at a crucial juncture. He had a steady stream of
visitors, and he knew that those who clambered to bid him welcome
would, if sufficiently alarmed by his health, refuse to bid him good-
bye. They would rush to care for him, making a well-intentioned
form of captivity with hovering attentions. His doctor had already
warned him not to leave his lodgings under any circumstances, but
he knew his best hopes for recovery lay in doing quite the opposite.

Propping himself upright, trying to control his coughing fits,
Holman mustered his best semblance of health as he entertained
his visitors. He was convincing, at least enough to earn a number
of invitations unlikely to have been extended to an obvious invalid.
A group of scientific gentlemen were departing on a survey expedition to determine the true height of Mount Corcovado; would
he care to join them? The director of the Imperial British-Brazilian
Mining Company would be leaving in a few days for an inspection
tour of the Gongo Soco gold mines in the mountainous Minas
Gerais district, deep in the northern interior. Perhaps the lieutenant might wish to come along?

He declined the surveying expedition, but eagerly accepted the trip to Gongo Soco. It meant at least a half-month astride a mule, winding through four hundred miles of either sparsely settled regions or outright wilderness, but Holman reasoned that a saddle would, for him, be more comfortable than a bed. More importantly, it was a ready means of extricating himself from civilization. While other travelers were content to cling to increasingly Europeanized population centers (with occasional day trips to take in local color), Holman had experienced in both Siberia and Fernando Po the exhilaration that came only from venturing off the maps. Hearing a foreign language spoken and eating exotic foods were no longer sufficient distraction from his afflictions. Henceforth his travels would usually comprise a cursory survey of cities, then a beeline for the wilderness.

One week later Holman was straddling a pack mule, listening as the vivid din of Rio fell away. The casual observer would not have noticed how tightly he held the reins, or how often his composed demeanor was interrupted by a sudden wince. Hidden underneath his jacket was Holman's one concession to the pneumonia: a mass of blistering plaster, intentionally inflicting second-degree burns, spread across his chest. He had allowed a physician not only to blister him, but to keep the blisters undressed for several days, on the theory that the open sores would bleed out some of the fluid in his lungs. He had surreptitiously applied a bandage just before starting out, and already it was chafing "like a red hot iron applied to the surface."

ON THE DUSTPATHS Holman maintained his convalescence in motion, basking in the ninety-degree heat and consuming little beyond castor oil, a purgative. Past the town of Qualos, the trail grew so steep that everyone dismounted and scrambled up alongside their animals—except for Holman. Although he felt sorry for burdening his mule, who splayed and staggered beneath him, he was still incapable of walking more than a short distance. His pneumonia had begun to abate, and the chest blistering was healing nicely, but taking their place was both simple exhaustion and the bane of travel in these regions, "jigger" larvae, painfully erupting in his skin. The tiny ticklike creatures, too small to be seen with the naked eye, swarmed through his clothes to where the skin was thinnest (ankles, armpits, crotch), then burrowed straight down to feast. Such infestations were commonplace, to the point that at bedtime travelers were routinely handed a *panela*, a bowl of hot water, for immersing one's feet in hopes of dislodging the parasites. Then a servant arrived, to inspect the flesh for signs of infestation and expertly prod them out with a needle.

After seventeen days they arrived in Gongo Soco, an incongruous sliver of England dropped down in the midst of the rain forest. The mining company, finding the local labor force cheap but inefficient, had hit upon the idea of importing professionals from the tin and copper mines of Cornwall in southwestern England. These transplanted Cornishmen brought along their families and set about transforming the settlement. The little valley was ringed by primeval trees, so huge that one could hold a picnic on a stump, but daily squads of machete-wielding boys held the jungle at bay for a patch of crisp white cottages complete with green lawns, vegetable patches, and formal gardens. Holman dutifully admired how everything was "fast acquiring a truly English appearance." Descending several hundred feet, he explored one of the gold mines without benefit of lantern—he was, he discovered, as immune to claustrophobia as he was to vertigo—but this was just a courtesy stunt, to oblige the miners who were his hosts. More exciting to him was an offer to join yet another mule train, this one winding through the *sertao*, the catchall Brazilian term for "inland places unredeemed by culture."

FROM THE MOMENT Holman joined the muleteers, he suspected he was traveling in hapless company. They set a strangely late departure time of three in the afternoon, and, sure enough, sunset found them chasing daylight, hurrying up hills so steep it took a firm grip to keep from falling off one's mule. By nightfall they were lost. "Some wandered to the right, some to the left, some stood still," he observed. "And so we went on making perplexity more perplexing until it was quite dark."

The entertainments of the night continued. One of the men, insisting he knew the way, plunged headlong into a river. The muleteers' leader, a young man, was forced to admit he had never actually traveled in this direction before. No one had thought to bring along blankets, bedding, food for the mules, or indeed any food at all beyond a single chicken and some ground cassava root. They would have to buy provisions from the next ranch they encountered. Holman, viewing these mishaps not as cause for complaint but "as little varieties calculated to quicken the stagnant blood and stimulate the nerves," maintained an arch optimism. The lack of a bed or breakfast, he noticed, made breaking camp a remarkably efficient process. When a flagging mule obstinately tried to pitch him to the ground, he speculated that the beast had found a promising vein of gold ore and was inviting him to inspect it. When his next mule proved unwilling to continue, he gamely pursued the local remedy:

> Upon such occasions it is usual for the muleteers to administer a bottle of cachaça, (common rum of the country) to the suffering animal as a sovereign remedy. Of this curious dose, a part is first poured into the creature's ears, and the remainder down his throat.

Other tribulations could not be borne so lightly. The dregs of his pneumonia still devastated his appetite, making his meal of preference a half-dozen hard-boiled eggs, of which he would eat only the yolks. The jiggers continued to burrow, and there were more fearsome adversaries to fight. He grew to dread the sound of a distant buzzing, followed by the cry that invariably sent his world topsy-turvy: "Marabundas, marabundas!"

The word was used to sound the alarm for any especially dangerous insect, but on this trip, it meant another sky-darkening swarm of wasps. Instantly, Holman was pitched from his mount;

all the mules instinctively rolled on their backs and violently flayed their hooves. He could only lie on the ground, making himself as still and small as he could, knowing his companions had already abandoned him at the first sight of the swarm. "The bravest travelers are not ashamed to fly the instant they perceive the terrific host," he observed. "Not without a good reason, for so severe is the torture inflicted by the pigmy assailants."

The strangest trial, for Holman, was walking through a blazing world. Then as now, the most brutally efficient way of clearing the jungle was by setting fires, often several miles in length. As these were entirely unregulated, it was a common occurrence for the party to find themselves suddenly lost in smoke, and flanked by flames on both sides of the roadstead for an unknown distance. They could only wrap scraps of cloth around their mouths and plunge on, with no assurance they would not be trapped just ahead.

The effect of an entire forest on fire both fascinated and dismayed him. The others could judge the distance of the flames' approach, but the chaos of sound and heat confused his sense of space.

There is something very awful in the sound of the distant crackling of the dry bamboos as the fire seizes them. They burst on the ear in rapid succession, like guns of a variety of caliber . . . the accumulating thunder, with its reverberating echoes in the depths of the forest, is like that of contending armies in the din of battle.

Now they were far enough afield to encounter the indigenous Botocudo, the people whose homes were systematically disappearing in that smoke. The Brazilian government had recently established a new, enlightened policy toward these rainforest hunter-gatherers. At first, on no evidence, they'd been declared cannibals and shot on sight. The shooting stopped when Christian missionaries arrived, but started up again as a "just war" when they were found to be impervious to conversion. After that they were hunted wholesale by the mining companies, who'd been granted the right to impose between twelve and twenty years of slave labor on each one they caught. That was abandoned as uneconomic, since they were indifferent workers. It was more cost-effective to purchase permanent slaves, which Brazil had in abundance.

Now they were left alone to wander at will, retreating further and further into the interior. Holman had hoped to leave his hapless muleteers behind and join them, but "the rainy season was fast approaching . . . I was therefore obliged to abandon the prospect of going on so interesting an excursion." In truth, the weather was the least of his worries. His health was rapidly deteriorating.

He remained in the mule train as it looped back toward Rio de Janeiro. Once in the city he was forced to spend "a very quiet week" in private lodgings, confining himself to his bed, attempting an accelerated recuperation from exhaustion, mild sunstroke, wasp stings, smoke inhalation, and "the wounds I had received on my feet from the venomous insects." Then it was time to confront the questions long stowed in the back of his mind. Where to go from here? And more importantly: how?

THERE WERE CHALLENGES to improvising a circumnavigation, particularly one that, as Holman hoped, would take him through some of the most isolated regions of the planet. Almost by definition, this meant destinations for which it was impossible to buy a ticket. The invitation to join the Fernando Po expedition had been an act of friendship from the unconventional Captain Owen. The passage on the Dutch ship was a chance encounter, and while the spur-of-the-moment arrangement had extricated him from Africa, it also sent him heading in the wrong direction: west, not east.

Other merchant ships were willing to take him on as supercargo, but these would stick to established trade routes. They would also charge dearly, and he was traveling, as he himself admitted, "under extremely limited pecuniary means." He'd boarded the *Eden* with letters of credit totaling only a hundred pounds. Back in England his books were accumulating royalties, but if his publishers were typical for the era they could be counted on to settle accounts very slowly, if at all. The nation's bestselling author, Sir Walter Scott, had just been forced into bankruptcy by the collapse of his publishing house, one of several dying or struggling in the wake of a British banking collapse that would later be called the Crash of 1826. He could expect no help from Windsor Castle, either. The trustees of the Naval Knights were likely to dock his annuity as long as he defied them by his absence. This put a time factor on his progress, too—there was only so long he could stay away without getting kicked out entirely. Based on their previous grumblings, he calculated their patience would endure five years, at most. He'd already been gone for one fourth of that time.

As he lay, sick and spent, on an indifferent bed in the Rua d'Ouvidor, he was forced to acknowledge that keeping the necessary pace would require more luck and energy than he'd mustered thus far—that his funds and health were likely to run out well short of his goal. The circuit of the world had once seemed like the grandest of all possible dreams. Now it was beginning to seem like an elaborate means of expending his strength, of summoning a death at once lonely, impoverished, and obscure. That he was contemplating abandoning the circumnavigation is evident in the choice of his next destination: Argentina, still in the wrong direction, but accessible by passenger service. He bought a ticket as soon as he could walk.

HE WAS SCRAMBLING to cash in that ticket the very next day. The news came at dawn that the HMS *Falcon* was dropping anchor in Rio Harbor, en route to South Africa. By midmorning, Holman was on board, requesting an interview with the captain. It was denied. When a lieutenant asked what he wanted, he told him: a berth and a seat at the mess table, as far as the Cape of Good Hope.

This was an audacious request, and an irregular one. Ships of the Royal Navy, as a policy, accepted as passengers only those necessary to the workings of government: diplomats on mission, soldiers (and their families) undergoing transfer to a new station, the sick and wounded going home. They were not a shuttle service for every half-pay lieutenant with wanderlust. A stranded sailor in an obscure port might hitch a ride by appealing to a captain's sympathies, but that was a small act of rescue. What Holman was asking for was the very opposite. The lieutenant told him to go ashore and await the captain's pleasure.

The *Falcon* was a small ship, only ten guns. The quarters were cramped, even by Royal Navy standards. Provisioning and lodging a passenger was not a simple task. There was every reason the request would be denied, which is why the next day Holman was delighted to receive a new visitor—the captain himself. Captain Pole not only invited him to come along, he offered to share his own cabin and table with him. That is, if Holman wished; the lieutenants were also eager to welcome him in the officers' mess and quarters. In other words, he would be the ship's most honored guest.

Thus a precedent was set. Although he was careful not to abuse the privilege, the ships of the Royal Navy thereafter accorded a special status to the Blind Traveler whenever they encountered him. He was welcomed aboard, and, at the very least, allowed the standard courtesies of an officer in transit back to England—which, as a circumnavigator, he was, by the very loosest of definitions. It was hardly an act of charity. His presence onboard was wonderful for morale. He was not only profoundly pleasant company—a gracious guest and gifted listener—but a nearly inexhaustible source of entertainment. In addition to his own adventures, which he recounted with a storyteller's flair, his eidetic memory allowed him to unspool a vast stock of poetry, prose, and even jokes.

Any pity directed toward him usually evaporated by the first week. On land, Holman's acquaintances were forever forgetting his blindness, but nowhere did his handicap disappear more thoroughly than at sea. He was a confident hand the moment he stepped on board, having lived on ships for most of his sighted years. It was a limited, orderly world, where everything was stowed in a specific place and a maxim held sway: *one hand for the ship, one hand for yourself*. Ships are built for the grip of sailors steadying themselves at sea. After a while, Holman's light but constant touch on the railings and ropelines faded from notice. Many people remembered his disability only vaguely, as he wrote:

> *Occasionally they have only had their recollection recalled by some unexpected movement of my hand overthrowing what they offered, as for instance, a cup of tea. Others, recollecting that I am suffering from some deprivation, mistake the sense, and begin to shout at me as if I were hard of hearing; in short this feeling is so general that almost every one who is not intimately acquainted with me elevates his voice when in conversation.*

Another factor easing Holman's ready acceptance was a long-held naval practice. For centuries, each Royal Navy ship had sailed with a certain number of "widows' men"—phantom members of the crew who existed only on the books, and whose salary and provisioning costs were donated to a pension fund for officers' widows. The rule of thumb was one such fictional crewmate to fifty actual ones. The tradition was on the wane (it would end in 1832), but most old hands were used to sharing a ship with a purely theoretical presence. Sharing it with the Blind Traveler was more rewarding.

Holman created his own tradition. He cured his shipmates of seeing him as a fragile invalid by beginning each voyage with a stunt. As soon as the ship was on the open sea he would make his way to the mainmast, remove his coat, and hand aside his cane. Then he would begin to climb. Ascending the ship's rigging for sport, a practice called skylarking, was usually the realm of young, thrill-seeking midshipmen. It was a dangerous diversion, frowned upon on some ships, banned outright on others. One miscalculation of the ship's roll and you were giving yourself a burial at sea.

Holman climbed to the uppermost point, where the sway rivaled the bucking of a horse. He would shout in triumph, wave his compliments to the crowd below, and spend a solitary moment in imaginary flight.

SOUTH AFRICA WAS a prize of war—of two wars, actually. Great Britain had seized the Cape of Good Hope from Holland in 1797, during a brief, lopsided conflict later labeled the Fourth Anglo-Dutch War. Then it occupied the adjacent Cape Town settlement in 1805, to keep Napoleon from getting a strategic foothold on the continent. But it was not a wanted prize. The region contained vast amounts of arable land and Africa's least-lethal climate, yet it also came with two groups unlikely to ever warm to British rule: the white Afrikaners, who proudly considered themselves natives, with roots in the land going back to 1688, speaking "Cape Dutch," a dialect on the verge of becoming the Afrikaans language; and the tribal peoples, whom the Afrikaners had been battling for generations, in a series of "frontier wars"—tribes whose demarcations were sketchily understood (Xhosa, Zulu, Bantu, Nguni, Bathoso, Khoisan), speaking languages and dialects (Ngqika, Gcaleka, Mfengu, Thembu, Bomvana, and Mpondomise) not yet fully comprehended. Rather than plunge into this tense multiplicity of cultures, the British overlords tended to ignore the interior, viewing South Africa instead as another home base for antislavery patrols, and a port from which to monitor the China tea ships—"Great towering castles," Holman's old shipmate Basil Hall would write, "in search of the westerly winds which were to sweep them half round the globe."

Holman had every intention of following those towering castles. But first he hoped to plunge deep into both Afrikaans and tribal territories, penetrating into the African interior as far as he could go. This meant mastering an appropriate means of independent overland travel. In his travels thus far, he'd relied on preexisting arrangements: public transportation, hired carts, expeditions planned by others. Now he wanted to go far beyond the reach of any such measures. As soon as he landed in South Africa, he set about teaching himself to ride a horse.

He'd ridden through Brazil on muleback, but this was a far more complicated proposition. Those were pack animals, soundly tethered and proceeding at an amble. Horseback is an active, not a passive mode of travel: even the most docile saddle horse expects a constant stream of commands from its rider, and can become upset when those commands are unclear or contradictory. Nor can horses be fooled by a false show of confidence.

Outside of Cape Town, Holman trotted a borrowed horse across a variety of terrain. It took immense concentration, but he persisted, gradually growing adept at using the sounds of hoofbeats as a sort of echolocator, not unlike the sharp metallic strike of his walking stick on stones. Another rider kept him in sight, but this was not the same as being led—a fact dramatically demonstrated. As they passed by a public house, a pack of barking dogs beset and chased them, so spooking Holman's horse that it bolted, careening wildly through the underbrush. "All I thought of was to keep my seat, and tug away at the bridle, without turning to the right or the left." It took a distressing while for his traveling companion to locate him, entirely disoriented and far from the trail. Clearly, it was a skill to be honed with practice. Holman kept at it, and grew in mastery until he could ride on horseback for hours without incident. Although he still relied on guides to point out particular trails, he needed no help on the trails themselves.

Asserting "that if I was once fairly in the saddle, I fancied I could contrive to keep there," Holman aimed himself at the wilderness. Leaving Cape Town, he wended inland, through the lands claimed for agriculture by the Boers (the Cape Dutch word for *farmer*), until he reached a frontier station called Caffre-Drift. There he recruited a young boy to ride along with him—a member of the northern tribe that called themselves Khoikhoi ("people people"), but whom the Afrikaners dubbed Hottentot, Cape Dutch for *stut-*

terer, in reflection of the clicking sounds used in their language. Holman and the boy appear to have shared not a word of common language, but together they forded the Great Fish River and rode beyond the protections of the Crown Colony, into the inchoate tribal lands known to whites as Caffreland.

This was a term of convenience, not a true cultural designation: *caffre*, or kafir (from the Arabic word for *pagan*), was the label stuck on any number of tribes that the whites had not yet seen fit to learn much about. He was, in fact, in the land of Gaika, chief of the Xhosa (Holman had grown weary of the white man's tendency to dub every chieftain a "king"). He paid his respects to Gaika and found him "so fond of rum . . . that both dignity and decency had so far merged into a brutal appetite." After witnessing Gaika's sad habit of offering up his wives in exchange for alcohol, he moved on.

It was territory that just a few months earlier would have been particularly hazardous to venture through, having been the scene of a series of vicious raids by warriors from the neighboring lands of the "Zoolah"—who were still, Holman noted, "in a very unsettled state." Their leader, the charismatic and indisputably brilliant Shaka Zulu, had been assassinated by his half-brothers just the year before, in large part because of his insistence on those raids. The recent death of Shaka's mother appears to have unhinged what was already a notoriously unstable personality. He perfected massacre as a form of mourning, multiplying his grief by commanding that all pregnant women be killed. Even cows were slaughtered, to teach their calves the pain of a mother's loss. Next, he banned all activities he considered even vaguely maternal: the drinking of milk, the planting of seed. But it was the ordering of one too many raids on Caffreland and the Cape Colonies that brought about his demise. In his frenzy, he had tried to eliminate his warriors' traditional season of rest.

Holman suffered on these open rangelands, but not at the hands of another. He had little choice but to ride what horses he could rent or borrow, and one day could only muster an immense creature "as large and heavy as a prize ox," a challenge for even a sighted horseman to control. He bravely took the steed to a full canter—an assured pace—but when the horse abruptly stopped in his tracks Holman pitched over the horse's head and hit the ground, instantly unconscious.

He awoke with blood streaming from his forehead, the skin peeled off of most of his nose, and a head-splitting pain so overwhelming that Holman—no stranger to agony—was certain that he was dying, or as he put it, at "the finale of all my adventures":

> *I must own that wanderer as I am, my* amour propre *was deeply wounded at the idea of dying, after all my sojourning, on the roadside, at a distance from any dwelling. . . . The slave boy, my companion, was indeed terribly frightened, but as he only spoke bad Dutch I could neither make him comprehend my wishes nor my fears.*

He recovered enough to stagger back onto the horse, then cling to the reins, still bleeding, for three hours, until the barking of dogs announced an occupied settlement. He nursed his wounds for three days. Then, finding his boy companion still jittery and shaken by the experience, he gently replaced him with another—equally young, equally incomprehensible to him—and continued on his way.

HIS ADVENTURES ACCELERATED. Holman, now confident in his overland mobility, maintained what he called "my dangerous and novel course" at a rigorous pace, staying only a matter of days in any particular place. Continuing to steer clear of the Zulus, he rode back to the Cape Colonies and quit the African continent, hitching a ride on the HMS *Maidstone* to the island of Mauritius in the Indian Ocean. There he was surprised to encounter a Dr. Lyall, the top British diplomat to nearby Madagascar. Lyall and his family had fled Madagascar the day before, escaping from a nerve-shattering captivity.

That island nation had been ruled by a King Radama, but Radama's recent death, under mysterious circumstances, had prompted some of the natives to level accusations of sorcery against Lyall. These triggered a trial by ordeal: the diplomat and his family were confined to a compound of huts, into which snakes, presumably venomous, were thrown. This went on for two weeks, until a member of the London Missionary Society extricated and evacuated them.

Lyall, also suffering from a "Madagascar fever" that would soon claim his life, warned Holman about the rampant unrest and anti-Westerner sentiment in the wake of Radama's death. Holman, of course, promptly departed for Madagascar.

It was by chance that he landed in the court of King Ramananoulouna, a stout man struggling to fit into an appropriated scarlet coat with golden epaulets. Ramananoulouna was claiming only a small part of Madagascar as his kingdom—the rest was firmly in control of Queen Ranavalona, Radama's widow, a woman a later traveler would call "one of the proudest and most cruel women on the face of the earth." Holman was tempted to make his way across the island to the queen's capital, but at the last minute opted to sail toward Zanzibar instead.

This was, by far, for the best. Ranavalona was rabidly, murderously persecuting every foreigner she came across. She had been behind the Lyall family's ordeal, and was, in fact, embarking on a bloodily xenophobic reign that would, over the next thirty-five years, execute or expel almost all Europeans.

NEXT WAS ZANZIBAR—a slave market, sadly well supplied with "pretty young girls, gaily dressed, decorated with flowers in their hair and painting on their persons," followed by the Seychelles Islands (wild pineapples, tortoise-shell traders, and leprosy). Then a memorable two-month passage southward on the *Constance*, a Dutch freighter laden with what promised to be a pleasant cargo of sugar and champagne. The champagne enlivened the voyage somewhat, but the sugar attracted all manner of infestation. "Mosquitos, and myriad of ants running over every part of my body; besides which there were cockroaches as large as a crownpiece that appeared to take particular pleasure in despoiling my hair and denuding the extremity of my toes."

It was a relief to arise one morning with the island of Ceylon announcing itself in the nostrils. Well before they made landfall, Holman "smelt Ceylon . . . the aroma of the spicy groves of this celebrated island."

Ceylon (present day Sri Lanka) was another ambivalently held bit of empire, like South Africa landing in the British lap as a consequence of the Fourth Anglo-Dutch War. It was the focus of few colonial ambitions. The fields ringing the capital of Colombo were, indeed, a feast of fragrances—old groves of evergreen cinnamon trees (Ceylon cinnamon, a distinct species from the Indonesian variety, is generally considered the finest in the world), surrounded by thickets of mango and experimental transplantations of nonnative black and golden tea. But beyond was land unsuitable for European-style agriculture, and an interior Buddhist kingdom, fiercely independent, centered on the Sacred City of Kandy—a kingdom that had only begrudgingly acknowledged the primacy of British rule in 1815.

Throughout the island, areas of settlement were separated by wide swaths of jungle, through which even the natives proceeded with trepidation. They were, respectfully but rightly, fearful of the wild elephants that still roamed the country. When Holman, brushing his hand, noticed that many of the roadside trees bore deep notches in their bark, he learned it was "for the more ready escape of such travelers as may chance to be attacked." He could visit the Buddhist temples in the mountains only by consenting to being carried in a palanquin, surrounded by bearers "continually hallooing, and making as much noise as possible, to keep the elephants at bay." This was hardly his style, and at first opportunity he jumped on horseback and joined a party hunting the most dangerous elephants of all. As he described their quarry:

> *A rogue is either a large male who has been driven from the herd, after losing a contest for the mastery of the whole, or a female, wandering from it in quest of her calf . . . they thus acquire an acquaintance with mankind, which only renders them more cunning and daring . . . . they become a plague and a terror to the neighborhood in which they prowl, especially to those who work late in the paddy-fields.*

Once these renegade elephants discovered they could intimidate humans into dropping their loads of food, they tended to stalk a particular patch of road. One had rampaged almost daily outside a town for more than thirteen years, escaping capture all the while. The sportsmen Holman took up with hoped to target a few known rogues, but were in general not too particular about which elephants they shot. They were also out for alligators, and wild peacock.

If there had been any objections to bringing a blind man along, they disappeared on the first day, when Holman proved that he could keep up with the hunt, under his own power, no matter what the terrain. Even so, there was genuine danger when the entire party sought to dispatch two elephants—not an easy or safe task, given that the guns of 1829 had unrifled barrels and little penetrating power. The wounded cries brought another fifteen elephants barreling out of the underbrush at near-stampede speeds, taking the hunters by surprise and sending them scattering on horseback. Holman managed to ride clear with the rest.

Impressed, the hunting party awarded him a gun of his own on the second day—a gift he was prudent enough to use not in the heat of the hunt, but during target practice. He'd point the gun, listen to his companions' shouted advice on aim—*Lower! To the left!*—then pull the trigger, usually with respectable results. On the third day, he was showing off a bit, astonishing his companions by pointing out approaching features that he could sense but not see. "Look at those fine coconut trees," he would say, with an easy authority and wry smile.

THE NEXT STOP was India, a day's sail across the Bay of Bengal. There, for the first time since leaving England, he did not make a beeline for the wilderness, because it did not exist in the sense he was seeking. This was a deeply British-dominated land, still titularly belonging to Mughal emperors but controlled, openly and ruthlessly, by the British East India Company for well over a century. Deference to Englishmen was instilled as a cultural imperative. Even in the most remote reaches he could expect a formalized reception, a reflexive insulation from unvarnished experience. The Indian people—their scents, their hypnotically melodic languages and unmelodic music—were fascinating, but he would never be allowed to lose himself among them. Travel in the subcontinent felt like tourism, not adventure.

Instead he gathered strength, making a slow northeast arc across the land, relaxing as a houseguest of the Rajah of Punganoor in the Yelagiri Hills and flirting his way through the British colonial community ("Though my pen is silent, my heart speaks."). He was a guest of honor at a grand society ball, but he found it unpleasant to attend; the swirling voices of the dancers made him dizzy and disoriented. His mind was elsewhere. He was still hoping to gain at least one original insight about India, one topic not already essayed upon to tedium by generations of travelogue writers. Intrigued by the touch of the plaster walls in Madras, he took pains to learn and document every step of their manufacture. The secret was the addition of clarified butter.

Arriving in Calcutta, he found the harbors shutting down. Monsoon season was about to begin, and most seafaring traffic chose to wait out the rain. But the last commercial ship to China had yet to set sail, and he hastened to book passage. Holman had acquired a pocket watch suitable for the blind, with hands he could touch without disturbing, and he marked the exact time of their departure. It was one o'clock in the morning on August 9, 1830, and the winds filling their sails were unmistakably the beginnings of a monsoon. "The night was dark, the sea running high, and the weather very squally," he noted, beginning to feel again the precipice-edge thrill of enveloping uncertainty.

CHINA INSPIRED FRESH effusions of poetry from Holman. Here at last was the most populous nation on earth, the Celestial Kingdom whose northern borders he'd been so tantalizingly close to in Siberia. But China would prove an even greater frustration than India: a thoroughly Anglicized subcommunity, apart from the native culture as a whole, in this case isolated to the point of quarantine by the host government itself. The Chinese did not welcome foreigners, just their business. Europeans were forbidden to venture far from the proscribed limits of the official residential district for *Ta-pi-tze* (Westerner; literally *big nose*) in the port of Canton (present-day Guangzhou). As one historian described it,

> At Canton itself the permanent Western trading community, fewer than 200 British, 50 or so Americans . . . occupied a strictly controlled area with an 800-foot seafront, divided into 13 houses, each extending inland about 130 yards. There was a fetid ditch on each side, and two streets, China Street, on which the houses opened, and Hog Lane, full of spirits shops—"nothing so narrow or so filthy," wrote one visitor, "exists in a European town."

Furthermore, Western residents were subject to a maddening set of rules. Each had to be transported by rickshaw, not by their own feet. Each was assigned a comprador, a local official who monitored their every movement. To make that task easier, all servants had to be hired not by the European master but by the comprador himself. The law dictated that "Foreigners are not to row about the river at pleasure but to take the air only on the 8th, 18th, and 28th day of the month; foreign barbarians may visit the flower-garden but no more than ten at a time."

Here Holman had little choice but to remain within strict confines. He experimented with the cooling benefits of wearing a bamboo shirt, and with smoking opium, which he found he detested almost as much as tobacco. Even after two pipes he registered no narcotic effect, only a profound headache. Unable to explore the Celestial Empire he immersed himself in studying its language and history instead, exulting in the complexity of both. Cantonese, an inflected language in which tones conveyed meaning, was, he noted, easier for the blind to learn than the sighted, as he had long been "obliged to trust to oral acquisition, to the sound of the voice, and the subtle transitions of its varying tones." While the written language was highly ornate, the spoken one was streamlined and highly contextual, without tenses, number, or gender. One syllable might have as many as a hundred different meanings. He relished the challenge of navigating through the ambiguity of a single phrase, as if it were an open field taken on horseback. He was amused to learn that the colloquialism for foreign money was "little wigs" (for the portraits on the banknotes), and that the term for American translated as "second-rate Englishman."

He lingered long enough to have his portrait painted by the well-known expatriate artist George Chinnery, on a modest, easily portable canvas. It shows a hearty but contemplative Holman, still surprisingly youthful at forty-six, sporting a ginger-blond beard and fingering his well-worn walking stick. Smiling was not the fashion in portraits of that era, but the subject is clearly deeply at ease with himself and the world. It is not the portrait of an important man, but a happy one.

He made a deep and lasting impression on one young Englishman, also confined to China Street and Hog Lane. James Brooke would go on to become Sir James Brooke, the famed "White Rajah" of Sarawak, personally ruling a large chunk of the island of Borneo (and inspiring Joseph Conrad's *Lord Jim*). But at the time he was an invalided soldier passing through the commercial settlement, just beginning his fascination with the Far East. "Yesterday I was much pleased with meeting Holman, the celebrated blind traveler," he wrote in a letter to his mother.

> *He has a fine and, [in] spite of his blindness, an expressive countenance; decision of purpose is stamped on every feature, but his beard and thick moustache probably give him a sterner air than he would otherwise have. His manners are gentlemanly and animated, his conversation both copious and instructive, and his observation apparently very penetrating. I was struck with his descriptions. One was of a Chinese lady's pipe. The mouth-piece, he said, was ivoery richly carved, the pipe a thin cane, the bowl silver also carved, and a bag attached to the stick to contain the tobacco was of crimson velvet richly embroidered in gold. Speaking likewise of a Hong merchant's daughter, he said, "She is beautiful, and what splendid eyes she has!"*

IF THERE WAS one constant in these travels, it was the sought-after presence of women. Holman delighted in the company of them all. As he put it, "The heart of woman, in every clime and in every region, overflows with tenderness, compassion and sensibility."

Whenever propriety allowed, he would ask permission to add to his growing haptic knowledge of the varieties of female beauty, a request so sensitively posed it was rarely denied. It did, however, lead to some embarrassment. In Clarence, one Fernandian woman had made sure she'd be recognized by Holman by clapping his hand, in public, to her breasts.

The curiosity was occasionally reciprocated. One morning on the Calabar coast, he submitted to a routine bath, only to find him-

self overwhelmed by the number of hands scrubbing and caress-
ing him clean.

"I had detected a good deal of giggling from the beginning, and
objected to the presence of so many persons," he wrote. He did
not renew his objections when informed that the informal crowd
of attendants were all women, "many of whom, although black,
were both young and handsome."

But it was rare that his interactions with women were tinged by
even the slightest lasciviousness. He was simply alive to their presence. "Oh, how dearly precious the breathings of female sympathy!"
he enthused. "Are there any who imagine that my loss of eye-sight
must necessarily deny me the enjoyment of such contemplations?"

Although he'd long benefited from the notion of the blind man
as eunuch, he now felt compelled to draft a defense of his powers to perceive, and enjoy, the charms of the feminine. In fact, he
argued that his blindness enhanced rather than diminished the
experience.

*The feelings and sympathies which pervade my breast when in the
presence of an amiable and interesting female, are such as never
could have been suggested by viewing a mere surface of colored
clay, however shaped into beauty, or however animated by feeling and expression. The intelligence still allowed me by a benefi-
cent Providence is amply sufficient to apprise me of the existence
of the more real—the divine beauties of the soul; and herein are
enjoyments in which I am proud to indulge. A soft and sweet voice,
for instance, affords me a two-fold gratification—it is a vehicle of
delight, as operating on the appropriate nerves, and at the same
time it suggests ideas of visible beauty, which, I admit, may by
force of imagination be carried beyond reality. But supposing I am
deceived, are my feelings any less intense? And in what consists my
existence, but in those feelings? Is it otherwise with those who see?
If it be, I envy them not.*

In other words, he was perfectly aware that some of the women he found beautiful would not be considered conventionally attractive. This was not delusion on his part but the ability to tap into a deeper aesthetic, much as a master musician ignores the ornateness of an instrument in favor of the music it produces. "How much more do I pity the mental darkness which could give rise to such an error," he concluded, "than they can pity my personal calamity!" He was inspired by the subject to write a poem:

> The beauties of the beautiful
> Are veiled before the blind,
> Not so the graces and the bloom
> That blossom in the mind.
> The beauties of the finest form
> Are sentenced to decay;
> Not so the beauties of the mind,
> They never fade away.

AMONG BOTH WOMEN and men, his reception was by now almost universally one of welcome, if not awe. People regularly requested a souvenir of the Blind Traveler. He obliged them by taking out his Noctograph and inscribing not only his signature but the personal motto he'd composed on Vesuvius. If the encounter called for something more, he'd expertly dive his hands into his bags and draw from a small stock of engravings: a limited edition of his last book's frontispiece portrait, the one with the blank globe of the world. It hardly resembled the bearded, road-weathered Holman of the present day (one recipient marked his "not a good likeness"), but it was kept as a fond memento. Holman was clearly gifted with the power of making instant attachments, and, just as importantly, deftly shaking off those attachments when the time came to move on alone.

Nowhere was Holman greeted with more effusive attention than in the former New Holland, now loosely known as the "australian" colonies of the crown. In Hobart Town, capital of Van Diemen's Land (present-day Tasmania), he was fêted, followed, and even imitated, to the point that he inadvertently started a bizarre trend. As a local reporter wrote:

> *A curious instance of the force of example, and the proneness of the human race to imitation, has been innocently introduced among us by this gentleman, who, since traveling as he does without an attendant, has almost necessarily been compelled to allow his beard to grow, which is very becoming to Mr Holman. Many of the boys of Hobart Town however, anxious to imitate so interesting a feature . . . many now be seen wearing the tails of opossums, and other bush tailed animals, tied around their chin in imitation of the blind traveler.*

In New South Wales, his arrival was breathlessly announced in the press, as were most of his daily movements ("the celebrated blind traveler intends, should the weather be propitious, to commence his journey up the country this week"). The denizens of Sydney were fascinated by his relaxed, lighthearted manner, which belied a power of orientation now honed to split-second sharpness.

> *On Sunday week Lieutenant Holman, the blind traveler, was seen on horseback with a party of gentlemen quite at ease and riding as if possessed with every faculty; on coming to a corner of a street, the word was given to him, and he turned the animal in a sharp trot with the upmost confidence to the no small astonishment of the spectator.*

Unfortunately, Holman's heralded presence in Sydney came just days too late for what would have been a most unusual reunion. Laurence Hynes Halloran, the scoundrel whose flight from Exeter had set Holman's naval career in motion back in 1798, had died two weeks previously. He was mourned as one of Sydney's more eminent citizens.

Transported to the penal colony in 1819, Halloran had finally given up on confidence games and stamp forgery in favor of a respectable profession. Looking back fondly on his time as head-master of the Alphington Academy, he founded a free school for "Classical, Mathematical and Commercial Education," the first of its kind on the continent. It was a struggle to establish, considering the founder's stigma (his criminal past was not held against him, just his lack of legitimate credentials), but he persevered. The school continues to this day as the venerable, prestigious Sydney Grammar School. Halloran is honored as the father of public education in Australia.

Holman appears to have learned of his old teacher's recent passing with at least a small measure of regret. He would have enjoyed trading Latin quips with him, and showing off his now encyclopedic command of English verse. He might even have expressed his thanks for being so inadvertently freed from a cleric's or apothecary's life.

The pleasures of celebrity soon wore thin, and Holman, as usual, began to cast about for an exit. His last appearance in the Sydney papers came on November 28, 1831:

> Lieutenant Holman, the blind traveler, is at present with an exploring party in Bateman's Bay.

IT WOULD TURN out to be "an adventure much more romantic and perilous than we had any idea of when we started our expedition." Bateman's Bay and Jervis Bay were two inlets several hundred miles to the south of Sydney, accessible by sea but ringed by high hills and coastal range. There were no known overland paths— even Aborigines' trails had yet to be discovered—but cattlemen in the interior Narriga station could climb the steepest of those hills and catch a glimpse of sea-blue on the horizon. If a path could be cut in anticipation of an eventual road, then arable land presently considered too remote for settlement would seem within reach. An expeditionary force had been assembled, consisting of two free whites, one convict-servant, and two Aborigines, the latter of which were called "guides" only as a label of convenience;

they freely admitted to never having set foot in those hills. Holman was a welcome addition to their number.

They set out on horseback and foot, stabbing eastward "through trackless and stony gullies, in which our way was greatly by jungle, and creepers of extraordinary size and length." Holman slept little, kept awake by the howl of dingoes that seemed to surround them in the darkness. The spooked horses soon broke their tethers and disappeared into the night. The party laboriously tracked down all but one of them the following day, just in time to get caught in the open during a thunderstorm of "awful grandeur." Soaked and short on rations, they took refuge in a cave. "My companions gave way under the depressing effects produced by the storm," Holman noted, "and all my efforts to induce them to push on, in hopes of finding some stockman's hut, were used in vain."

When they emerged they found that nothing lay ahead but deep gullies, then an increasingly soggy stretch more water than land. The horses were soon more of a burden than a boon, each "sinking almost up to their middle in this marsh." When they could no longer be ridden, they were slowly eased through the mud on tethers, by a dismounted Holman and company. The men were reduced to hopping from reed clump to reed clump, then finally climbing on individual stalks of submerged reed. The marsh had given way to a full-fledged swamp.

Clearly, this was not a promising course for a trail, much less a potential road. The dispirited party, soggy and hungry, began to fall apart. Most decided to stay with the fatigued and injured horses, then retrace their steps. Holman and one of the natives opted to keep going.

They slept in improvised *gunyers*, or native lean-tos of sticks and bark. They subsisted on fish, squirrel, and opposum, all speared by the guide without complaint, or even comment. Holman was gaining a sincere respect for the Aborigines. At the time, the dominant prejudice among whites was that the natives were subhuman at best—"the *last* link in the long chain of humanity"—but he thought otherwise.

It appeared to me that they have, on the whole, been misrepresented. If it were not for the illicit intercourse which is maintained by the whites with the native women, there would be but little ground for censure or animadversion, with the exception of the petty thefts which the blacks commit in the locations of the settlers, the natural and inevitable consequence of being brought into a communion which, affording them but a scanty subsistence procured by begging, exposes them to all the vices of civilization.

That respect would grow when they reached the coast at last. There he learned that the white men had long been overriding the Aborigines, and that "had we taken the line recommended by our guides, we should have found a comparatively easy and much shorter road to Jervis Bay, instead of being exposed to a variety of mishaps and *deságrements* that cast no little gloom over our journey."

He left the bickering remnants of the exploring party behind to perform a private ritual. A few miles down the shore lay the River Muroo, the boundary of the colony of New South Wales. The territory on the other side was the recognized possession of no one.

The river was running high and fast, but he forded it on horseback. Then he paced and paused for a moment on the opposite bank, just long enough to savor what he called "this favorite intention"— that of venturing beyond the reach of all known governments, into truly untamed terrain.

Six weeks later he was back in Sydney, alone. It was Christmas Eve.

HOLMAN HAD GIVEN himself exactly five years for his circumnavigation—he couldn't dare to be an absentee Naval Knight much longer. In Hong Kong he'd learned of the death of King George IV, who in recent years had taken to emulating his father, shambling through the halls of Windsor a virtual recluse with an increasingly tenuous grasp of reality. An opium addict, an alcoholic, and severely obese, the formerly high-living king had died in his delusions, convinced he was a soldier, who had fought in the Battle of Waterloo.

There was yet another royal funeral with Holman absent from the procession. The new king was George's brother, the former duke of Clarence and lord high admiral who had given his blessing to the Fernando Po expedition, and in whose honor the settlement had been named Clarence. He was crowned William IV, but the public soon called him the Sailor King.

Now it was January, high summer in Australia. The inversion of seasons served to remind him that, with his self-imposed deadline fast approaching, he was still half a world away from England. It took the bulk of his remaining funds, but he booked passage on the *Strathfield Saye*, named incongruously after the manor house of the Duke of Wellington. Formerly a transport ship specializing in women prisoners, it was one of the fastest ships on the route, having been fitted out to protect the female convicts by making as few interim stops as possible.

During three months of uneventful sailing through the Tasman Sea, the Indian Ocean, and finally the Atlantic, there was one flash of excitement. During a provision stop on the isolated isle of Flores, Holman and other members of a shore party found themselves stranded when a squall blew the *Strathfield Saye* to sea. They idled about for two days, taking bets as to whether they were now castaways. The ship, of course, reappeared to retrieve its passengers, but "It was a matter of indifference whether she returned or not," was Holman's opinion. "My mind was more devoted to adventure than to the regular course of the homeward voyage."

In a typical fit of modesty, he described the now-resumed voyage as "not marked by any incidents worth recording." In truth it contained a milestone both personal and historic. Somewhere in the Atlantic, approaching England, Holman at last completed his circuit of the world.

Frontispiece portrait of Holman's *Voyage Round the World*.

FIFTEEN

Assuming a More Alarming Character

IN AUGUST OF 1832, Holman returned to a London that was at once familiar and strange. There were new scents and sounds in the air, new textures to recognize and comprehend. The venerable but decrepit London Bridge had been torn down, and a new one, of granite from Holman's native Devonshire, erected one hundred feet upstream. Where the king's stables had stood was now cleared ground, in the process of becoming Trafalgar Square. The busiest streets were no longer cobblestone, but covered with wood to combat the rising noise of horse-drawn traffic. That traffic now included a new kind of vehicle: the omnibus, "the novel form of the carriage . . . a handsome machine" pulled by a team of horses three abreast, holding up to eighteen passengers and making regular stops through the city on four runs a day. London had launched the rudiments of a public transportation system.

But for Holman, the biggest changes were the novel presences now crowding him on the sidewalks. An Englishman walking did not squeak and rustle quite so much as before. The fashionable were abandoning crisp, smooth textures like silks and brocades in favor of sober wools and linens. Instead of form-hugging breeches and hose, they wore loose-fitting trousers. In contrast, Englishwomen were noisier than ever, and well on their way to becoming pedestrian hazards. Up until recently, women's fashions had not changed markedly since before he'd lost his sight—he remembered women, fondly, as wearing thin, shape-revealing, high-waisted dresses. Now the female form was being buried under increasing layers of petticoats and lace and ballooning skirts. Holman could hear them approach more readily, but it was harder to give them the necessary wide berth.

Everyone had to make way for another phenomenon introduced in his absence, the "sandwich men" bearing advertising placards, often accompanied by even more elaborate street spectacles—oversized walking hatboxes, stoves, boots, and coffee grinders. There was a new, commercialized cacophony to the streets. This was the London that a twenty-one-year-old court reporter named Charles Dickens was just beginning to capture in fiction (his first short story would be published the following year). It was an era that would soon be dubbed Victorian.

The Blind Traveler made his way to the home of his cousin, Dr. Andrew Holman. A thirty-five-year-old surgeon, Andrew was his closest relation in the city, a supportive friend and source of a forwarding address, who looked after Holman's affairs and correspondence during his long absences. There he learned that, this time, years of unauthorized leave would not be easily forgiven.

The Visitors of Travers College had long since grown impatient of waiting for their wandering Naval Knight to return. Giving up on contacting him directly, they had tried interceding through Andrew, sending him an admonitory letter, then a follow-up, asking "if you have conveyed to your Cousin the purport of it." Finally, the dean of Windsor's secretary wrote that the trustees were "much disappointed" that all correspondence had been roundly ignored, by both cousins. Awaiting at Windsor would be a daunting backlog of what Holman later characterized as "frequent warnings, and threatening messages from the Visitors of the College, of the loss of my situation."

Holman couldn't understand the uproar—or, at least, he affected not to. As he pointed out, the Naval Knights had only two elected offices: treasurer and auditor. Since both "are of a nature which I cannot execute; consequently my absence from the College does not impose any additional duty on the other Members." He did not mention the mutual obligation of prayer in Saint George's Chapel, since that practice had predictably already dwindled to a trickle, just as it had with the Military Knights. As records in the Knights' Check Book show, only three of the members were showing up for services with any regularity. Of those, only the newest Naval Knight, Lieutenant George Bland, was consistently racking up the cross marks that indicated twice-daily attendance.

Holman chose not to dispute the censure. It served his purpose to settle in at Windsor, as he had a half-decade's worth of adventures to dictate. He took a great deal of time and care in crafting his new manuscript, which grew voluminously, and for which he had great hopes. The resulting book was long enough to warrant publication in phases: the first two volumes appeared in 1834, the final two the following year.

The work was remarkable at first glance, for two reasons. The first is summed up in the title page, which bears what was, for the era, a streamlined title. *A Voyage Round the World, Including Travels in Africa, Asia, Australasia, America, etc, etc.* More importantly, there is no subtitle at all—no reference, as in the previous books, to the author's "total blindness" or "total deprivation of sight." The portrait on the facing page also does nothing to convey Holman's affliction. Earlier portraits had dealt with his sightless gaze by having him stare off to one side. In the new one, he clearly, and for the first time, makes eye contact with the reader. One eye is sharp and clear—the other is just slightly unfocused, as if that portion of the portrait was done while Holman was lost in thought. To the casual viewer, the subject seems perhaps mildly cross-eyed, but not blind.

In the text Holman was not coy about his blindness, but he did seek to get the subject out of the way as quickly as possible. His preface was a brisk assertion that far from being a handicap, it made him a superior investigator of novel cultures. "Freed from the hazard of being misled by appearances, I am the less likely to adopt hasty and erroneous conclusions," he wrote. "I always vividly remember the daily occurrences which I wish to retain, so that it is not possible that any circumstances can escape my attention." After that, the reader is reminded of the author's blindness only when absolutely necessary.

But the book is also extraordinary on its own merits. It is a dense yet engrossing hybrid of genres—mostly a travelogue, but this time around, Holman did not feel bound to cling to day-to-day descriptions of his own adventures. His previous books had their share of digressions and appendices, but *Voyage* aspires to the encyclopedic. "My object has not been to make a book, but to furnish the results of long and arduous journeys of investigation," he explained.

Anecdotes of his sojourn in China are followed by an exhaustive survey of Chinese history, hundreds of pages that could have comprised a scholarly work in and of themselves. In addition to the first ever Fernandian-English dictionary, there are precise instructions for preparing soy sauce, hunting kangaroos, and plastering walls in the Indian fashion. For a blind man, he describes vividly the appearance of Aborigines in mourning ("They daub and plaster their heads and bodies over the white earth, and scarify their heads until the blood trickles down their faces"). There are meticulous surveys of local ecologies and real insights into native cultures, passages that would be gratefully read by future generations of botanists and anthropologists. One section, on the flora and fauna of the Indian Ocean, would become source material for one of the greatest scientific treatises of all time.

But significantly, the narrative also veers regularly to places where Holman had explored only slightly, and in some cases, not at all. One of the most colorful chapters is devoted to New Zealand, a place the *Strathfeld Saye* had skirted without landing on the passage back to England. As he was "aware of the interest which all the accounts of the New Zealanders that have been hitherto published have excited," he hastened to add another, compiled from interviews he'd conducted in Australia. It relied heavily on the accounts of an anonymous sea captain "trading amongst the natives in different parts of the island," and it hardly skimped on spectacle, with description of casual cannibalism and human sacrifice. But those were not the passages that would prove controversial. It was this one:

> *There is not a woman in New Zealand who is not scarred in the face, arms, and body; these wounds being often inflicted for joy as well as grief. The women frequently exchange their children, and nurse those which they adopt with great care. They are also often seen to suckle puppies and young seals.*

INITIALLY, THE AMBITIOUS scope of *Voyage Round the World* seemed to be paying off. He was allowed to dedicate it to the queen, and there was no lack of initial critical enthusiasm. "We have seldom met with any work so replete with interesting information," wrote the *London Observer*. "Mr. Holman's book, of which the concluding volume has not yet appeared, would do credit to any traveler," said *Frasier's Magazine*. "Considered as the production of a blind man, it is quite wonderful." The *London Literary Gazette* predicted another bestseller: "For this work we cannot but anticipate a circulation as wide as the author's *Travels*." The Siberia book was then in its fourth printing.

But other critics were not so kind. They tended to begin with an elaborate disclaimer, such as, "We never ranked ourselves in the number of those who censured or ridiculed the peripatetic tendencies of our interesting and enterprising traveler." But then they proceeded to join that number, responding dismissively, with occasional gusts of open derision. Cochrane's old condemnation—that a blind man's insight was automatically secondhand and suspect—was now taken as a given. "A want of verification . . . renders the work almost if not entirely useless," wrote one. "Deprivation of sight bears along with it a physical barrier to investigation in foreign lands, which no talent or judgement can surmount."

Another was blunter still:

> *Surely if sight (as it must be confessed) is indispensably necessary to the publishing discipline of travel, the Lieutenant would act wisely were he to direct his energies and contemplation to some other object more beneficial to the public, and more suitable to his physical powers.*

Such displays of prejudice were nothing new. But other critics were, for the first time, attacking his factuality—not his firsthand facts, but those he'd reported in the accounts of others. As *Gentleman's Magazine* scornfully remarked:

> *In p. 312 we have a fine study for the craniologist: it is the head of Confucius, the Lycurgus of the Celestial Empire; the crown of whose head we are informed, was of the form of a hillock: and the naturalist will find ample amusement in p. 494, where we are seriously told "the New Zealand women suckle puppies and young seals."*

In his zeal to produce a definitive guide to the world, Holman had overreached himself. He knew that the unnamed Sydney sea captain's account of New Zealand life, dripping as it was with human sacrifice and assorted cruelties, had been "so revolting as to appear incredible"—he acknowledged it as such in the book itself. But he had taken pains to confirm it through independent sources, and noted that "if the interests of civilization were not concerned in its publication, I would gladly omit from the pages of my travels."

In his defense, the vast majority of the statement does accord with other eyewitness accounts of the period: cannibalism *was* a part of New Zealand culture, although rapidly on the wane. As to the shape of Confucius's head, Holman only conveys the traditional story that the sage's childhood nickname was *E-kew*, or "hillock," "in consequence of the formation of the crown of his head." In his survey of Chinese history, he also reports that the Emperor Yu, who ruled in 2191 B.C., was nine feet two inches tall, and ascended to the throne at the age of ninety-three. It is maliciously disingenuous to imply that Holman took any of this literally, or meant for his readers to do so. There *are* errors of fact—when visiting Penang in the Straits of Malacca, he mentions that "there had been an eclipse of the sun and moon two days previously," an unknown astronomical phenomenon. But any massive work, spanning four volumes and the globe, could be expected to contain a mistake or two. This was a flaw not of blindness nor even blind faith, but simple humanity.

With sighted authors, such mistakes were not fatal to their career. But coming from a blind man, they could be seized upon as proof of "a physical barrier to investigation." It only took a few errors to undermine what many already considered a tenuous authority, and to dovetail neatly with the view of him as being inherently, ludicrously removed from actual experience. Another critic landed what must have seemed like a decisive blow.

> *If the observation were not fraught with sarcasm, we might remark that a residence in London would equally have fitted him for the task! . . . We should imagine that the studious garrets of our Metropolis could have collated every interesting fact he has recorded, without those alloys of trifling nothings which his diary affords.*

BUT THERE WAS more than malice behind the critics' unwillingness to forgive a few factual slipups. In light of a very recent scandal, all travel accounts were under increased scrutiny. For the time, criticism and skepticism seemed intertwined.

In 1827, the same year Holman had launched his circumnavigation by way of Fernando Po, another renowned traveler, named Jean Baptiste Douville, a respected member of the Geographic Society of Paris, had departed for the deepest interior of Africa, by way of the Congo River. Douville's one-man expedition emerged four years later with acutely observed and exhaustively detailed notes, enough to publish a three-volume *Voyage au Congo et dans l'interieur de Afrique equinoxiale*, complete with an attached atlas of regions never before mapped. The book so impressed his fellow Geographic Society members that they awarded Douville a gold medal, then elected him secretary of the organization.

The critics were the ones who exposed him as a fraud. First the *Foreign Quarterly Review*, then the *Revue des deux mondes* began to point out internal contradictions, and details that were either inconsistent with, or disturbingly similar to, other travelers' accounts. Within a few months, Douville was resigning his post in disgrace, dogged by denunciations that his book was "romance and not verity." He *had* spent time in Western Africa—but only long enough to come across unpublished manuscripts from earlier Portuguese explorers, which he proceeded to rewrite and pad out with his own imagination.

His fiancée, a young woman named Audrun, was so ashamed she committed suicide. A shunned Douville tried to salvage his reputation by launching a legitimate solo expedition, this time into the heart of the Brazilian rain forest. He'd departed just as Holman was returning from his circumnavigation, and would never be seen again (he is presumed to have perished on the Amazon). For a time at least, all extraordinary travelers' accounts would be viewed with a skeptical eye. It's worth noting that the Raleigh Club of world explorers had, in Holman's absence, been absorbed by a new, larger organization, the Royal Geographic Society. Although the RGS would later claim to "trace its descent" from the elite dining club, at the time it did not see fit to extend membership to the Blind Traveler, one of the Raleigh's founders.

•   •   •

HOLMAN WAS STILL a celebrated figure. The less-literary London journals carried long profiles of him, marveling at the highlights of his adventures: the mad elephant hunt in Ceylon, the amblings through Zulu territory, the friendship with Cut Throat ("a gentleman between whom and us we are glad some thousand leagues of ocean extend"). An anonymous female poet was moved to write an ode "on seeing Holman's first volume ornamented with the Globe":

A book,—the world! a traveler blind!
How strange the world has grown!"
Why strange? No need of eyes he'd find;
Who uses now their own?

Throughout the universal parity
Of wise creation's rules,
Perfection still remains a rarity,
Ne'er found except by fools.

So gifted spirits mythological
Partake the just decree;
And so by reasoning purely logical
Our Holman should not see.

But there was no mistaking the fact that sales of *A Voyage Round the World* were disappointing. The original publisher—Smith, Elder—accounted for only a middling "600 or 700 copies" sold, neither an abject failure nor a success. In contrast, their most successful title, a saccharine anthology called *Friendship's Offering*, was selling about 10,000 copies a year, and would continue to do so for a total of two decades.

More importantly, the book was not the vehicle Holman had hoped it would be—a *tour de force* work to catapult him out of the ranks of literary novelties and into the role of a trusted observer of "the world and its multiplying delights." There would be a second edition in 1840, but thereafter it was not reprinted so much as repackaged. A series of publishers obtained the plates to one volume or another, ignored or deleted the references to the larger work, and printed them cheaply as *Travels in Sierra Leone* or (inaccurately enough) *Holman's Voyage to New Zealand, etc.* Ironically, these budget-minded houses were making the same gamble that the author had made—that readers would forget Holman was blind.

THE DISHEARTENING RECEPTION of *Voyage* did not keep him from contemplating further voyages. On the contrary, rootedness was already beginning to gnaw at him. Even as he was completing his *magnum opus* he was musing on "the traveler's rest," which, he pointed out, "is not altogether a life of idleness and dreams . . . It is part of the constitution of a traveler to look back with unsettled feelings, and to yearn for the time to come, which he believes to contain the great purpose of his life."

He went on, breaking into blank verse:

> *He cannot be quite at ease. A thousand memories crowd upon him.*
> *He again treads the shore of a remote land, and feels the breath of an unaccustomed climate.*
> *He hears the sounds of an unknown language for the first time, and struggles through a cloud of novelties with the energy of one who is resolved to succeed.*
> *He indulges in the sanguine but natural prophecy that there remains for him a wider field, and a more glorious work.*

But the trustees of Travers College were doing their best to extinguish any hopes of traveling at all. Even though he was once more attending services—fitfully, but unprotestingly—they made it clear that the penance for his prolonged absence would be permanently imposed. Other Naval Knights were now routinely receiving leaves of absence for a broad range of reasons, but Holman's applications were just as routinely denied.

With straining politeness, he asked the reasoning behind the rejection. He was informed that he would be untethered from Windsor only for reasons of health. And given his past, loose interpretation of "medical leave," he'd need a detailed physician's certificate before the matter could even be considered.

This wasn't difficult to obtain. By the summer of 1836, after five consecutive leave rejections, he was genuinely suffering from the effects of idleness. No less than Dr. William Fergusson, the august and eminent Inspector-General of Military Hospitals, paid a personal visit to Holman's quarters, accompanied by local surgeon William Hammond, "who had long attended him, and been well acquainted with his constitution." As they jointly certified,

> *We find him much out of health, being greatly emaciated, and in a state of nervousness, approaching to melancholy. All these complaints we attribute to the sedentary habits and confinement of his College residence . . . and for which we have no hesitation in recommending him immediate change of air and scene.*

To Holman's amazement, this moved the trustees not at all. His sixth request was not denied but summarily ignored, until he fired off a final plea.

> *I beg to assure you that I can no longer support, with any degree of equanimity, the state of suspense which I have hitherto been induced to bear up against, in the expectation that motives of humanity alone might, ere this, have prompted you to grant the leave I solicited.*

The response was a single terse sentence: *I hereby give you leave to be absent from Travers College for four months.* As was no doubt calculated, so brief a leave was almost as infuriating as no leave at all. He hastened as far away as he could, to the northern reaches of Ireland, and wandered himself back to a certain degree of health. But by the following year, he was again restless and pining, and declining in strength. On the advice of Dr. Hammond, he stopped attending chapel. The physician would later testify that he considered "the life of the said James Holman to be in imminent danger."

THEN A STRING of chance developments seemed to hold out new hope. William IV, sixty-five when he succeeded his brother, had viewed himself as a caretaker monarch, assuming his reign would be short. He had many children, but none of them legitimate (an Irish actress had given birth to at least ten), so his heir apparent was a very young niece, a girl he called Drina, who playfully called him "Uncle King." He hoped to avoid another regency by living until she reached her majority, and he succeeded, dying of pneumonia in 1837, one month after her eighteenth birthday. For the first time in his quarter century as a Naval Knight, Holman was at last present to play his role in a royal funeral, then a coronation. Drina ascended the throne as Queen Victoria.

The new queen, "a very short, very slim girl in deep plain mourning," brought sweeping changes to the court. Her mother had chosen to raise her quietly, as far from the vices and mistresses of the recent kings as possible. Victoria's private life was described as "that of a novice in a convent: hardly a human being from the outside world had ever spoken to her." Not once had she ever been allowed to be alone with anyone other than her mother or her governess (a no-nonsense Lutheran pastor's daughter). The result was a brisk young woman without a coquettish thought in her head, prepared to move quickly and decisively into action.

One of her first acts was to appoint a royal physician. She chose a very unconventional medical man, one who had long ago abandoned a small, unsuccessful practice to research the healing effects of mineral water, and the influence of climate on disease. James Clark, the doctor who had tended the dying Keats and befriended Holman on the Spanish Steps of Rome, was now holding the most prestigious medical office in the land.

As he was far from ambitious, Clark's rise had been a happy accident. His interest in mineral springs had led him to a German spa where one of the other guests was Prince Leopold, the future king of Belgium, who had married into the British royal family. Though described as "lazy and easy-going," Clark must have inspired confidence, since Leopold promptly named him his personal physician. After a few years, he moved on to fulfill the same role for Leopold's sister the Duchess of Kent, who happened to be Victoria's mother. Now he was the Queen's medical attendant, soon to be knighted Sir James, deeply trusted as the doctor who had presided over her girlhood. No one thought it prudent to point out that he had trained as a naval surgeon, not a gynecologist. Of women's medical concerns, he had almost no knowledge at all.

Despite his elevated status, Clark greeted Holman as an old friend. When he heard about the dispute with the Visitors, he didn't hesitate to take advantage of his access to the queen. Even though Victoria had yet to arrive at Windsor Castle (which, thanks to her sequestered upbringing, she had never even seen), the matter was promptly brought before her at Kensington Palace in London.

On July 27—exactly one month and one week since Victoria had learned she was queen—her secretary sent a succinct letter to the Visitors:

I am commanded by Her Majesty to acquaint you that it is Her Majesty's Pleasure to dispense with Lieutenant James Holman's residence at Travers College.

A jubilant Holman paid a professional scribe to pen a beautifully elaborate letter of thanks to Her Majesty, effusive with appreciation for "that generous act of benevolence so necessary to your

Memorialist's health and enjoyment of life, under his melancholy privation."

Why did the fledgling queen, during her earliest weeks of rule, take action on this surpassingly minor dispute? Why did she bestow such an unequivocal mark of favor to a blind man she'd never met? Clark was an important personage, but dozens of vastly more important men were clamoring for her attention on far more urgent matters. While she may have heard of the Blind Traveler or been passingly familiar with his work, it's likely her sympathy had more personal origins.

Next in the line of royal succession was her cousin, Prince George of Cumberland, only slightly younger than she. He'd lost sight in one eye in early childhood. When he was fourteen an accident on horseback had claimed the other, and now Prince George was completely blind.

There had already been one Blind King of England, their grandfather. Victoria knew that until she married and gave birth to an heir of her own, her cousin could very well be the next. In fact he was bound to rule the one hereditary realm that she would lose. As succesor of the house of Hanover, she inherited the thrones of Great Britain and Ireland, but the dynasty's namesake kingdom of Hanover, in what is now northwestern Germany, could not pass to a woman. Victoria was fond of her cousin (he also called her Drina), and perceptive enough to grasp that he, too, would chafe under constraints such as those imposed on Holman. This kindness was not just an indulgence of a favor, but a privately resonant act of empathy.

CONFIDENT THE MATTER was settled, Holman began planning his departure in earnest. But as he was soon to learn, the queen's command was no guarantee of freedom—on the contrary, it served to sweep him into the machinations of politics and power.

The death of a monarch automatically triggered new parliamentary elections, and the communiqué of Victoria's decision happened to arrive at Travers College just two days after a bitterly fought election for Windsor's seat in the House of Commons. Although the queen was officially above the fray of politics, the general assumption was that she favored the more liberal, reform-minded Whig party (her closest advisors were prominent Whigs). This concerned the more conservative Tories, who feared she would try to influence the elections in progress.

The Reverend Henry Hobart, dean of Windsor and therefore one of the two Visitors of the Naval Knights, was a dedicated Tory. And he assumed that Lieutenant Holman, the thorn in his side for these many years, was naturally a Whig sympathizer. To him, the timely appearance of the royal dispensation confirmed his darkest suspicions. Queen Victoria was not only a Whig but a corrupt one, purchasing Holman's vote by granting him his fondest wish. In a fit of anger, Hobart took up the document and scrawled across it *Election for the Town of Windsor*, as if it were a receipt for services rendered. Then he flung it back at the man who delivered it, shouting "There, Sir. You may make what comment you please on this!"

The other Visitor, Joseph Goodall, provost of Eton College, was watching. "Sir, Her Majesty has been ill advised," he piped in, revealing his own Tory sympathies.

The stunned messenger later testified on this moment, describing it in the present tense:

> *The inference His Reverence means to draw is that the Government granted the dispensation to Lieutenant Holman as* a bribe *to him for having voted for Mr. Robert Gordon M.P. for Windsor, hence the calling into question the Queen's prerogative.* [emphasis in the original]

Dean Hobart would never be celebrated for tact (years later, when Victoria at last bore a son, he congratulated her for "saving us from the incredible curse of a female succession"). At first, he opted to ignore the edict entirely, just as he had Holman's multiple requests. When pressed on the matter, he decided to protest. His refusal to comply was not, he maintained, an act of political spite. It was the principle of the thing. What right did the queen have to tinker with the rules of an autonomous fraternal order— an organization of which she was not, and could never be, a member?

It was an unusual position for a Tory to take, since the party generally favored increasing, not decreasing, the power of the sovereign. But it went to the heart of the central issue of constitutional monarchy: where, exactly, was the dividing line between power and glory? When is the ruler merely a figurehead, and when a true leader to be obeyed? While there were many clear demarcations, there was also a large gray area. Dean Hobart considered himself loyal to the queen, but he was determined to send a message to her Whig advisors: that gray area could not be claimed, and exploited for political purposes, without a fight. Secure in his lifetime appointment as a Visitor, he dug in his heels. What had begun as a simple application for leave now threatened to become a legal and policy crisis, one that could ultimately influence the scope of Victoria's ability to rule.

THE LIMITED POWERS of the Crown, under the United Kingdom's constitution, are known collectively as the Royal Prerogative. These are the technical powers. The ones the monarch can actually wield are smaller still. For instance, the Prerogative gives monarchs the right to approve all acts of parliament, but by Victoria's reign that power had long since devolved into a rubber stamp: no sovereign had dared withhold approval for well over a century. It also grants the ruler personal immunity from all prosecution, making him or her, in a sense, literally above the law. But had Victoria begun openly committing crimes—mowing down pedestrians in her carriage, shoplifting at Covent Garden—she would have been quickly stripped of that immunity. It existed only in theory, not in application.

Hobart's contention was twofold. The dispensation was not, he argued, specifically within the queen's Prerogative powers. And if the language of the Prerogative was being interpreted so loosely that the queen could claim such power, then it was time for more specific language to hem in such abuses. He had a point. There was, strictly speaking, no exact precedent. Had Holman been a criminal, the matter would be clear-cut: the Prerogative gave the queen the power to pardon convicts. But he was guilty of violating not laws, but rules—the rules first set forth in Samuel Travers's 1726 will.

Victoria was not seeking to free Holman from the Naval Knights, only from its terms of membership. And if the queen could suspend an institution's standards of eligibility at will, that had potentially far-reaching implications. What if she wanted to install a nonartist in the Royal Academy of Arts, or a nonsurgeon in the Royal College of Surgeons? What if, heaven forfend, she wished to appoint a female Knight of the Garter?

Hobart's reasoning (and his willingness to argue loudly and publicly) carried the day. Victoria herself went mute on the matter, but Lord John Russell, her secretary of state, issued an official finding. He did not void the dispensation—that would have the appearance of backing down—but he declared it "no longer in force, unless it receives the sanction of the Visitors."

This was a face-saving way of killing it. Everyone knew no such sanction was forthcoming. Neither Lord Russell nor the queen wanted the dispute to go to court—they could very well lose, and trigger an overhaul of the entire Prerogative. At the beginning of her reign, the last thing Victoria needed was a perception that she was overstepping her authority. That could force her to set a more timid tone for years to come. Any plans for further intervention in the plight of the Blind Traveler were quietly dropped.

•　　　•　　　•

VICTORIA ABANDONED HOLMAN, but Holman did not abandon Victoria. He wrote to her, acknowledging "that doubts have since arisen respecting the right of your Majesty . . . to dispense with the obligation of any rules." But he also ventured to suggest another tack on the matter. Instead of giving him immunity from the rules of the Naval Knights, could she not modify the rules themselves? He was bold enough to submit language ready for insertion into the order's charter:

> That any Knight, whose state of health or whose infirmities require a Dispensation as to residence and attendance, may have such Dispensation direct from the Crown.

As a legal strategy, this was surprisingly astute. It deftly countered all of Hobart's objections, while exposing a crucial flaw in the organization of Travers College: the bylaws were not only unchanging, but unchangeable. The knights were expected to march perpetually to the instructions of a man now dead for over a century, with no recourse for adapting to the times. Samuel Travers's bequest spelled out many things, but one thing he'd forgotten was to spell out any set of rules for changing the rules.

If an institution had no internal means of modifying itself, then who should bear the responsibility for enacting changes when necessary? Holman cannily pointed to the Royal Charter. The order's official life dated from the moment that document was signed—which meant the Naval Knights of Windsor was, legally, a creation not of Travers but of the Crown. By extension, that meant the Crown had the creator's right of amendment.

It was an inspired bit of logic, particularly coming from a man whose debilitating illness was now, in the words of his doctors, "assuming a more alarming character." Whether Holman had legal guidance in drafting this proposal is unknown. The letter itself, written plaintively and without legalese, seems to suggest otherwise. It was not even drafted by a professional scribe but by the uneven hand of a sighted friend, a rare lapse in formality for a document intended for the eyes of the queen.

Victoria's counselors were quick to recognize not only the strengths but the political advantages of Holman's argument. It had the effect of expanding the Prerogative without looking like a power grab; it put forward a legitimate solution to an unaddressed need. Yet winning them over was only the beginning of the battle. The matter would have to be submitted to the courts, but not by the queen—she needed to avoid any further allegations of politicking by remaining as aloof as possible. It would be Holman's burden to act as plaintiff, to pursue the case in the High Court of Justice. The legal fees would have to come out of his pocket. He would even have to pay to track down and notify the surviving descendants of Samuel Travers, so that their opinion might be heard.

An aide to the secretary of state wrote a letter to Holman, instructing him in the steps of filing a formal lawsuit. Then, in a second letter, marked *Private*, he sounded a note of warning:

> *I am now directed by Lord John Russell to inform you, that you must follow your own course; but that he advises you to be very cautious and circumspect in what you do.*

It was sound advice. The Tories had swept the elections of 1837, and, much to the queen's distaste (she was, indeed, a secret Whig), she would soon be forced to accept a government dominated by that party. The Whig politicians who encouraged Holman to proceed did so as their own small act of farewell.

HOLMAN HAD HOPED for help in fighting the petty bureaucrats of Travers College. Now he was entangled in the most daunting bureaucracy of all, and the stakes had widened from winning his personal freedom to a redefinition of the powers of the Crown.

But he was on his own. Lord Russell was out of office, and, to make matters worse, his channel of private communication with the queen was no longer open. Doctor Clark had fallen victim to the reign's first scandal.

Lady Flora Hastings, one of the queen's ladies-in-waiting, was young, flirtatious, and daring. When, on a trip to Scotland, she shared a carriage with a man who was someone else's husband, tongues twittered. They twittered louder still a few months later, when her abdomen began to swell. Victoria sent in her physician for a diagnosis. Clark drew on his scanty knowledge of female physiology and announced that the unmarried woman was indeed pregnant—despite her adamant protests that she was still a virgin.

This was a monstrous scandal, but soon the outrage shifted to Clark himself. Lady Hastings demonstrated her innocence in the most extreme way possible: she died, of what proved to be a massive stomach tumor.

The grave mistake should have cost Clark his job, but firing him would have meant a public enquiry and further airing of dirty laundry. The press was already having a field day, calling him the "court physician with his cringing back." Victoria chose to keep him around, still holding the office but, for all practical purposes, a pariah. His reputation was damaged to the point that years later, when he finally resigned to launch a private practice, it almost collapsed for lack of patients.

Although his influence with the queen had disappeared, Clark was still able to help Holman by adding his voice to the chorus of physicians now raising alarms about Holman's health. In June of 1839, he examined his old friend and submitted a sworn testimony that "James Holman is fast sinking, and that change of scene and climate is absolutely necessary for his restoration."

This opinion was seconded by another of England's most prominent doctors, Peter Mark Roget, a colleague of Holman's in the Royal Society. He was blunter still, noting that the patient was notably emaciated, racked by violent spasms and "defective digestion," concluding that "unless the remedial measures . . . shall be speedily adopted the constitution of the said James Holman will soon be irreparably shattered." He prescribed a specific course of treatment, one that thankfully coincided with Holman's deepest desires:

> *The only chance remaining to the said James Holman of ultimate restoration to health would be afforded by a continual change of scene and of climate, together with the unrestrained exercise of his mental and physical powers prolonged for a period of at least three years.*

These medical assessments, from Fergusson, Clark, and now Roget, were far more than called-in favors. They were sincere diagnoses. Personal sympathies aside, three of the most prominent physicians in the nation would not take such firm stands—under oath and in the face of an escalating controversy—unless they honestly concurred. Mysterious as Holman's ailment was, the one seeming certainty was this: it was fueled by sedentary ways, and prolonged exposure to the familiar. The only known treatment was travel.

DESPITE DWINDLING HEALTH and finances, Holman pressed on with the case. There were setbacks—it was rejected by the Chancellor Secretary of Petitions on the grounds that it constituted a personal complaint against Hobart and Goodall. This required further argument that it was "a mere statement of facts, not impugning any one." If the trustees' own actions made them look ridiculous, that was not the fault of the plaintiff. The case was accepted on review, and slowly matters began to tilt in Holman's favor.

Their party's dominance in Parliament dictated that the prime minister should be a Tory, but Victoria kicked up enough of a fuss over the transition that Sir Robert Peel, the prime minister-designate, relented and withdrew. She was permitted to restore

Lord Melbourne, her original prime minister, an old family friend and a dyed-in-the-wool Whig. Back in office, Melbourne was in a position to nudge along the proceedings. He dispatched a letter to Baron Lyndhurst, who as Lord High Chancellor presided over both the House of Lords and the national judiciary:

> *I bring to your notice the case of Lieutenant Holman, a naval Knight of Windsor, whom you may perhaps have heard of as the "Blind Traveler." If, therefore, it would not be giving you too much trouble, would you be so good as to enquire . . . whether the Government have not the power to make a rule which shall give effect to Her Majesty's benevolent intentions, without subjecting Mr. Holman to the expense and delay of having the case brought in a Court of Law?*

Baron Lyndhurst was probably the prime minister's greatest political adversary. He was an impassioned Tory, given to unabashed obstructionism in the House of Lords and fiery speeches denouncing the evils of Whig ascendancy. But he was also a quirky, resolute individualist. Lyndhurst was a Bostonian by birth—in fact, he was the son of John Singleton Copley, the portraitist of Paul Revere, generally acclaimed as the greatest American painter of the colonial period. Trained as a painter himself, he had rebelliously declared that he would sooner head up the House of Lords than follow in his father's footsteps, then set about single-mindedly to do exactly that. He was an early advocate of women's rights, divorce reform, and the admission of Jews to Parliament (he had, in defiance of genteel society, married a Jewish woman).

Lyndhurst was, in other words, a man who trod his own path. Lord Melbourne, his old opponent, was gambling that he would empathize with Holman, and take up his cause. Melbourne knew his enemy. The Lord High Chancellor does not appear to have gone on record in favor of Holman—that would have been politically imprudent—but the case was quickly placed before one of his judges, who just as swiftly handed down a decision:

No doubt I should think, the object having been to grant Lieutenant Holman an indulgence, that indulgence having failed owing to a matter of form, that the Crown would be advised to carry into effect the intended indulgence by these means.

Holman had won. He was sicker and poorer than ever, but eight years of compelled confinement were indisputably at an end. The other Naval Knights wasted no time in piggybacking on his success, filing their own petition to grant them all a minimum of five months' freedom each year. They should have heaped Holman with praise for setting the precedent, but they could not. He was already gone.

Detail from Viennese map of "European Turkey"—
the Continental extent of the Ottoman Empire.

SIXTEEN

The Arrival of an English Traveler

FOUR YEARS LATER, a young Scotsman far from home had a memorable visitor.

At thirty-three, Andrew Archibald Paton was beginning to regret his career as a diplomat. Intelligent, meticulous, and adept at languages, he had committed the unfortunate error of becoming an expert field officer—too expert, in fact, to warrant pulling him out of the field. That meant a wearying procession of fact finding missions and minor functionary roles, each of which seemed to push him farther to the periphery of the world stage—aide de camp in the Egyptian mission, deputy assistant quartermaster general in Syria. His latest assignment could hardly be farther removed from the corridors of power. He was the acting consul general for Serbia, charged with monitoring conditions on the westernmost extent of the Ottoman Empire.

Taking stock of his post in Belgrade, the capital of Serbia, he wondered if it was too late to launch a second career, perhaps a literary one. He cut a fresh quill and began confiding to the page:

I have been four years in the East, and I feel that I have had quite enough of it for the present. Notwithstanding the azure skies, bub-

*bling fountains, Mosaic pavements, and fragrant narghiles, I begin
to feel symptoms of ennui, and a thirst for European life, sharp air,
and a good appetite, a blazing fire, well-lightened rooms, female society, good music, and the piquant vaudevilles of my ancient friends.*

As he quickly surmised, this small city on the upper reaches of
the Danube was even less visited by Westerners than it had been
in centuries past. The "high road to Constantinople" used to wend
through Belgrade, but now the steamship routes had rendered
that overland passage superfluous.

*No mere tourist would now-a-days think of undertaking the fatigu-
ing ride across European Turkey, when he can whiz past Widdin
and Roustchouck, and even cut off the grand tongue at the mouth
of the Danube, by going in an omnibus from Czernovoda to Kus-
tendgi; consequently the arrival of an English traveler from the interior, is a somewhat rare occurrence.*

In August of 1844, Paton was startled by just such an arrival.
While leaving the gates of the city, he noticed the approach of "a
strange figure, with a long white beard and a Spanish cap, mounted
on a sorry horse." He recognized the man at once.
"How do you do, Mr. Holman?" he said.
"I know that voice well."
"I last saw you in Aleppo." Before Paton could give his name,
Holman plucked it from memory. Their encounter in that Syrian
city was at least two years in the past.

*I then got him off his horse, and into quarters. This singular indi-
vidual had just come through the most dangerous parts of Bosnia
in perfect safety; a feat which a blind man can perform more easily
than one who enjoys the most perfect vision; for all compassionate
assist a fellow-creature in this deplorable plight.*

The next day, Paton walked with Holman through the town. At first, he kept up a steady stream of description, pointing out the public statues Holman could not touch, expounding on their history. Then, on the esplanade overlooking the river, Holman made an unusual request.

They came to a standstill. Holman stood straight and quiet. Paton placed his hands on the older man's shoulders and gently repositioned him, four times.

I turned his face to the cardinal points of the compass, successively explaining the objects lying in each direction, and, after answering a few of his cross questions, the blind traveler seemed to know as much of Belgrade as was possible for a person in his condition.

IN HIS LATEST years of absence from England, Holman had been a study in perpetual motion. From Malta he'd swept through the Ionian Islands, then on to the Greek mainland, across the Hellespont to Turkey, and over the border to Syria, then Beirut. Plunging eastward on to Al Qahirah, or Cairo, he paused just long enough to ready himself for the long, parched crossing of the Arabian Desert. That trek took him over the Sinai peninsula, to Al Arish and the threshold of the Holy Land, where he fell in among pilgrims at the climax of their pilgrimage.

Jerusalem, Bethlehem, Nazareth. Then another desert crossing, from Amman to Damascus. Next he trod the edges of the Adriatic Sea, tracing a rising arc up through northern Italy and into the Slavic lands. In Montenegro the ruling *vladika*, or prince bishop, welcomed him with a formal reception. Holman told Paton that the territory after Bosnia and Sarajevo was some of the roughest he'd encountered thus far, "nearly all forest, with here and there the skeletons of robbers hung up in chains."

This succinct accounting does no justice to the true exhaustive extent of Holman's wanderings. To properly trace his route, one must take a map of Europe, Africa, and the Middle East, and reduce it to a mass of scribbles. There were sightings of him in Tyre and Tripoli and Tunis and Trieste, in Alexandria and Antioch and Apulia and Anti-Lebanon. He was seen ascending Mount Sinai, thrusting his walking stick at the Well of Moses. He was spotted inside Saint Mark's Cathedral in Venice, "examining its various details, and ascertaining by the touch the most minute admeasurements."

A twenty-one-year-old American named Francis Parkman was visiting Sicily when he met Holman. "I walked home with him through the streets, admiring his indomitable energy," he eagerly recorded in his diary. "I saw him the next morning sitting on his mule . . . his strong frame, his manly English face, his gray beard and mustaches, and his sightless[ness] gave him a noble appearance in the crowd of wondering Sicilians about him."

Young Parkman had a very personal reason for his fascination. His own vision was "sadly impaired by some obscure trouble of the brain, which affected also the action of the heart and the control of the limbs." It was difficult for him to walk, and increasingly difficult for him to see. Like Holman's decades earlier, his presence on the Mediterranean was intended as a convalescence.

Francis Parkman would go on to become one of the most respected historians of the century, despite his condition, which progressed to the point of intermittent total blindness. Each time the darkness descended, he feared it would be permanent. The fear was blunted by memory of his brief acquaintance with the Blind Traveler.

HE WAS FIFTY-EIGHT years old, more of a commanding presence than ever, but the trials of traveling so far on so little funds had begun to show. He was, as Paton noted, riding a sorry horse. His well-worn suit of unadorned dark blue was now so out of date most observers would scarcely recognize it as a naval uniform. Technically, it no longer was: contemporary British lieutenants wore shiny-buttoned coats dripping with epaulets. Still, the acting consul general—who had himself walked from Naples to Vienna in his youth—couldn't help treating this slight acquaintance as both an old friend and a figure of awe.

Their time together would be brief, for Paton was preparing to embark on a journey of his own, an official reconnaissance tour of the borderlands. On the morning of his departure, there was a tapping on his door—Holman had come to bid him farewell. Soon they were joined by another man of letters: Sima Milutinovich, known as the "bard of the Balkans," the nation's greatest living poet.

When Milutinovich, "who looked upon his own journey to Montenegro as a memorable feat," realized he was in the presence of the celebrated Holman, he launched into transports of rapturous admiration. He had read of the Blind Traveler in the Augsburg *Gazette*, and considered him a marvel of the age. Shyly, "with a reverential simplicity," he begged Paton to convey a request. Might he have the honor, the exquisite honor, of kissing his beard?

> *Holman consented with a smile, and Milutinovich, advancing as if he were about to worship a deity, lifted the peak of white hairs from the beard of the aged stranger, pressed them to his lips, and prayed aloud that he might return to his home in safety.*

HOME IF HOLMAN COULD be said to still consider England home—was still very far away, and Holman took no pains to shorten the distance. The scribbling on the map continued: Bucharest, Transylvania, Hungary. In time, he was crossing his own path, returning to Austria and the environs of Vienna, places he had first explored two decades earlier, after his expulsion from Russia. He had long pursued a policy of never retracing his steps if he could help it, but now he discovered that time had rendered the territory sufficiently different, almost new. This was an Austria crisscrossed with the tracks of team-driven "horse railroad" lines. Vienna was bursting out of its seams, nearly twice the size of the city he'd known two decades earlier. He promptly moved on to the scenes of his first journey: Nice, Nîmes, Montpellier. If he learned the fate of the once fatally beautiful Clementine, now well into her forties, it is not recorded.

As he neared the Channel, there were a few disquieting signs that back in England, not everyone would wish to kiss his beard. It wasn't hard to detect an air of not-so-faint patronization in his encounters with other British travelers, as was soon the case in a hotel dining room in Lyons, in central France.

Thomas Noon Talfourd was a member of Parliament with literary leanings, and a close friend of Charles Dickens. In 1846, he was passing through France and Italy on his way to stay with Dickens in Switzerland, when a waiter approached him. A blind gentleman had heard the sound of English voices, and wondered if he might have the pleasure of conversing with a fellow countryman.

> *I went to him; and found a venerable man with a long beard, who introduced himself to me as "Mr. Holman, the blind traveler." He was, he said, on his way to Egypt, and averred that he experienced gratifications akin to those of travelers with eyes in his visits to celebrated places—that, in the vicissitudes of the atmosphere, and the feelings suggested by unseen objects, he perceived all the varieties of nature and art that they saw.*

This amused Talfourd to no end—a blind man piteously insisting his experience was equal to the sighted. What's more, upon learning that Talfourd would soon be squiring his family through Rome, this piquant character presumed to give him traveling advice.

"Go to Rome, my dear sir, in September, and you will die as surely as you now live," Holman said.

Talfourd was startled, but not so much as to let his reply go unlaced with sarcasm. "Why, I suppose, there are *some people* at Rome in September—and they do not *all* die—why may we not perchance escape?"

"Oh, no! You must not go to Rome." With the sounds of Talfourd's children in the background, Holman summoned as much authority as he could. "If you go, you will all die there—I am sure of it; go to Sicily—that is charming, delicious, divine; but Rome in September is death."

Talfourd, who thought the dialogue droll enough to record it, italics and all, declared himself "staggered by his prophetic emphasis" and made a quick exit, no doubt barely repressing a smirk. As he was later proud to report, he conducted his son and daughter to Rome forthwith, and "although we actually beheld the malaria rising, like an exhalation, from an opening of its great sewer, it harmed not us!" He might have struck a less derisive note had he known that the Blind Traveler was not conveying his own opinion but that of the former physician to the queen. A quarter of a century earlier, James Clark had warned Holman of "the injurious effects of the malaria arising from the Pontine marshes," and earnestly bade him to stay off the road to Rome at that time of year.

Holman, who had known several malaria victims in Rome, who had witnessed the death of hundreds from malaria and had almost died of it himself, finished his meal alone.

HOLMAN WAS DOUBTLESS sincere when he told Talfourd of his intent to return to Egypt, probably as the first stage of a deeper plunge into Africa or Arabia, but, in fact, his peregrinations were almost at an end. Just one month later—scarcely time to visit Vichy, Moulins, Macon, Chalons-sur-Saône, Dijon, Chalons-sur-Maine, Rheims, Saint, Quentin, Valenciennes, Lille, Dunkirk, Calais, and Bolougne—he at last boarded the Channel packet.

His pace had clearly not slackened, but there were financial realities to face. His royalties were long spent, and to explore the few portions of the planet still unfamiliar to him would require new reserves of cash. It was, he realized, time to work a fresh supply of carbonated paper through the Noctograph, to restore both his bank account and his literary standing in the public mind.

He had every reason to believe a new book would be eagerly received, since the mere fact of his return garnered coverage in the press. As the *Liverpool Mercury* trumpeted upon his arrival,

> *The celebrated blind traveler, Lieutenant Holman, returned to this country on Thursday week, after an absence of upwards of six years, during which time he visited Portugal and Spain, Algeria, and all the places in the Mediterranean, penetrated Egypt and Syria, crossed the desert to Jerusalem, and finally made an extensive tour through the least frequented parts of the southeast of Europe . . . as on all former occasions, this extraordinary man traveled perfectly alone. He has returned in perfect health and spirits.*

The notice was notable for what it did not contain. It was far from Holman's nature to boast. But somewhere in these peripatetic years, he had become the most accomplished traveler of all time.

LET US DISTILL the definition of *traveler* to its purest form. Not a sea captain or surveyor, someone whose passages and movements are a function of career. Not a merchant or diplomat, whose entrance into foreign cultures is purpose-driven. Let us apply it to those who venture forth on their own initiative, to their own itineraries, seeking, like Holman, only to "explore distant regions, to trace the varieties exhibited by mankind."

Nowadays, the term applies to almost all of us, at least at some point in our lives. The impulse toward the exotic fuels a significant portion of the global economy. It is the force that propels Tahitians to Texas, and vice versa. It crowds the lanes of Kathmandu with backpacks, compels a need for traffic management at the South Pole, and makes Prince Edward Island in the Canadian Maritimes a popular site for Japanese weddings.

But before technology simplified the transit of great distances into an act of leisure, very few could risk, or survive, vast and sustained journeying. For centuries, the world's most prolific traveler was thought to be the eponymous author of *The Travels of Sir John Mandeville*, written in French around 1357. The writer describes himself as an English knight bedridden by gout, then goes on to describe an incredible series of jaunts and encounters. Literally incredible—his lands are populated with phoenixes, with crocodiles crying over their prey, with "men whose heads did grow beneath their shoulders." It now seems likely that the travels were not only fictitious, so was the traveler; "Sir John Mandeville" was probably a device for amalgamating an anthology of far-flung, far-fetched tales.

As far as modern historians can determine, the true longstanding record was held by a man known variously as Shams ad-Din or Abu Abdullah Muhammad Ibn Battuta, who lived at the same time some medieval Frenchman was concocting Mandeville. Born in Morocco in 1304, Ibn Battuta left his native land at twenty-one and returned three decades later, whereupon he dictated to a scribe a reasonably accurate account of the entire Islamic world and much beyond. Not only had he completed the *hadj*, or sacred pilgrimage to Mecca, no less than seven times, he had ventured as far south as Ceylon, as far east as Peking, as far north as the Ukraine, and as far west as Spain. All told, Ibn Battuta's adventures by land and sea led him through approximately two dozen distinctly different cultures, and over approximately seventy-five thousand miles. To put that in perspective, his rough contemporary Marco Polo probably traveled a little more than fourteen thousand miles.

Ibn Battuta is deservedly remembered as history's greatest traveler prior to the age of steam. Holman's travels belong to that age but only to its infancy, when steam-powered vehicles were just emerging from novelty into practicality. He had taken steamboats into the interior of Australia, and from Carthage to Malta, but that was a minute fraction of his various routes. There is no record of his boarding any railroad, nor of him being in a place where a railroad could have taken him more than a very modest distance. The overwhelming preponderance of his travels were accomplished by the same means as Ibn Battuta's—on foot and on horseback, in whatever passed for a carriage or cart, and in vessels driven only by the wind.

As best as can be reconstructed, by October of 1846, when Holman stepped off the Channel packet, his travels totaled no less than a quarter of a million miles. While other contemporary, professional travelers, such as Cochrane, had racked up impressive mileages, none could even approach the achievements of the Blind Traveler. He could claim a thorough acquaintance with every inhabited continent, and direct contact with at least two hundred distinctly separate cultures. Of the handful of nations he hadn't passed through, many of them, like Japan or Vietnam, were "hermit states," where entrance was forbidden to Westerners, or at least to British nationals. Alone, sightless, with no prior command of native languages and with only a wisp of funds, he had forged a path equivalent to wandering to the moon.

SEVENTEEN

The Pleasure of His Intimacy

MANY THINGS WERE unchanged. His fellow knights were still grumbling their way up and down the Hundred Steps. His apartment was his to reclaim. Above, on the castle hill, the royal standard of Victoria Regina still flew. But other things had altered profoundly in his six years' absence.

Queen Victoria and her consort Prince Albert had been giddy honeymooners when he departed. Now they were the parents of five children. The queen had only just glimpsed her first locomotive (declaring it "a curious thing indeed"). Now she regularly departed from London on her royal railway carriage (complete with crown on the rooftop) or her royal steam yacht, the cozily named *Victoria and Albert*. Her words traveled even faster. In 1840, the world's first commercial use of electricity had been England's one telegraph line, only thirteen miles long; citizens paid a shilling for the novelty of transmitting a message, even when there was no one they knew on the other end to receive it. By 1846, the wires stretched out from London in a growing radius of almost a hundred miles, and the queen's address to Parliament was telegraphed to the public. That was something of a publicity stunt—the service was still too limited and expensive for general use—but the trend was clear.

Holman in old age, "much esteemed and loved."

Wire above, tracks below. The future of England and empire was being laid out in parallel lines.

Holman was untroubled by the rapidity of change. He'd always been more interested in newness than familiarity, and his studies at Edinburgh had thoroughly acquainted him with the principles of harnessing both electricity and steam. He took an active interest in the innovations of the day, becoming a regular, quietly attentive presence at the Royal Society, particularly during the *conversaziones*, members-only events in which the latest discoveries were both lectured upon and convivially discussed. It was among his fellow natural philosophers—or "scientists," as a new coinage went—that Holman received his most heartfelt welcome, and marks of real respect. Peter Mark Roget, one of the physicians who had testified on his behalf in his court case, was now the Society's secretary and a would-be author, immersed in the manuscript that would become *Roget's Thesaurus*. Among the younger members was Charles Darwin, who had published his own first book only two years earlier. He had a particular debt to pay to the Blind Traveler. In 1832, as a neophyte naturalist, Darwin had sailed to the isolated Cocos Islands in the southern Indian Ocean. Upon returning to England to write *The Voyage of the Beagle*, he'd found that Holman's *Voyage Round the World* already included an extensive report on this remote location, comprehensive enough to quote at length in his own text. They had plenty of notes to compare, both professional and personal: Holman was familiar with the HMS *Beagle*, and its captain, Robert Fitzroy, was an old friend. In fact, back in 1828, the two had celebrated Fitzroy's promotion to that command.

Almost all members of the learned society, eminent or otherwise, enjoyed their encounters with Holman. "As many among us can bear testimony," one would write, "he was a most cheerful and agreeable companion, full of information and anecdote on a great variety of subjects." Another colleague called him "patient, gentle and firm . . . beloved," concluding that "the character of Lieutenant Holman was eminently calculated to command respect and conciliate attachment."

J. P. Knight, an acclaimed professor of perspective at the neighboring Royal Academy of Art, asked him to sit for a portrait. The resultant canvas captures him as a lively raconteur, getting on in years but neither bent nor stiffened with age. His military bearing is still evident in his comfortable occupation of an overstuffed chair. His lips are slightly parted, his left hand risen in a gesture of emphasis. He is clearly telling a story.

YET OUTSIDE THE walls of the Royal Society, those stories were meeting with mounting indifference. Making the rounds of his former publishers—George Routledge; Smith, Elder & Company; George Whittaker; the House of Rivington—had become an exercise in cordial frustration. He had been a profitable author for most if not all of them, but the critical dismissal of *Voyage Round the World* had not faded from their memory. They no doubt greeted him with real warmth and listened attentively to his adventures, duly marveling at both the teller and the tales. But in no case did the admiration extend as far as an actual offer to bring those tales into print.

If anything, the public's willingness to accept a blind person writing authoritatively on almost *any* subject, had declined in his absence. It was now more negligible than ever. Since 1834, a new organization, the Indigent Blind Visiting Society, had become an increasingly high-profile charity, raising funds "to visit the blind in their own homes, relieving them and administering to them the consolations of sympathy and religion." Still reflecting the popular suspicion that blindness was somehow a punishment from God (a notion reinforced by the fact that syphilis was still a leading cause), their priority was spiritual. They provided Scripture readings and escorts to church services, but little in the way of financial assistance. While well-meaning, the IBVS promoted a deeply patronizing view of the blind, treating them as pitiable creatures, unenlightened in every sense. This was reinforced in the popular press. The previous Christmas, Charles Dickens had published the latest in his series of bestselling holiday-themed novellas, *The Cricket on the Hearth*. The plot's main engine of pathos was the plight of character Bertha Plummer, otherwise known simply as The Blind Girl. She lived in squalid poverty with her toymaker father Caleb, in a "little cracked nutshell" of a hovel. But Caleb, too tender-hearted to burden her with the truth, spun tall tales about their circumstances: the house was glorious, the clothes they wore fashionable, cruel acquaintances actually tender friends. She, of course, had no choice but to believe him utterly.

> *The Blind Girl never knew that ceilings were discoloured, walls blotched and bare of plaster here and there, high crevices unstopped and widening every day, beams mouldering and tending downward. The Blind Girl never knew that iron was rusting, wood rotting, paper peeling off; the size, and shape, and true proportion of the dwelling, withering away. The Blind Girl never knew that ugly shapes of delft and earthenware were on the board; that sorrow and faintheartedness were in the house; that Caleb's scanty hairs were turning greyer and more grey, before her sightless face.*

Despite such predominant, profoundly incorrect notions of what blindness meant, Holman had faith in the value of his work. But he also realized that publishers would be better swayed by a persuasive third party. He sought out a man well suited for the task: Robert Bell, a forty-six-year-old congenitally feisty Irishman, who would become his strongest champion and closest literary friend. Bell lived in Manor House, a stately home in the green and peaceful London suburb of Chiswick. It was a lunatic asylum.

Bell was not insane —just a freelance journalist and "miscellaneous writer" of anthologies, popular histories, and comic plays, supplementing his income by purchasing and operating a madhouse. It was a popular investment of the day. Care of the insane was a highly regulated industry, subject to the 1832 Madhouse Act and the Metropolitan Commission in Lunacy, but it was an easy enough business to run profitably, particularly in the case of Manor House, which specialized in clients of independent means, often with aristocratic pedigrees. Bell and his wife Elizabeth lived, genteelly enough, in the midst of sixteen licensed lunatics.

Warmhearted but contentious, Bell was a man born for causes, and no cause evinced more vigorous action than another writer in need. He was a director of the Royal Literary Fund, a charity administering assistance "to authors of merit and good character who may be reduced to distress by unavoidable calamities." While he was seemingly a perfect choice to act on Holman's behalf, his charitable background was, in fact, something of a drawback. The Royal Literary Fund doled out its funds in secret, to maintain the dignity of the writers it was helping. That meant that from the publishers' perspective, the first sign that an author had become a hard-luck case was the fact that Robert Bell had taken up an interest in his career. For Holman—who didn't need charity, just connections—an association with Bell may have proven more hindrance than help.

On the first anniversary of his return to England, the popular magazine *People's Journal* prominently featured a profile of "Lieut. Holman, The Celebrated Blind Traveler." Its pseudonymous author ("An African") declared himself a longstanding admirer of this man of "indomitable will, combined with a large portion of good solid common sense." But while the piece, accompanied by a full-page engraving adapted from the recent J. P. Knight portrait, was clearly celebratory in spirit, it could not resist painting its subject as a faintly comical character. Its most vivid depiction was of Holman in Malta, sniffing in wait for his elderly servant and calling him a "dirty sneaking little rascal." And even when doling out praise, it betrayed what had come to be an overriding sentiment: "Lieutenant Holman must be considered one of the most remarkable men of his age."

His age, not *our modern age*. As the *People's Journal* made quite clear, Holman now had an aura of anachronism.

THE RAILWAYS REACHED Windsor in 1849. It had been something of a race. Approaching from different directions, two firms—the Great Western and the Windsor, Staines & Richmond company, or WS&N—had rushed to build their tracks across the Berkshire ground and on trestles over the Thames, until they extended to the very perimeter of the chalk hill of Windsor Castle. Each opened impressive stations just a few months apart. The WS&N's terminal, complete with private entrance for the queen, arose in red brick directly across from Travers College, and the Naval Knights had something else to complain about. Their intended life of quiet devotion, never too devoted, was now also hardly quiet. Both routes to the castle, Thames Street and the Hundred Steps, had to be shared with the ruckus of passengers and porters. Soot settled on the windowpanes, in the garden, everywhere.

Holman was more discomfited than the other knights. The grounds now had a high wall to block their view of the trains and retain some privacy, but for him, the wall only slightly softened the new sounds he heard around the clock: steam in compression and escape, the roar of open boiler doors, the chuff of coal shovels, the thumps of baggage and cargo.

A few years earlier, a friend recorded Holman's confidence that his voyages still continued, after a fashion, in his dreams, "that often, when first waking in the morning, he forgot in what part of the world he was." Now the soundscape fixed him instantly in a sort of limbo: on the periphery of the journeys of others, neither arriving nor departing.

HOLMAN TOOK ADVANTAGE of the railroad to spend more time in London than ever. He was an unusual sight on the city

streets, not only for his jarring contrast of naval uniform and tapping cane, but for his beard. In time, most proper Victorian men
would sport a full set of whiskers, but at the moment, the dominant fashion was for clean-shaven faces, interspersed with the occasional mustache. Described as one "that would have done credit to
the Chief Rabbi of the Jews," his beard had not been a conscious
affectation. Back in 1827, after Fernando Po, he'd simply stopped
shaving because lather, hot water, and unrusted razors were too
often in short supply. In one Royal Society *conversazione* hosted
by the marquis of Northampton, his fellow natural philosophers
were not above staging a small spectacle at his expense. One of the
few who "fancifully adopted the same patriarchal style" of facial
hair was the geriatric James Ward, once a respected painter of animal scenes, forced to abandon his profession by age and failing
eyesight. William Jerdan, the editor of the *Literary Gazette* (which
had long ago favorably reviewed Holman), noticed both men and
could not resist the symmetry. As he recalled the scene,

> Beards had not come into fashion yet, and the two were alone in
> their glory. Knowing them both familiarly, I took an opportunity
> to introduce them to each other, and as one was blind and the other
> could not see, advised the cultivation of a further intimacy by the
> mutual stroking of beards—a ceremony they performed with hearty
> laughter, and to the no small amusement of a little circle of admir-
> ing spectators.

There was little chance of hurting Holman's feelings. Everyone
knew his appetite for humor, and his far from self-serious nature.
He was, as Jerdan acknowledged, a phenomenon of conviviality, a
deeply agreeable soul.

> In his conversation he was lively and interesting; under all circum-
> stances, accommodating and good-natured. He was consequently
> much esteemed and loved by those who enjoyed the pleasure of his

intimacy, and met with a mingled feeling of sympathy and respect from general society.

ESTEEMED AND LOVED as he was, the presence of the feminine was slowly slipping from his life. There was little room for striking up new female friendships in the all-male worlds of Travers College and his London scientific circles, and a new sense of Victorian propriety had brought about the rising social segregation of the sexes. In Georgian England, an evening of mixed company could remain mixed without stigma; Holman had been as welcome to relax among the ladies as among the men. Now he was likely to be whisked away the instant dinner was concluded, into an exclusively masculine enclave where brash, loud voices and (even more dismayingly) cigars and pipes held sway.

Any dreams of advancing from flirtation to courtship, of establishing an enduring bond, were now also part of the past. Holman's failure to marry, particularly at the height of his fame, must be seen as a conscious choice—had he set his mind to matrimony, it's hard to imagine him not achieving it—even though the long-standing taboo against intermarriage of the blind meant that he, like François Huber, would have had to win the heart of a sighted woman. But supporting a wife would be a precarious matter, especially since marriage would force his resignation from the Naval Knights of Windsor. And there was the inescapable fact of his unique condition, which still seemed to respond only to frequent immersions in the unfamiliar.

He still embarked on new journeys, but within the range of his dwindling funds. He wandered through rural Scotland, traveling as far as the Scilly Islands in the rough North Sea. He ventured to Paris, then back again.

HIS AURA OF anachronism grew stronger with each passing year. By 1851, if Holman's writings were mentioned at all, it was

by means of insulting another writer. That was the year an anonymous critic in *The Living Age* panned the politician Lord Holland's
memoir *Foreign Reminiscences*, casting the withering aspersion that
it should "claim only its proper place on the same shelf with the
descriptive tours of Mr. Holman, the Blind Traveler."

Worse still was the renewed, and now public, patronization of
Thomas Noon Talfourd, the man who had disdained Holman's
earnest warnings against exposing his family to malaria. Talfourd's
own travel book, *Vacation Rambles*, had sold well enough to warrant a sequel, so he wrote *Supplement to Vacation Rambles*, based on
his notes of a journey now eight years in the past. To pad out the
anecdote of their encounter in Lyons, he took the trouble to read,
and weigh in on, at least some of Holman's books. His verdict was
airily dismissive, both of "Mr. Holman's felicities as a phenomenon" and "as a workman-like author."

> I wish his practical intuition may be as real as his belief in it . . . but
> the works of "the blind traveler" do not prove it. They are elaborate
> accounts of countries he has visited, compiled with industry and
> care; but they are such as may be written without either visions or
> a miracle . . . For what aspects of land and sea and sky, exquisitely
> various in each momentary being of light and shadow, does one epi-
> thet often stand! What virtual representation of a thousand things
> may one good word comprehend in its duty!

Talfourd had considerable influence in the publishing world.
He was a bosom friend of Charles Dickens, who had dedicated *The
Pickwick Papers* to him. As a member of Parliament, he'd drafted Britain's first international copyright law, giving publishers the right to
quash pirated foreign editions of their work. Coming from him,
this sort of open derision could prudently be read as the death
knell of a career. It was a sign of Bell's loyalty and tenacity that he
did not wash his hands of the Blind Traveler. It was a sign of Holman's optimistic faith that he not only continued to compile the

manuscript of his most recent travels, but also launched a second, even more ambitious work.

"Perhaps a time may come when I shall be enabled to resolve the history of these inward associations into a more definite and tangible shape," Holman had written in *Voyage Round the World*, referring to the world that only he knew. Not the one he'd interpreted for public consumption by a sighted readership, but the more complex one of his sensory experience. For the first time, he wrote in forthright detail about both the world that blindness had closed to him and the one it opened up. The work took shape as an autobiography. He struggled to recall the name of his teacher at the Exeter day school, finally describing her only as "an old woman." He told the story of Laurence Hynes Halloran's scandalous flight from Alphington Academy, and the subsequent appeal to John Graves Simcoe. He recounted proudly his three bold petitions to Lord Bridport, and his years on the North American station. He described the failure of his joints, of his eyes, of his doctors, of his own medical education. Then he retold the stories of his travels, this time more frankly, from his unique perspective. There was much to add. As he had explained in *Voyage Round the World*:

> All the transitions following upon travels of many years, are as fresh to me as if they were but of recent occurrence: and I can recall with ease the most minute personal events, dates, and names, that lie scattered through the whole. Indeed, my recollection is so strong of every thing I have witnessed, that I believe I could orally recount, without reference to my diary, the entire of my wanderings from first to last.

The year of Talfourd's attack, 1851, was the year the English Channel Submarine Telegraph Company ran its wires underwater to the Continent. They marked the occasion with a special salute to the Duke of Wellington—a cannon in Dover, fired by remote control in Calais. It was the year of London's Great Exhibition, held in a new, sparkling Crystal Palace of soaring steel and more than a million square feet of glass. Over six million flocked to view the marvels of the Industrial Revolution on triumphant display: a Jacquard loom, a mechanical reaper, an envelope machine. Their overarching sentiment was less of wonder than satisfaction, of the certainty growing to smugness that the British Empire dominated both the world and its future. There were still a few blank spots on the maps of the globe—Africa's deepest interior, the North and South Poles—but the great era of exploration had ended.

That year marked the final turning point of Holman's literary ambitions. Contemporary audiences were resoundingly less interested in marveling at earthly variety than taming it. A blind traveler was not a phenomenon, but a joke. He diligently kept to his Noctograph, but now he was clearly writing for future generations, for posterity.

IN THE SPRING of 1852, he went abroad once more, tramping through Norway and Sweden. It's tempting to conclude that he hoped to get another book out of the journey. A Scandinavian travelogue had launched the career of another novelty author, a widow named Ida Louise Pfeiffer, who was now setting out to become the first solo female traveler to circumnavigate the world (the route she was taking bore a strong resemblance to Holman's). It's also true that this was the shortest route to Arctic latitudes, and the home of the Lapps, Europe's last indigenous nomadic culture, still only sketchily studied. But, in truth, his motivations were likely less ambitious: Norway and Sweden completed his list. There was now no European country he hadn't thoroughly explored, or, for that matter, any country in that quadrant of the globe.

That same year, a cuttingly ironic honor issued from America. In upstate New York, two advocates for the education of the blind, one of whom was blind himself, compiled and self-published the inspirational tome *Beauties and Achievements of the Blind*. It was an anthology of the lives and works of the blind throughout history, from Homer and Ossian (the Celtic bard, also traditionally blind, perhaps an incarnation of the same myth) through John Milton and the Irish musician Turlough O'Carolan. There was a chapter on the naturalist Huber and his bees. And there was a chapter on "A Celebrated Blind Traveler . . . a sketch of whose life we have the honor of publishing for the first time in this country, together with some excerpts from his writings."

There followed a breathless recounting of Holman's captivity in Russia, a condensation of his musings on female charms (and his ability to perceive them), and an appreciation of "the exquisite delight with which his inner vision drank in scenes of beauty." While sincere in their desire to find him an American audience at last ("We may, at some future time, favor the reading public in this country with Mr. Holman's entire work"), the anthologists made an unfortunate assumption: that the Blind Traveler was already dead. Their biography reads as a eulogy.

It is to be regretted that Mr. Holman did not give to the world more of his own observations and reflections . . . Our author's peculiar situation and comparative helplessness might have opened up to him an endless field of useful labor. We are, however, not disposed to find much fault with the course Mr. Holman pursued. His writings have amused and interested the public, and have gained for their author a high character in the literary world.

HOLMAN DID NOT yet belong to the ages—he was, in fact, working hard to give the world as much of his observations and reflections as possible. But time was not a commodity to be wasted. After returning from Scandinavia, he eliminated his Windsor-London commute, not relinquishing his Travers College apartment but establishing a boardinghouse in the city as his chief residence.

Those who knew him were startled at his choice of neighborhood. Even given his financial limitations, there were far more respectable cheap establishments than that of Miss Clementina Bourne, numbers 10 & 11 in the shallow lane called Crutched Friars. With an almost audible sniff of disapproval, one friend wrote, "nor can I imagine what took him into that quarter."

Crutched Friars was on Tower Hill, in the shadow of the Tower of London on the city's eastern extreme. It was far from the Strand publishing houses and literary coffeehouses of Soho, and further still from the Westminster addresses of Royal Academy and the Linnean Society. Tower Hill was, frankly, a notoriously dodgy neighborhood. In *The Old Curiosity Shop*, Charles Dickens underscored the marginality of the villain Daniel Quilp by giving him a Tower Hill address. It was on the fringes of the raucous, near-lawless district called Ratcliff Highway (after the main thoroughfare), where respectable society ventured only to seek a covert thrill. Street life there had a distinctly nautical flavor, thanks to the proximity of the Pool of London, the terminus of merchant shipping up the Thames. One writer of the time, a correspondent for Dickens's magazine *Household Words*, affected a rakish tone when describing what happens "when I emerge on Tower Hill":

> *A row of foreign mariners pass me, seven abreast: swarthy, ear-ringed, black-bearded varlets in red shirts, light-blue trousers, and with sashes round their waists. Part of the crew of a Sardinian brig, probably. They have all their arms round each other's necks; yet I cannot help thinking that they look somewhat "knifey," "stilettoey." . . . were you to put an indefinite quantity of rum into them, they would put a few inches of steel into you.*

Another anonymous Londoner conveyed his slumming experiences by lacing indignation with genuine fear:

> *Either a gin-mad Malay runs a much [amok] with glittering kreese, and the innocent and respectable wayfarer is in as much danger as*

the brawler and the drunkard; or the Lascar, or the Chinese, or the
Italian flash their sea knives in the air, or the American "bowies" a
man, or gouges him, or jumps on him, or indulges in some other of
those innocent amusements in which his countrymen delight. Day
by day we are horrified and disgusted—night by night the "shrill
edged shriek" of a woman "divides the shuddering night." Where
are the police?

Seedy and boisterous as it was, its appeal to Holman can be discerned in the jumble of nationalities mentioned: *Sardinian, Malay, Lascar, Chinese, Italian, American.* In 1856 alone, a total of 826 merchant marine vessels, hailing from all quarters of the globe, docked by day in the Pool of London. Their crews were roaring through Tower Hill by nightfall, dropping months of pay in the beer shops, pubs, and "houses of infamy," chattering, slurring, and singing in dozens of languages and dialects. Close by were opium dens, for those who had acquired the habit in the Far East. For homesick Yankees, tattered panoramas of the American landscape, painted on reels of canvas, unspooled each night in the penny theaters.

In short, Tower Hill was a highly irregular home for a gentleman of scientific and literary standing. But seedy and dangerous as it was, it amply fed an appetite for the exotic. If he could no longer afford grand forays out into the world, at least he could let the world come to him.

HOLMAN STILL HAD the power to astonish. One day he received an invitation to dine with an old friend, a former navy messmate visiting London and staying in a fashionable hotel. They made plans to meet in the hotel's large and busy restaurant, and the friend was already seated against the dining room's far wall when he noticed Holman entering, alone. Watching him across the bustling room from the seclusion of a booth, the friend whispered to a companion, "Be quiet; see what he will do."

They sat in a conspiratorial silence. It seemed like a case of mistaken identity when the spare, bearded, elderly man "walked up past several tables, as if blessed with the clearest of sight." But he stopped at the proper booth, and "softly put both his hands on that where they were seated."

It was uncanny. "There was no voice here," the friend recalled, "and it is impossible to account for an act so closely resembling the highest animal instinct." It was, he declared, nothing less than a demonstration of "second sight." Patiently, Holman explained that where others heard noise, he heard a rich matrix of sounds he could comprehend simultaneously. It was no trouble to extract even a faint whisper from the matrix of a crowded room, and he knew "see what he will do" pertained to him, since he recognized his friend's voice, even though he hadn't heard it in at least forty years. His acoustic sense of space was precise enough to pinpoint the table. Navigating the busy restaurant with unhesitating confidence required a bit more concentration, but he knew he was being watched. He couldn't resist the challenge.

Most evenings were not so dramatic. As another friend was surprised to find, the Blind Traveler had acquired a taste for quiet domesticity. On nights when there were no *conversaziones* at the Royal Society, Holman left his Tower Hill boardinghouse and walked a few blocks north to one of the district's few pockets of demi-respectability, a cluster of townhouses called America Square. There, Dr. Andrew Holman, his surgeon cousin, lived in rented quarters with his wife, Louisa, and their four daughters— Mary, Louisa, Edith, and Ellen, all in their twenties, all destined to never wed. With his abiding appreciation of feminine company, Holman was a welcome, fussed-over presence in their home. Evenings usually culminated in a few relaxing board games played by the fire, with Holman memorizing the position of each piece. The friend affectionately described the scene.

And so the traveler who had traversed the globe under circumstances
of unexampled difficulty, solaces the evenings of his life-days, when
not otherwise engaged, with the vicissitudes of backgammon in his
cousin's home.

HE WAS STILL a traveler. But the excursions dwindled in fre-
quency and scope, until they became occasional, recuperative forays to Bath, to Devonshire and—most refreshing of all—to the
nearest foreign shore. If you had wandered through the coastal
town of Bolougne-sur-Mer, just across the Channel in northern
France, you might have encountered an elderly military gentleman pacing in a similar direction, authoritatively tapping a cane.
If your voice held a hint of distant origins—if you spoke Quebe-
cois French, or Portuguese with a Brazilian lilt, or English with an
American accent—the gentleman was likely to veer closer, pay his
respects, and do his best to launch into a conversation. If he introduced himself as the Blind Traveler, he would not wait for a mark
of recognition in response. These days, he expected none.

You'd notice he was blind, of course. If you were particularly solicitous, he'd humor you by letting you link your arm in his.
But as he fell into an alongside step you'd be more struck by how
wholeheartedly he listened, how easily you found yourself pouring out stories—your origins, your travels, the news of your homeland. When he parted ways, he'd do so apologetically. He had to
catch the ferry for England, then the London train.

In 1857, even the day trips stopped. Then Holman disappeared
from the chambers of the Royal Society, and, soon after, from the
sight of his friends altogether. They pondered the significance of
his absence, knowing both his lifelong health issues and his pen-
chant for sudden, unannounced departures. Inquiries were made
at Tower Hill, and the report came back: Holman was still a ten-
ant of Miss Clementina Bourne, but he was "secluding himself
completely from all society, occupying himself wholly in writing."

He'd chosen to channel all energies into his autobiography, which now had a working title *Holman's Narratives of His Travels*. Possessing, in the words of one friend, a "very natural longing for fame beyond the grave," he'd come to believe this was the document that would, in time, fix his place in history. His other books, now long out of print, had been an attempt to ply a trade; these pages were his legacy, and he was filling them with scenes drawn vividly from his photographic memory ("whatever I retain, I retain permanently").

As the work progressed, the exertion began to show. Those who kept tabs on him later blamed the intensity of this period for "materially injuring his health." But it is difficult to imagine that Holman's decline was prompted by fervent writing—rather, the other way around.

In the last weeks of July 1857, Parliament was debating the possibility of building a canal in Suez, linking the Mediterranean and the Red Sea. A few miles down the Thames, a battered old warship called the HMS *Agamemnon* was being loaded with an unprecedented cargo: a strand of seven copper wires, wrapped in gutta-percha, hemp, and yarn, all overwound in iron wire and wrapped on giant spools.

It was enough submarine telegraphic cable to reach halfway across the Atlantic, where the *Agamemnon* planned to meet the USS *Niagara*, the largest ship in the American navy, reeling out a similar length from the opposite direction. The Old World and the New would be bridged with a single splice.

In Crutched Friars Street, 70-year-old James Holman, R.N., K.W., F.R.S., laid down his stylus, and drew one last sheet of carbonated paper from his Noctograph. His life's work was complete, ready to be entrusted to the care of Robert Bell. But the triumph was tempered with the certainty that he was now indisputably ill, and weakening.

The strength flew from him quickly. On Tuesday, July 28, less than a week after finishing his manuscript, the Blind Traveler's exquisite sense of the world dimmed, then departed. The most restless man in human history was finally at rest.

•   •   •

HIS PASSING WAS not reported in the popular press. There was no official mourning at Windsor, despite his entitlement to a Saint George's funeral (an occasion that usually prompted both the Naval Knights and the Military Knights to dust off their best uniforms). If there was a memorial service for him at all, in London or elsewhere, no record of it survives. It was left to Andrew Holman to make the arrangements, and he quietly buried his cousin in Highgate Cemetery, a recently opened cemetery on the city's outskirts.

Highgate would come to be known as the Victorian Valhalla. Baron Lyndhurst, the American-born lord chancellor, would join him there, as would such luminaries as George Eliot, Michael Faraday and, most famously, Karl Marx. At the time Charles Dickens was maintaining a family plot on the same grounds, which he hoped to occupy himself (though he assumed, correctly, that fame would reroute him to Westminster Abbey). It was a sprawling, peaceful, partially forested place, even in 1857 a popular site for a mildly morbid afternoon's ramble. Mausoleums, obelisks, and other ornate testaments to eternal memory were rapidly sprouting up, so much so the cemetery had recently doubled in size. Here the art of mourning through marble was reaching new heights. In addition to an army of dolorous angels, there were displays of professional success (a bookseller's tombstone in the shape of a book), commemorative statues (complete with sleeping pets), even an Egyptian Avenue with exotic-themed decor. Holman's grave was conspicuous in its simplicity. Only a modest headstone marked the Blind Traveler's final destination.

The parting wishes of his will were carried out. The mass of manuscripts went to Robert Bell, in his Chiswick madhouse, "as a token of my regard." This was intended as much more than a souvenir—Holman was anointing Bell, already his literary executor, as his primary heir. The writings were not just entrusted to him but given outright, a strong financial motivation to see them eventually published. The oil portrait of Holman in China, painted by Chinnery, was bequeathed to the Royal Society. A handful of friends were given mementos: his Noctograph, his naval sword. There was, curiously, no disposition made for the unique collection he'd compiled from his travels, which lay dusty and uncatalogued back in Windsor. The Naval Knights awarded Holman's apartment in Travers College to one Lieutenant Thomas Salkeld, late of the HMS *Undaunted*. It was probably his task to decide what to do with an indigenous model of an Arctic dogsled, a Roman-era mosaic from Pompei, and a stuffed menagerie that included a Siberian flying squirrel and a white baboon.

There were a handful of obituaries. The one in *Zoology*, the proceedings of the Linnean Society, was notable for its valiant attempt to tally just the major population centers Holman had visited. It is exhausting simply to read, running on for four pages, petering out just shy of a four-hundredth destination. The *Gentleman's Magazine* struck a more emotional note, bidding farewell to Holman but looking forward to seeing his final works in print.

> *His last employment was in preparing for the press his final journals, which experience and matured observation had rendered more valuable than any of his former records of travel. The whole of these journals, completed, and a large mass of miscellaneous papers, are in the hands of his friends, and it is to be hoped that they will be given to the public, accompanied by an adequate biography, of undoubtedly one of the most remarkable men of our time.*

The hope was not fulfilled.

NINE YEARS LATER, William Jerdan—the man who had encouraged Holman to engage in mutual beard-stroking—was compiling an anthology of his personal acquaintances, to be titled *Men I Have Known*. It occurred to him that the Blind Traveler would be an interesting character to include, although he admitted that "circumstances led to my seeing little of Holman for several years prior to his death." The eighty-five-year-old author published a biographical sketch in *Leisure Hour* magazine, wondering aloud about the "journals and much literary material in the hands of his executors and relatives; but of these nothing farther has been heard."

Having read the sketch, Robert Bell stepped forward from his asylum to explain. He'd given it his best effort, but had "found no encouragement in the trade for fulfilling this hope or promise." After several years of buttonholing uninterested publishers, Bell had finally given up.

When including Holman in his anthology, Jerdan added a coda eulogizing not the man, but the unpublished work. He concluded that "probably it has gone to rest for ever, even for partial realization."

The only known photograph of Holman,
undated but probably taken in the last year of his life.

EIGHTEEN

Raise the Soul to Flame

"THIS IS WHERE he would have walked," my guide says. "Right down through here."

Thousands of tourists wend through the public-access portions of Windsor Castle each year. I had expected to queue up and join them, but Jude Dicken, assistant archivist for Saint George's Chapel, is demonstrably kind to overawed, jet-lagged Americans. She moves aside a length of chain and takes me on an impromptu tour of the castle as James Holman had known it.

He could navigate these corridors today, without a moment's hesitation. Little has changed in the nearly two centuries since his first climb up the Hundred Steps. Those stone stairs still rise up the hill, and through the castle walls to the Canon's Cloister. From there a covered passageway leads past wooden buildings built half a millennium ago. A few more steps take us to a peaceful, arcaded quadrangle built of limestone block, adjacent to the chapel. Here is the only difference he would have noticed: the arcade echoes a little differently now, as much of the limestone has been supplanted by marble. The task of commemorating the dead has spread to the chapel's perimeter, and the closer we get the more we are surrounded by memorial plaques, busts, and niches.

Although neither one of us mentions it, this tour is something of a consolation prize. The Archives of Saint George's Chapel are also the archives of the Naval Knights of Windsor, but of the order of the Seven Gentlemen there is precious little to preserve. They offer up all that remains with a slight air of apology—a boxful of papers, mostly attendance records and scattered correspondence. The institution was formally dissolved in 1892, after decades of Dissent had rendered it permanently dysfunctional.

The other knights had not been as patient as Holman. When their petition for five months' leave each year was denied, they divided into two camps: those who left anyway, in defiance of the rules, and those who stuck around to grumble. Of the absentees, many did their best to beat Holman's record for truancy. Knight Fredrick Henslow stayed abroad for nine years, on the strength of doctor's notes attesting that it would "not be prudent to attempt the voyage to England." The last of these excuses was postmarked from Tasmania.

Those who remained at Windsor found many things to argue about. The declining condition of the building, the less than friendly common table and, always, the compulsory attendance at chapel. After years of what the Visitors characterized as "wretched and long-standing disputes," a policy of quiet attrition was put into effect. When one member died, there was no longer an effort to recruit a new one.

The remaining Naval Knights were pleased with the thinning ranks, because it accordingly increased their proportion of benefits from Samuel Travers's endowment. But it also spelled the inevitable death of the order. By 1890, the Seven Gentlemen were four in number, and the Admiralty was drafting a bill to dissolve Travers College.

In keeping with their capacity for quarrel, the members strongly resisted dissolution. Three were eventually placated, with financial settlements. But Cecil Sherlock Wale Willis, the very last Naval Knight held out to the end. On January 20, 1893, a squad of policemen descended on the building, and read out a warrant of eviction. They forced open a window, and overcame "resistance from within"—Willis and a lone loyal housekeeper. Then it was over.

The one place I most fervently wish to visit is Holman's apartment in Travers College, but Assistant Archivist Dicken cannot conduct me there today. Immediately after the order's ignominious end, the grounds were taken over by Saint George's School, the centuries-old academy for the boys of the chapel choir. The student body has long since expanded to include nonchoristers of both sexes, most notably members of the royal family. At present two of the latest generation of Windsors are matriculating there, the Princesses Beatrice and Eugenie, the youngest grandchildren of the queen. For security reasons, I am not allowed to watch them—or any of the more than three hundred boys and girls, aged three to thirteen—as they bound noisily, happily up the Hundred Steps toward chapel.

Despite its musical roots and aristocratic aspects, the school honors its previous occupants, in a small way. A nautical flair has been retained, becoming a beloved part of the school's culture. The bell in the cupola is transplanted from the HMS *Saintes*. The classrooms and dormitories are named after the great sailors of the Empire: Drake, Raleigh, Nelson. As recently as 1974, each student belonged to competitive subsets named after Royal Navy ships. The pupils of the *Revenge* group would vie with the *Victory* and *Vindictive* units for academic distinction.

Late at night, the children pass on a story of the ghost that haunts the grounds. They've awarded him a posthumous promotion—he's called the Admiral, an exalted title for a specter who in life would almost certainly have been a lieutenant. Although he particularly troubles the disobedient, this appears not to be his primary purpose. He is described as a clanking, creaking old man, not particularly overjoyed to be sharing his home with children, but determined nonetheless to never leave Travers College.

I content myself with a glimpse of colonnades and yellow brick through the hedges. If the Admiral exists, he sounds likely to be the long-lingering Cecil Sherlock Wale Willis, or another of the twilight Knights. He is most certainly not Holman, the man who fought hardest to free himself from these walls, the man who took joy in quoting Oliver Goldsmith's "The Traveler"—a poem in which the title character gently pities those who choose comfort over experience, who bind themselves to place:

> *Unknown those powers that raise the soul to flame,*
> *Catch every nerve, and vibrate through the frame.*
> *Their level life is but a mouldering fire,*
> *Unquenched by want, unfanned by strong desire.*

IT IS EXCEEDINGLY difficult to invoke the spirit of the Blind Traveler anywhere in Great Britain. His boyhood home, the apothecary shop at the hub of Exeter, has long disappeared, although the family business survived, as Holman & Ham, until the early twentieth century. Also gone is Miss Clementina Bourne's boardinghouse on Tower Hill, a victim of renovation in the wake of the Blitz bombs of World War II. The area is now the skyscraper-encrusted heart of the city's financial district.

Even Holman's final resting place conveys only the faintest sense of the man. Highgate Cemetery, which fell into decades of disrepair—it was the setting for several low-budget horror films in the sixties and seventies—is now lovingly tended by a nonprofit organization that has done much to restore it to its former dignity. But the vines and underbrush grow quickly on the Blind Traveler's grave. Despite its nearness to the main path, it is easily missed. Andrew Holman's limited funds could pay for only a stub of a headstone. There are no decorations, only these words:

> In Memory of
> The Celebrated Blind Traveler,
> Lieut. James Holman, R.N., F.R.S., &c,
> Of Travers College, Windsor
> Who died 28th July, 1857, age 70 years.

Holman would have been disappointed in the stone. Not because it lists none of his publications and achievements—or even because whoever wrote it appears to have been ignorant of the date of his birth. A lover of the epigram, of the apt quotation, he would have wanted the inscription to end with a last blaze of poetry. *Some difficulties meet, full many. I find them not, nor seek for any.*

WHAT WAS THE fate of Holman's unpublished writings? After their delivery to Robert Bell, the trail immediately goes cold. They are not among his surviving papers, nor does it appear that Andrew Holman's family reclaimed them at any point. As early as 1890, scholars were posting notices in *Notes & Queries*, the Oxford journal of literary investigation, noting that the obituaries of the Blind Traveler made reference to numerous documents he'd left behind. "Were these journals ever published?" they asked plaintively. "Where are the miscellaneous papers?"

Even under the best of circumstances, the long-term, intact survival of a large collection of writings is largely a matter of chance. But Holman's work had two unique factors that may have accelerated its obliteration. The first was Mr. Bell's vocation as a madhouse-keeper.

Bell was clearly a believer in art as therapy, for almost all that remains of the Manor House as an institution are a number of sketches and writings created by the patients, archived in the Wellcome Library in London. When he died in 1867, he left behind a multitude of papers—his own, those of his literary charity cases, and these productions of the deranged. Someone had to winnow down the piles. If Holman's autobiography had been discovered in these heaps, it would have been easy for the casual reader, glancing at these pages with their tortured script, to mistake them for a far-fetched work of fiction, or the fevered imaginings of a delusional soul.

The other factor was the Noctograph. Holman appears to have relied increasingly on his writing machine in his last years, when finances minimized his access to hired scribes. He'd been among the first to use the device, and seemingly one of the very last as well; the invention had ceased manufacture decades earlier. How, then, did he keep a supply of the "carbonated paper" necessary for its operation?

That product, now known as carbon paper, had begun to come into common use on its own, as a cheap and easy means of duplicating documents. While his writing was once strikingly unique, a faint gray that stood apart from the rich blacks, browns, and greens of conventional inkwork, it became indistinguishable from a sea of equally faded-looking papers. Anyone coming across a Holman manuscript could be forgiven for assuming it was not an original but a discardable copy, of little value.

Given both the papers and the context in which they were found, the most likely last location of Holman's life's work was a fireplace in Chiswick.

WHAT OF HIS other mark on posterity—the Holman River, named in his honor by Captain Owen? It exists only on faded Admiralty maps. The British government doggedly maintained the settlement of Clarence on Fernando Po until 1835, despite an inexorably mounting death toll so grim the London *Times* declared it "the most pestiferous land which the universe is known to contain." When they finally withdrew, the island reverted to Spanish rule. There was a predictably disastrous 1858 attempt to colonize it with Spaniards (one-fifth of them died in the first five months). The next idea was to convert it into a penal colony, but that notion was abandoned as inhumane, "the equivalent of a death sentence."

The native Fernandians (later classified by ethnologists as the Bubi) withdrew into the interior, trading with the whites only occasionally and out of necessity. By 1861, Clarence was reduced to "a scattered line of about a dozen whitewashed and thatched bungalows," according to the man who would become its most famous resident, the explorer and translator Sir Richard Francis Burton.

After his failed expedition to discover the source of the Nile, Burton was so desperate to remain in Africa he accepted the post of British consul to Fernando Po, despite the daunting mortality rate. He called the job "a plank-lined coffin containing a dead consul once a year," and found the fearsome tornado season so furiously wet the air seemed "without atmosphere." Burton never mentions if he knew Holman was one of the settlement's founders, but he was certainly familiar with his predecessor's works. He would later conclude his ten-volume translation of *Arabian Nights* with a "Terminal Essay," describing, as Islam's central doctrine, "sympathy and tolerance of others . . . which teaches the vulgar Moslem a dignity observed even by the 'blind traveler.'" Holman had enthusiastically attended several Siberian mosques in 1821, the year Burton was born.

Fernando Po remained a Spanish colony until 1968, when it joined with a neighboring island and a small patch of the mainland to form the independent nation of Equatorial Guinea, not to be confused with Guinea or Papua New Guinea. You can find it on your world map between Gabon and Cameroon, although a close examination is usually called for: it is the second-smallest country in Africa. Most traces of the pioneering British have been obliterated by time and politics: almost all of the place names were replaced by Spanish counterparts, and in many cases replaced yet again by African coinages. Fernando Po is now Bioko. Now the nation's capital, Clarence was renamed Santa Isabel, then Malabo.

Some of names bestowed by Owen have managed to endure—there is a Punta Owen, named by the captain not after himself but in honor of his half-brother. But the Holman River has been known for generations as the Rio Biady. The massive formation at the mouth of its estuary, once christened Holman's Rock, now has no official name at all.

•　　　•　　　•

SINCE THE BEGINNING of my research, I've harbored dreams of solving the mystery of Holman's blindness. But that task has proven, paradoxically, to be both simple and impossible. The simple part was finding a likely diagnosis, based on modern medical knowledge. The experts I consulted quickly reached a consensus: optic nerve death, a result of what is now called uveitis, the inflammation of the middle tissue of the eye (the layer which includes the color of the iris). No act of historical forensics can be assumed to be entirely correct, but in this case, the symptoms as documented are all too familiar to modern opthalmology. In the United States, uveitis remains the third-leading cause of blindness, after diabetes and macular degeneration. It still claims, more or less suddenly, the eyesight of an estimated thirty thousand people a year.

Rheumatic syndromes, such as Holman's afflicted joints, are suspected to be a common cause of uveitis. But the key word is "suspected." The sight loss is usually triggered by another, pre-existing condition, and the identity of that trigger is consistently elusive. The vast majority of all cases are diagnosed as "idiopathic uveitis"—"idiopathic" being a clinical term for *of unexplained origin*. As the American Academy of Ophthalmology acknowledges, "Uveitis can have many different causes, including viral infections, fungal infections, toxoplasmosis, bacterial infections, arthritis, autoimmune diseases and as a result of eye injuries. However, the cause in most cases of uveitis remains unknown." If Holman were alive today, he'd have no new opportunities for truly understanding the nature of his blindness.

HOLMAN'S OBSCURITY HAS become almost total. But the blind remember the Blind Traveler. In 1970, at the annual convention of the National Federation of the Blind, the organization's president Kevin Jernigan exhorted his assembled membership to proudly claim the Blind Traveler as part of their shared heritage. "To be sure, many blind persons have been cowed by the

myth of helplessness into remaining in their sheltered corners,"
he told them. "Holman's story is important for its demonstration
that blind people could wear such seven-league boots almost two
centuries ago—before Braille or the long cane, before residential
schools or vocational rehabilitation."

There will never be another James Holman, a sightless person
dedicating a lifetime to ranging the entire world "alone, without
counsel, and without attendance," as he put it. Life on the planet
has speeded up, to the point where even the most extraordinary
nonvisual perception cannot be relied upon.

The modern age of blindness began in 1918, after the use of
mustard gas in World War I claimed the sight of thousands of soldiers. These blind were actively discouraged from relying on compensatory senses, at least when it came to navigating the outside
world. Rubber-soled shoes had muffled the footsteps of pedestrians. Horses were rapidly giving way to automobiles, running swiftly and lethally on rubber tires and smooth asphalted streets. They
were issued canes, ones usually silenced with rubber tips and too
short for effective sweeping—shorter still than Holman's walking
stick. These were painted white, to warn the sighted of their status
(the American version adds one red stripe for the blind, two stripes
for the blind and deaf). When crossing the street, they were taught
to hold the cane straight out in front of them at arm's length—
to maximize its visibility to motorists—then trust that traffic had
come to a stop. Mobility became a matter of the eyes of others: if
not passersby, then "seeing eye" dogs, which were introduced in
America in 1929, in Britain in 1931.

Yet by the second half of the twentieth century, the blind were
beginning to reassert their independence. The "long cane" that Ken-
neth Jernigan spoke of made an appearance—a slender, flexible pole
for sweeping, much like the switch Sir John Fielding had used two
centuries ago, only now made of fiberglass, in collapsible segments.
In the late 1960s, mobility-supporting laws began to mandate tactile aids to navigation, such as raised crosswalks, dipping curbs, and

beeping traffic signals. But it wasn't until the 1990s that a spiritual successor to James Holman emerged.

Daniel Kish, executive director of World Access for the Blind, is a contagiously enthusiastic young man, with a lifestyle that is quintessentially, if not stereotypically, that of a native Southern Californian. His hair is longish, and tousled. His wardrobe runs to the informal: comfortable slacks, colorful short-sleeve shirts. He's fond of mountain biking, and mountaineering. He multi-tasks relentlessly on a cellphone as he strides through the sunshine of Orange County. His greenish brown eyes are beautiful, as well they should be—they are the product of a talented prosthetic art-ist. His organic eyes were surgically removed at the age of three, as part of a treatment for cancer.

Pity was not an element of his childhood. Encouraged to keep pace with his active, sighted siblings, he climbed fences, explored trees, played sandlot games—all situations where a cane was use-less. To keep from lagging behind, he began to experiment. He discovered that sounds, when decoded carefully, carried their own form of spatial perception.

Where Holman used the tap of his walking stick, or the strike of his horses' hooves, Kish used a simple clicking noise made with his tongue against the roof of his mouth. The sharp sound bounced off objects, and with practice he learned to "read" the landscape through the nature of the echo. It was, he recognized, a form of echolocation, the same technique used by radar, and bats in flight.

This realization not only added a new dimension to his mobility, it became his life's work. After earning two masters' degrees, one in developmental psychology and one in special education, he began a pilot research project to see if echolocation could be success-fully taught to blind children. The results were impressive. Now Kish lectures internationally on the subject. He works with the National Institute of Health, studying the methods by which the brain processes acoustic input into physical awareness. He's part of a team designing an enhancement technology called Sound-Flash, "which will triple echo efficiency." But he's best known as the founder of this nonprofit organization, devoted to "developing and using a comprehensive approach to replace vision with other ways of seeing."

It is uncanny, how much of the world Kish and his students have learned to extract from a spark of sound. When a television crew asks him to describe his surroundings on camera, he emits a few quick tongue-clicks, as if they were a nervous habit. Then he gives accurate positions for everything in a fifteen-foot radius: the boom microphone overhead, the light reflector behind him, even a tree in the background. He's confident enough to reach out and tap the camera directly on the lens.

Yet the most impressive aspect of Kish's work is the organization's Team Bat. If there is a modern version of James Holman riding horses across the wilds of Africa, it is the members of this team riding mountain bikes at exhilarating speeds through the dirt trails of Southern California foothills. With clicking devices attached to their bikes, striking the spokes as the wheels turn, they listen to the unfolding terrain, to the approach of obstacles, to the bends of the path.

As was the case with Holman, the team rides with a sighted companion. But that person is decidedly not the leader—if anything, he or she does their best to keep up. The blind bikers are not reckless, but it is thrilling how deeply they abandon themselves to the ride.

"We are interested in more than just the meeting of minimal requirements for functioning and life satisfaction," Kish says. "We believe there should be no limits."

GROWING UP IN a multiethnic, multilingual household in Argentina, the poet Jorge Luis Borges always conceived of himself as a citizen of the world. As a boy he traveled the pampas of South America, drifting into Uruguay and Brazil. As a young man he lived in Switzerland and Spain, and as he grew older he ventured afield farther still, even when his congenitally weak eyes had failed entirely, leaving him blind. In his last years, he could be found rambling through ancient ruins on the Adriatic coast, or going triumphantly aloft in a hot-air balloon over California. These acts were perfectly natural to him, the only sort of life he could imagine. But he found himself having to explain his unchanged appreciation of the gifts of travel.

> *To discover the unknown is not a prerogative of Sinbad, of Eric the Red, or of Copernicus. Each and every man is a discoverer. He begins by discovering bitterness, saltiness, concavity, smoothness, harshness, the seven colors of the rainbow and the twenty-some letters of the alphabet; he goes on to visages, maps, animals and stars. He ends with doubt, or with faith, and the almost certainty of his own ignorance . . . I have shared the joy and surprise of finding sounds, languages, twilights, cities, gardens and people, all of them distinctly different and unique.*

Conscious, sensory-rich travel—a process of awareness, not a means of conquering distance—is beginning to make a comeback. In the last century, the race was to provide speed and comfort in ever increasing quantities, to make journeying a sort of blank spot between destinations. But that race ended in a sonic boom. The fastest commercial jets in the world are mothballed, for lack of passengers. Each summer, the Italian countryside now plays host to people exploring it as Holman had with his friend Colebrook, at a companionable walking pace. When necessary, arm in arm.

There will never be another James Holman. But there will always be people who must summon the courage to plunge, wholeheartedly, into a world complex beyond our illusions of comprehension. It was to them that Holman addressed his most unguarded words. Contemplating his circuit of the world, he confessed that the most profound moments left him feeling not blind, but mute.

*On the summit of the precipice, and in the heart of the green woods
. . . there was an intelligence in the winds of the hills, and in the
solemn stillness of the buried foliage, that could not be mistaken. It
entered into my heart, and I could have wept, not that I did not see,
but that I could not portray all that I felt.*

Time, if not space, renders all of us travelers. Cling as we might,
we are ultimately compelled to let go of the familiar, to forge affin-
ities with the new, and to sense the approach of the more unfamiliar still. We feel our way. If we are as fortunate as the Blind
Traveler, we are given the grace to listen, with equal attention, to
the intelligence of winds and the solemnity of silence. To remain,
joyfully, awake to the path itself.

Acknowledgments

This book was inescapably a global undertaking. I'm deeply grateful to everyone, everywhere, who contributed to the quest.

In New York: Foremost and heartfelt thanks go to Michelle Tessler of Tessler Literary Agency (who believed, and didn't hesitate) and Courtney Hodell of HarperCollins (whose sparks of insight illuminated my trail). Thanks also to Rachel Safko, Lila Byock, Jonathan Burnham, Kathy Schneider, Christine Boyd, and Clive Priddle.

Absolutely everyone at the San Francisco Writer's Grotto: Daniel Kish and World Access for the Blind; Cathryn Ramin and Aparna Sreenavasan.

In the UK: Andrew Gordon, Roger Barrington, Fiona Sinclair, Jude Dicken, Jean Pateman, and Susan Norton of Highgate Cemetery, and Craig Stanton of Hordem House Rare Books.

In Australia: Jenny Fawcett, Evelyn Wier, Don Yorath, Ken Gibb, and Doug and Jan Oldaker.

In Hong Kong: Geoffrey Bonsall, former director of the Hong Kong University Press and deputy librarian of the University of Hong Kong, who graciously volunteered Holman documents from his private collection and undertook illuminating local research on his own initiative.

Elsewhere: Crucial expertise was provided by Paul Collins in Iowa City, David J. Clark in Portland, Rob Bustos in Vancouver, and Lisa Rosner of the Historical Studies Program in Stockton State College, New Jersey.

And my family: Moana in Truckee, Gloria in Arizona, the Mixons of New Iberia, the Plummers of Capistrano Beach, Kal in Cowboy Heaven, Eden Elise, Jesse Eli, and (always, always) Patricia, *ma jolie.*

Notes and Sources

Orthographic note: Both spellings of the word *traveler,* or *traveller,* are considered correct, although the latter as a dominant spelling is limited primarily to the United Kingdom. I first attempted to employ them both, using the spellings encountered in my sources. But this introduced a jarring irregularity to early readers of these pages, and I've since opted for consistency. The word is rendered *traveler* in this edition of the book, and *traveller* in the UK edition.

INTRODUCTION: THE WORLD AND ITS MULTIPLYING DELIGHTS
"more thoroughly than any other traveler": William Jerdan, *Men I Have Known* (London: George Routledge and Sons, 1866), 262.

Darwin cites him as an authority. Charles Darwin, *The Voyage of the Beagle,* Harvard Classics edition (New York: P. F. Collier & Son, 1909-14), chapter XX, fn. 2.

pays tribute to both the man and his fame: Richard F. Burton, *The Book of the Thousand Nights and a Night* (electronic text of 1886 edition: www.gutenberg.org), v. 10, section IV ("Social Condition"), subsection A ("Al-Islam").

"one of the greatest wonders of the world": Jerdan, *Men I Have Known,* 264.

"something incongruous and approaching the absurd": Diary of Thomas Giordano Wright, Newcastle, entry circa 1826 (collection Tyne and Wear Archive Services, Newcastle upon Tyne).

PRELUDE: I SEE THINGS BETTER WITH MY FEET
the blind man paused to feel the end of his walking stick: James Holman, R.N. & K.W., *The Narrative of a Journey, Undertaken in the Years 1819, 1820 & 1821, Through France, Italy, Savoy, Switzerland, etc.* (London: F. C. and J. Rivington, 1822), 226. Holman reports the flames "shriveled the ferrule, and charred the lower part."

I accompanied to the mount the celebrated blind traveler (and subsequent excerpts): R.R. Madden, *The Literary Life and Correspondence of the Countess of Blessington* (London: T. C. Newby, 1855), v. 1, 10.

above middle height: Henry Maull and Polyblank, *Photographic Portraits of Living Celebrities* (London, 1857–59). Comparison based on multiple subjects sitting in the same studio chair.

"I see things better with my feet": Madden, *Blessington*, v. 1, 12.

Vesuvius was at its most violent in living memory: Ibid: "[T]he disemboguing volcano, of the greatest violence that had occurred in recent times." Madden and Holman were witnessing the eruption cycle of 1796–1822. As measured by volume of tephra (solid matter ejected into the air), this cycle was the most violent since the 1708–1723 cycle (source: Global Volcanism Program, Smithsonian National Museum of Natural History, www.volcano.si.edu).

"Some difficulties meet, full many": Holman, *Narrative of a Journey,* 230.

CHAPTER I: THE CHILD IN THE COMPASS
"conscious from my earliest youth of the existence of this desire": James Holman, *A Voyage Round the World, Including Travels in Africa, Asia,*

Australasia, America, etc, etc. (London: Smith, Elder, & Co., 1834), v. I, 1.

an apothecary in the very latest mercantile fashion: This description of the store's inventory is drawn from advertisements in Exeter *Flying Post* dated January 17, 1783 and February 21 and June 12, 1788.

"the ships come now quite up to the city": Daniel Defoe, *From London to Land's End,* first published in 1714 (electronic text of 1888 edition: www.gutenberg.org).

a large phaeton carriage: the vehicle ("with harness compleat, and in very good condition") was advertised for sale in the Exeter *Flying Post* on June 13, 1777.

a seat on the Exeter city council: Ibid., October 1, 1773.

"Chymist & Druggist" or "Surgeon and Apothecary": Ibid., September 6, 1782 and November 12, 1779.

Samuel, who was to be a soldier: War Office, Printed Annual Army Lists 1754–1879, National Archives (UK) catalogue WO 65.

the one destined for the sea: William R. O'Byrne, *O'Byrne's Biographical Book on Serving Royal Navy Officers* (London, 1855), 531.

already attending day school: Zoology: *Proceedings of the Linnean Society of London,* v. 3, 1859, xxvii.

"all the Polite Arts": George McCall Theall, *Records of the Cape Colony, Volume XXXIV* (Cape Colony Governmental Publication, 1905), 169.

"sons of petty tradesmen in Exeter": Anna Eliza Bray, *A Description of the Part of Devonshire Bordering on the Tamar and the Tavy* (London: John Murrary, 1836), 203.

"If his legal advisor had not stopped his mouth": Ibid., 203.

Lumsden's New Map of the World, from the latest discoveries: This particular map (London, 1785) was incorporated into editions of

Thomas Salmon's *Geography*. Far from reflecting the state of the art of geography, it depicts the low level of accuracy to be expected in popular texts of the time (it also labels the east coast of North America as "British Empire"). A similar map, the anonymous *The World from the Best Authorities* (London, c. 1790) identifies Tahiti as the Sandwich Isles and places a "Pike's Lake" in the Rocky Mountains.

his verse is still anthologized today: Roger Lonsdale, ed. *The New Oxford Book of Eighteenth Century Verse* (Oxford: Oxford University Press, 1989), 780.

An ode (attempted in Sapphic verse): Laurence Hynes Halloran (Exeter: private publication, printed by T. Brice, 1789).

accused of acts of "immorality": J. Kerrison, *Australian Dictionary of Biography* (Melbourne: Melbourne University Press), CD-ROM.

Halloran was a fraud: Ibid. Kerrison describes him as a "bogus clergyman, schoolmaster and journalist."

commander of the greencoats: This period in Simcoe's life is well enscapsulated in chapters 3 through 7 of Mary Beacock Fryer and Christopher Dracott's *John Graves Simcoe, 1752–1806: A Biography* (Toronto: Dundurn Press, 1998).

expected to line up before the gates in double file: Ibid., 226.

money which she borrowed from William Pitfield: Ibid., 26. The loan may not have been directly earmarked for the commission, but Simcoe's mother died owing Pitfield 100 pounds.

both charitably active: Fryer and Dracott name Pitfield as "responsible for drugs at Exeter Hospital" (p. 27). John Holman was elected cotreasurer of Devon and Exeter Hospital on March 17, 1796 (Exeter *Flying Post*, March 24, 1796).

a new naval rank, the Volunteer First Class: Brian Lavery, *Nelson's Navy* (Annapolis: Naval Institute Press, 1989), 88.

"crammed with geography, astronomy, algebra": Zoology.

a private naval preparatory school: The name of the school is not documented, but it must have been one of the three or so institutions operating in Gosport at the time, as Holman was too young to attend the Royal Naval College, across the harbor in Portsmouth.

"destined to the naval service": James Holman, R.N. & K.W., *The Narrative of a Journey, Undertaken in the Years 1819, 1820 & 1821, Through France, Italy, Savoy, Switzerland, etc.* (London: F.C. and J. Rivington, 1822), vi.

a brilliant early-morning display of shooting stars: Astro Info Base Web site (members.tripod.com/astro1000).

a war that would prove to be the deadliest in human history: T. N. Dupuy, *The Evolution of Weapons and Warfare* (New York: Bobbs-Merrill, 1980), 314.

John, the eldest, died suddenly: Exeter *Flying Post*, December 13, 1798.

one of his apprentices, John Ham: Ham's former apprenticeship to Holman is noted on the Exeter Roll of Freemen dated April 11, 1811. The business was advertised as "Holman and Ham" in the Exeter *Flying Post* of June 30, 1803.

"I felt an irresistible impulse": Holman, *A Voyage Round the World*, v. 1, 2.

CHAPTER 2: SCARCELY WORTH DROWNING

The Royal George *was vast:* Brian Lavery, *Nelson's Navy* (Annapolis: Naval Institute Press, 1989), 73.

"scarcely worth drowning": (quotation of Sir Edward Pellew): C. Northcote Parkinson, *Britannia Rules: The Classic Age of Naval History 1793–1815* (London: Weidenfeld and Nicholson, 1977).

oxymoronically enough, "open blockade": Lavery, *Nelson's Navy,* 300.

carved it into decorative boxes: G. E. Manwaring and Bonamy Dobrée, *Mutiny: The Floating Republic* (London: The Cresset Library, 1987), 44.

a round of "Rule Britannia": James Dugan, *The Great Mutiny* (New York: Signet Books, 1967), 170.

the intercepted invasion plans had been a hoax: William Laird Clowes, *The Royal Navy: A History from the Earliest Times to the Present* (London: Sampson Low, Marston and Company, 1898), v. IV, 387.

"equally an old woman": (Edward Pellew): C. Northcote Parkinson, *Edward Pellew, Viscount Exmouth* (electronic text of 1934 edition: www.pellew.com).

a face-to-face audience with the admiral: Zoology: Proceedings of the Linnean Society of London, v.3, 1859, xxvii: "after two unsuccessful applications to Lord Bridport to be allowed to join cruising frigates, [he] was placed on board the *Cambrian.*"

Holman's first battle: Laird Clowes, *The Royal Navy,* v. IV, 388.

traced back to a traffic accident: The Hood Peerage Pedigree (www. hoodpedigree.co.uk), notes for Alexander Hood (ref 951).

CHAPTER 3: THE VERY HEIGHT OF EXPECTATION

an accidental battle with a lighthouse: Captain Basil Hall, R.N., *The Log-Book of a Midshipman* (London: Blackie & Son, undated edition of work first published in 1831), 109.

living quarters larger and better supplied with light: James Henderson, *The Frigates* (Ware: Wordsworth Editions Limited, 1998), 19.

the growing collusion of "broken voyage": Peter P. Hill, *Napoleon's Troublesome Americans: Franco-American Relations, 1804–1815* (Dulles: Potomac Books, 2005), xii.

the going rate for reflagging a ship: Hall, *Log-Book of a Midshipman.*

arresting the progress of all the vessels we saw: Ibid.

The happy but anxious young prize-master: Ibid.

"the constant play of hopes and fears": Ibid.

"directly under the shadow of the flag itself": Ibid.

"Once an Englishman, always an Englishman": "Wage theory," *Encyclopedia Britannica,* 2005.

"sundry trespasses, wrongs, and unlawful interruptions": President Jefferson's Proclamation of Cambrian Ship and Other British Armed Vessels, dated December 20, 1806.

" . . . still held in detestation": Hall, *Log-Book of a Midshipman.*

"as if I was walking on my eyeballs": (quotation of Reverend Sidney Smith): Roy Porter and G. S. Rousseau, *Gout, The Patrician Malady* (New Haven: Yale University Press, 1998), 3.

"a glass of generous wine": Dr. William Buchan, *Domestic Medicine; or, the Family Physician* (London: Balfour, Auld and Smellie, 1785).

"whether I am to remain here": British Public Records Office reference ADM 1/2927, dated July 21, 1807.

plaintively petitioning the Navy Pay Office: British Public Records Office reference ADM 1/2928, dated April 28, 1808.

the Guerriere, *a prize of war:* Michael Phillips, *Ships of the Old Navy: A History of Sailing Ships of the Royal Navy* (online database: www.cronab.demon.co.uk/E.HTM).

he took up residence in Bath: Zoology: *Proceedings of the Linnean Society of London,* v.3, 1859, xxvii.

"exceeding ill health": Horatio Nelson, short autobiographical "Statement of His Services" (circa April 1795), manuscript collection, National Maritime Museum.

"strong flavour o' warm flat-irons": Charles Dickens, *The Pickwick Papers*, chapter 37.

the affliction progressed rapidly: Zoology.

"Some hope was entertained": *Annual Register, Appendix to Chronicle*, 1857, 322.

CHAPTER 4: NOR SUN NOR MOON

"impossible to describe the state of my mind": James Holman, *A Voyage Round the World, Including Travels in Africa, Asia, Australasia, America, etc, etc.* (London: Smith, Elder, & Co., 1834),v. 1, 3.

"It is sufficient to say": James Holman, R.N. & K.W., *The Narrative of a Journey, Undertaken in the Years 1819, 1820 & 1821, Through France, Italy, Savoy, Switzerland, etc.* (London: F.C. and J. Rivington, 1822), vi.

Buchan's Domestic Medicine: Dr. William Buchan, *Domestic Medicine; or, the Family Physician* (London: Balfour, Auld and Smellie, 1785).

I will even appoint over you terror: Leviticus 26:16.

the West of England Eye Infirmary had opened: P. M. G. Russell, *A History of the Exeter Hospitals, 1170–1948* (Exeter: James Townsend & Sons, 1976), 102.

Thereupon a needle is to be taken: De Medicina (On Medicine): A. Cornelius Celsus, Loeb Classical Library, 1938, translated by W. G. Spenser.

Dr. Samuel Barnes, its brand-new chief physician: Russell, *A History of the Exeter Hospitals,* 104.

Old Ugly: Rootsweb genealogical database (http://freepages.gene alogy.rootsweb.com).

Animal Magnetism, or The Pseudo-Philosopher Baffled: Lonsdale, ed. *The New Oxford Book of Eighteenth Century Verse,* 780.

Revisit'st not these eyes, that rowle in vain: Paradise Lost, Book III, line 23.

CHAPTER 5: THE SEVEN GENTLEMEN

a strangely nautical will: Peter Clissold, "Samuel Travers and the Naval Knights of Windsor," *The Mariner's Mirror* (Society for Nautical Research), v. 60, No. 1, February 1974.

"grown more fit for prayer than war": Edmund H. Fellows, *The Military Knights of Windsor 1352–1944* (Windsor: Oxley and Son, 1944).

"Poor Knights" of Windsor: The traditional name was officially eradicated in 1833 by order of William IV. But the term lives on. In many parts of England, "poor knight of Windsor" is a breakfast dish, analogous to French toast

positions filled by tailors, victuallers: Fellows, *Military Knights,* xliv.

"as I am now getting on in years": Clissold, *Mariner's Mirror.*

the application itself: British Public Records Office reference ADM 106/3535.

annual share of the Travers trust: Knights' Pay Record, British Public Records Office reference ADM 80/194.

harboring his own secret: Genealogical compilation by Cheryl Silvestrin, Orkney Genealogy: Family Heritage of the Orkney Islands of Scotland (www.cursiter.com).

"to old and rheumatic limbs": Clissold, *Mariner's Mirror.*

Knights' Check Book: Saint George's Chapel Archives, Windsor Castle.

the centuries-lost bodies: Peter J. Begent, *The Romance of St George's Chapel* (Windsor: Friends of St. George's Chapel, 2001), 36.

"an undefinable power": James Holman, R.N. and K.W., *The Narrative of a Journey, Undertaken in the Years 1819, 1820 & 1821, Through France, Italy, Savoy, Switzerland, etc.* (London: F.C. and J. Rivington, 1822), viii.

CHAPTER 6: A SMATTERING OF PHYSIC

"you might smoke bacon": Paul Johnson, *The Birth of the Modern: World Society 1815–1830* (New York: HarperCollins, 1991), 183.

"so narrow that you can lay a hand on either wall": Robert Louis Stevenson, *Picturesque Notes* (electronic text of 1879 edition), chapter II.

no entrance requirements: This and many other details of this chapter are drawn from Lisa Rosner's *Medical Education in the Age of Improvement* (Edinburgh: Edinburgh University Press, 1991).

a woman masquerading as a man: Brian Lalor, ed., *The Encyclopedia of Ireland* (Dublin: Gill & Macmillan, 2003). Barry would go on to pioneer Cesarian surgery and become inspector general of British hospitals in Canada. Her gender was discovered only after her death in 1865.

"whatever I retain, I retain permanently": James Holman, *A Voyage Round the World, Including Travels in Africa, Asia, Australasia, America, etc, etc.* (London: Smith, Elder, & Co., 1834), v. 5, 7.

"this protracted day of darkness": James Holman, R.N. & K.W., *The Narrative of a Journey, Undertaken in the Years 1819, 1820, 1821, Through France, Italy, Savoy, Switzerland, etc.* (London: F.C. and J. Rivington, 1822), vii.

smattering of physic: Holman, *Travels in Russia,* v. 1, 288.

"any of the flowers of oratory": Robert Christison, *The Life of Sir Robert Christison* (Edinburgh: William Blackwood and Sons, 1885), 75.

"the tempting field of chemical research": Ibid., 58.

"knew almost all that was then known": Ibid., 111.

"unnecessary to mention": Holman, *Narrative of a Journey,* viii.

"in the cultivation of those pursuits": Holman, *Voyage Round the World,* v. 5, 513.

"At the time my health was so delicate": Ibid., v. 1, 3.

Admiralty records show: British Public Records Office, reference ADM 6/208.

"Behold me, then, in France!": Holman, *Narrative of a Journey,* 3.

CHAPTER 7: A WHIMSICAL INVALID
Unless otherwise specified, details and quotations are drawn from James Holman, R.N. & K.W., *The Narrative of a Journey, Undertaken in the Years 1819, 1820, 1821, Through France, Italy, Savoy, Switzerland, etc.* (London: F.C. and J. Rivington, 1822), vii.

at the very head of the procession: Times of London, February 17, 1820, 2.

CHAPTER 8: THE EXPERIMENTAL CITIZEN
Unless otherwise specified, details and quotations are drawn from James Holman, R.N. & K.W., The Narrative of a Journey, Undertaken in the Years 1819, 1820, 1821, Through France, Italy, Savoy, Switzerland, etc. (London: F.C. and J. Rivington, 1822), vii.

their lives had long run in parallel: Dictionary of National Biography (London: 1887), v. X, 401.

"the experimental citizen": James Holman, *A Voyage Round the World, Including Travels in Africa, Asia, Australasia, America, etc, etc.* (London: Smith, Elder & Co., 1834), v. 4, 513.

"Mr. C—l—b—k": Holman, *Travels Through Russia,* 21.

a beehive that folded open and closed: François Huber, *New Observations on the Natural History of Bees (translated from the Original)* (Edinburgh: John Anderson, 1806).

"the Injured Queen of England": Flora Fraser, *The Unruly Queen: The Life of Queen Caroline* (Berkeley: University of California Press, 1997).

CHAPTER 9: A CIRCUIT OF THE WORLD
"a plain and faithful statement": James Holman, R.N. & K.W., *The Narrative of a Journey, Undertaken in the Years 1819, 1820 & 1821, Through France, Italy, Savoy, Switzerland, etc.* (London: F.C. and J. Rivington, 1822), xi.

Bruge I saw attired in golden light: William Wordsworth, *Memorials of a Tour on the Continent* (London: Longman, 1822).

few readers who are not fond: J. Arago, *Narrative of a Voyage Round the World in the* Uranie *and* Physcienne *Corvettes* (London: Treuttel and Wurtz, 1823).

will command for him the admiration of future ages: William Jerdan, *Men I Have Known,* (London: George Routledge and Sons, 1866).

"My motives for concealing": Holman, *Travels in Russia.*

"secret geographical and astronomic expedition": Leonid Sverdlov, "Russian Naval Officers and Geographic Exploration in Northern Russia," *Arctic Voice,* no. 11, November 27, 1996.

CHAPTER 10: TRUE SENTIMENTS AND POWERS

Unless otherwise specified, details and quotations are drawn from Holman, *Travels in Russia, v. 1 and 2.*

the illegitimate son of the black sheep: John Keay, *Explorers Extraordinary* (New York: Tarcher, 1986).

"the fighting Cochranes": Robert Harvey, *Cochrane: The Life and Exploits of a Fighting Captain* (New York: Carroll & Graf, 2001).

One cousin, now Lord Cochrane: This was Thomas Cochrane, whose career and exploits would later serve as the inspiration for two well-known fictional captains: C. S. Forrester's Horatio Hornblower and Patrick O'Brian's Jack Aubrey. He would also later be Holman's colleague in the Raleigh Club.

"in some servile capacity": This and all subsequent Cochrane quotes drawn from John Dundas Cochrane's *Narrative of a Pedestrian Journey Through Russia and Siberian Tartary*, fourth edition (London: Charles Knight, 1825).

CHAPTER 11: THE SLEEPING LAND

the path-swallowing marshlands: The *Encyclopedia Britannica* characterizes the area as "exceptionally swampy, with many lakes." In his novel *Michael Strogoff*, Jules Verne describes it as "ponds, pools, lakes, and swamps, from which the sun draws poisonous exhalations, that the road winds, and entails upon the traveler the greatest fatigue and danger."

Alexy Kolovin, a feldjager: Holman refers to his captor only as "the Feldjager," but his name is given in an account published, of all places, in *The Iowa Recorder*, Greene, Iowa, June 4, 1904.

CHAPTER 12: A SALVO UPON ALL DEFECTS
Holman details and quotations are drawn from *Travels in Russia, v. 2.*

"What object he can have, without a servant": Monthly Magazine, August 1, 1824.

"Great as my affliction may be": Letter to the editor of the *Monthly Magazine*, dated October 15, 1824.

"by her beauty and accomplishments": Quoted by Mervyn Horder in his postscript to an abridged edition of *A Pedestrian Journey* (London: The Folio Society, 1983), 215.

a very amusing volume: Diary of Thomas Giordani Wright, Newcastle, entry circa 1826 (collection Tyne and Wear Archive Services, Newcastle upon Tyne).

as far as human observation and selection can fix: Uvedale Price, *On the Picturesque* (London: J. Robson, 1796).

I am constantly asked, and I may as well answer: James Holman, *A Voyage Round the World, Including Travels in Africa, Asia, Australasia, America, etc, etc.* (London: Smith, Elder, & Co., 1834), v. 1, 4.

"The world was to be mapped out into so many divisions": Clements R. Markham, *Major James Rennel and the Rise of Modern English Geography,* (London: Cassell & Co., 1895), 194.

"authoritative and generous": This and subsequent biographical details are drawn from E. H. Burrows's *Captain Owen of the African Survey* (Rotterdam: A. A. Balkema, 1979), 173.

in the present state of the island: Quarterly Review, October 1822.

"to test the effect of seawater on dry rot": Michael Phillips, *Ships of the Old Navy: A History of Sailing Ships of the Royal Navy* (online database: www.cronab.demon.co.uk/E.HTM).

the deadliest expedition of all time: Burrows, *Captain Owen,* 198.

CHAPTER 13: WHITE MAN'S GRAVE

Unless otherwise specified, details and quotations are drawn from James Holman, *A Voyage Round the World, Including Travels in Africa, Asia, Australasia, America, etc, etc. (London: Smith, Elder, & Co., 1834),* v. 1.

a Supernumerary Boy of the Second Class: Logbooks of the HMS *Eden,* British Public Record Office, reference ADM 37/8047.

Holman's Rock: Holman records only the naming of the river in his honor, but Holman's Rock appears on the Colonial Department map of 1829, British Public Record Office, reference CO 700/West Africa 9.

a notably dramatic disease: Details of malarial pathology are drawn from Mark Honigsbaum's *Fever Trail* (New York: Picador, 2003).

the marks of over one hundred liberated slaves: British Public Record Office, reference ADM 1/2273.

joking they had standing orders: E.H. Burrows, *Captain Owen of the African Survey* (Rotterdam: A.A. Balkema, 1979), 196.

valiant but losing battles: Burrows, *Captain Owen,* 197.

CHAPTER 14: MY DANGEROUS AND NOVEL COURSE

Unless otherwise specified, details and quotations are drawn from James Holman, *Voyage Round the World, Including Travels in Africa, Asia, Australasia, America, etc, etc. (London: Smith, Elder, & Co., 1834),* v. 1, 2.

the indigenous Botocudo: Hal Langfur, "Uncertain Refuge: Frontier Formation and the Origins of the Botocudo War in Late Colonial Brazil," *Hispanic American Historical Review,* May 2002.

widows' men: N. A. M. Rodger, *The Wooden World: An Anatomy of the Georgian Navy* (London: Fontana Press, 1988), 430.

"Great towering castles": Basil Hall, *Fragments of Voyages and Travels*, first series (Edinburgh: 1831).

"one of the proudest and most cruel women": Ida Pfeiffer, *The Last Travels of Ida Pfeiffer: Inclusive of a Visit to Madagascar*, translated by H. W. Dulcken (New York: Harper & Bros., 1861).

At Canton itself: Paul Johnson, *The Birth of the Modern: World Society 1815–1830* (New York: HarperCollins, 1991), 784.

"I was much pleased with meeting Holman": Sir James Brooke, *The Private Letters of Sir James Brooke, Rajah of Sarawak*, ed. John C. Templer (London: Richard Bentley, 1853), v. II, 24.

"A curious instance of the force of example": Sydney *Gazette and New South Wales Advertiser*, April 30, 1831.

"On Sunday week Lieutenant Holman": Sydney *Herald*, October 3, 1831.

"an exploring party in Bateman's Bay": Sydney *Herald*, November 28, 1831.

CHAPTER 15: ASSUMING A MORE ALARMING CHARACTER
oversized walking hatboxes: Paul Johnson, *The Birth of the Modern: World Society 1815–1830* (New York: HarperCollins, 1991), 454.

"if you have conveyed to your Cousin": British Public Record Office, reference ADM 80/189, logged copy of correspondence dates July 29, 1832.

"so replete with interesting information": Quoted in printed circular promoting the book, British Public Record Office, reference ADM 80/189.

"would do credit to any traveler": *Fraser's Magazine for Town and Country*, London, v. xi, June 1835.

"For this work we cannot but anticipate a circulation": Printed circular ADM 80/189.

"We never ranked ourselves in the number": *Gentleman's Magazine*, London, September 1834.

"A want of verification": *Gentleman's Magazine*, London, March 1836.

"Surely if sight (as it must be confessed)": *Gentleman's Magazine*, London, November 1835.

"romance and not verity": *Encyclopedia Britannica*, eleventh edition (1911).

so ashamed she committed suicide: Ibid.

"A book,—the world! a traveler blind!": Titled "Impromptu, by a Lady," this poem was included in the front matter of the second edition of *Voyage Round the World*. A footnote helpfully explains that "spirits mythological" means "Love, Fortune, Justice."

"600 or 700 copies": James Grant, *The Great Metropolis* (electronic text of 1837 edition: www.victorianlondon.org), chapter III: "Literature."

a girl he called Drina: Lyton Strachey, *Queen Victoria* (electronic text of 1921 edition: www.projectgutenberg.org). chapter II, Section I.

Uncle King: Grace Greenwood, *Queen Victoria, Her Girlhood and Womanhood* (electronic text of 1883 edition: www.projectgutenberg.org), chapter III.

"a very short, very slim girl": Strachey, *Queen Victoria*, chapter II, section V.

I am commanded by Her Majesty: Unless otherwise noted, all documents cited henceforth in this chapter are components of British Public Record Office, reference HO 44/52: *1838–1840, Naval Knights of Windsor, Papers re: Lieut. Holman's application, to a New Regulation dispensing with Residence.*

"the incredible curse of a female succession": "A Brief History of Nocton Church" (www.allsaintsnocton.co.uk).

the reign's first scandal: Christopher Hibbert, *Queen Victoria: A Personal History* (Cambridge, Mass.: Da Capo Press, 2000), chapter 10.

CHAPTER 16: THE ARRIVAL OF AN ENGLISH TRAVELER
I have been four years in the East: Andrew Archibald Paton, *Servia, the Youngest Member of the European Family: or, A Residence in Belgrade* (London: Longman, Brown, Green and Longmans, 1845), 1.

"I last saw you in Aleppo": Ibid, 75.

a study in perpetual motion: Holman's itinerary in these years is faithfully recorded in the *Zoology* obituary of 1859.

"examining its various details": The Living Age, v. 3, no. 27, November 16, 1844.

"I walked home with him through the streets": Henry Dwight Sedgwick, *Francis Parkman* (American Men of Letters series) (Boston: Houghton, Mifflin and Company, 1904), 87. Parkman's private diary entry for January 18, 1844, in which he misidentifies Holman as "Holeman."

"a venerable man with a long beard": Thomas Noon Talfourd, *Supplement to "Vacation Rambles"* (London: Edward Moxon, 1854), 57.

"injurious effects of the malaria": James Holman R.N. & K.W., *The Narrative of a Journey, Undertaken in the Years 1819, 1820 & 1821, Through France, Italy, Savoy, Switzerland, etc.* (London: F.C. and ·J. Rivington, 1822), 175.

"returned to this country on Thursday week": Liverpool Mercury, as cited in *The Living Age*, v. 11, no. 130, November 7, 1846.

Abu Abdullah Muhammad Ibn Batutta: Ross E. Dunn, *The Adventures of Ibn Batutta, a Muslim Traveler of the Fourteenth Century* (Berkeley: University of California Press, 1989).

CHAPTER 17: THE PLEASURE OF HIS INTIMACY

"a curious thing indeed.": Queen Victoria, February 1837, cited in *Queen Victoria's Empire*, Public Broadcasting System (www.pbs.org/empires/victoria).

"a most cheerful and agreeable companion": Zoology: *Proceedings of the Linnean Society of London*, v.3, 1859, xxvii.

"to visit the blind in their own homes": Rose, *Changing Focus*.

"The Blind Girl never knew": Charles Dickens, *The Cricket on the Hearth* (electronic text: www.pagebypagebooks.com).

it was a lunatic asylum: Andrew Roberts, *The Lunacy Commission, a Study of its Origin, Emergence and Character* (Middlesex University online resource: www.mdx.ac.uk/www/study/01.htm).

"indomitable will": People's Journal, no. 93, October 9, 1847, 197.

"he forgot in what part of the world he was": Ibid.

"the two were alone in their glory": William Jerdan, *Men I Have Known* (London: George Routledge and Sons, 1866), 264.

"claim only its proper place": The Living Age, v. 29, number 367, May 31, 1851.

"a workman-like author": Thomas Noon Talfourd, *Supplement to "Vacation Rambles"* (London: Edward Moxon, 1854), 57.

"an old woman": Zoology: *Proceedings of the Linnean Society of London*, v.3, 1859, xxvii. Owing to the amount of detail offered, it is clear that the anonymous author of this 1859 obituary had personally read at least portions of Holman's autobiography.

I can recall with ease: James Holman, *A Voyage Round the World, Including Travels in Africa, Asia, Australasia, America, etc, etc.* (London: Smith, Elder, & Co., 1834), v. 4, 518.

a cuttingly ironic honor: W. M. Artman and L. V. Hall, *Beauties and Achievements of the Blind* (Dansville, New York: Published for the Authors, 1854).

Miss Clementina Bourne: Post Office Directory, London 1856, facsimile CD-ROM edition (Archive CD Books, 2001).

"what took him into that quarter": Jerdan, *Men I Have Known*, 265.

"when I emerge on Tower Hill": George Augustus Sala, *Gaslight and Daylight, With Some London Scenes They Shine Upon* (London: Chapman & Hall, 1859), chapter IV: "Jack Alive in London."

"a gin-mad Malay": East London Observer, no. 4, October 10, 1857, 2.

"be quiet; see what he will do": Jerdan, *Men I Have Known*, 265.

"solaces the evening of his life-days": Ibid, 267.

Bolougne-sur-Mer: Zoology.

"secluding himself completely": Ibid.

"materially injuring his health": Ibid.

"His last employment": Gentleman's Magazine Historical Review (annual), 1857, 341.

CHAPTER 18: RAISE THE SOUL TO FLAME
"not be prudent to attempt the voyage": Clissold, *Mariner's Mirror*.

the ghost that haunts the grounds: Peter Clissold, *The Naval Knights of Windsor: A History* (unpublished manuscript), Saint George's Chapel Archives, Windsor Castle.

"Were these journals ever published?": *Notes and Queries*, v. s7-IX, no. 229, 1890.

"the most pestiferous land": As quoted in *The Living Age*, v. XIX, October-December 1848.

"a scattered line of about a dozen": "A F.R.G.S." (pseud., Richard Francis Burton), *Wanderings in West Africa From Liverpool to Fernando Po* (London: Tinsley Brothers, 1863), v. II, 294.

"a plank-lined coffin": *Telegraph* newspaper (UK), August 29, 2004.

"alone, without counsel": James Holman, *A Voyage Round the World, Including Travels in Africa, Asia, Australasia, America, etc, etc.* (London: Smith, Elder, & Co., 1834), v. 5, 515.

"Each and every man is a discoverer": Jorge Luis Borges (trans. Anthony Kerrigan), *Atlas* (New York: E. P. Dutton, 1985), 7.

"On the summit of the precipice": Holman, *Voyage Round the World*, v. 4, 6.

Illustration Credits

Frontispiece: 1834 portrait of Holman by William Brockedon, © National Portrait Gallery, London.

Prelude: from the anonymously authored *L'Italie, la Sicile, les îles Éoliennes, l'île d'Elbe, la Sardaigne, Malte, l'île de Calypso, etc.* (Paris: Audot, 1834-1837).

Chapter 1: from *Wood Carvings in English Churches, Volume 1: Misericords* by Francis Bond (London: Henry Frowde, 1910).

Chapter 2: 1795 portrait of Bridport by Lemuel Francis Abbott, National Maritime Museum, London.

Chapter 3: Depiction of *Cambrian* and *Leander* pursuing coasting sloop *Richard*, Library of Congress.

Chapter 4: Operation for cataract, Sir James Earle, Wellcome Library, London.

Chapter 5: Engraving, *Travers' College in 1804*, author collection.

Chapter 6: Personification of "chymical medicine," Wellcome Library, London.

Chapter 7: Anonymous engraving, *Discoveries, breaking up*, author collection.

Chapter 8: Illustration facing p. 330, *Travels Through Russia, etc.*, v. 1

Chapter 9: Illustration facing p. 195, Ibid.

Chapter 10: Author portrait, *Pedestrian Journey.*

Chapter 11: Illustration facing p. 164, *Travels Through Russia, etc.,* v. 2

Chapter 12: Engraved portrait of Holman, author collection.

Chapter 13: Illustration facing p. 262, *Voyage Round the World,* v. 1

Chapter 14: 1830 portrait of Holman by George Chinnery, The Royal Society.

Chapter 15: Author portrait, *Voyage Round the World.*

Chapter 16: Detail from *Carte der Europæischen Türkey in XXI Blättern* (Vienna: 1829).

Chapter 17: Adaptation of Knight portrait, circa 1854.

Chapter 18: Attributed to Maull and Polyblank, author collection.

Of Further Interest

To learn more about the Blind Traveler and his era, please visit:
www.jasonroberts.net/holman

There you'll find contemporary accounts, further images and commentaries, a bibliography, and even the complete online text of Holman's Voyage Round the World, Vol.1.

To learn more about World Access for the Blind, echolocative navigation, and the work of Daniel Kish, please visit:
www.worldaccessfortheblind.org